Journalism

Reference Sources in the Humanities Series
James Rettig, Series Editor

Journalism: A Guide to the Reference Literature. By Jo A. Cates.

Music: A Guide to the Reference Literature. By William S. Brockman.

On the Screen: A Film, Television, and Video Research Guide. By Kim N. Fisher.

Philosophy: A Guide to the Reference Literature. By Hans E. Bynagle.

Reference Works in British and American Literature: Volume I, English and American Literature. By James K. Bracken.

JOURNALISM

A GUIDE TO
THE REFERENCE
LITERATURE

Jo A. Cates
Chief Librarian
The Poynter Institute for Media Studies

LIBRARIES UNLIMITED, INC.
Englewood, Colorado
1990

LIBRARIES UNLIMITED, INC.
P.O. Box 3988
Englewood, Colorado 80155-3988

Library of Congress Cataloging-in-Publication Data

Cates, Jo A.
    Journalism :   a guide to the reference literature / Jo A. Cates.
      xvii, 214 p. 17x25 cm.
      ISBN 0-87287-716-7
    1. Reference books--Journalism--Bibliography.   2. Journalism-
-Bibliography.   I. Title.
Z6940.C38   1990
[PN4731]
016.0704--dc20   89-78335
                                                      CIP

To Joe Frank,
the best reporter I know.

Contents

Foreword

You are holding not only a valuable reference guide but, so much the better, a wonderful book. Jo Cates's *Journalism: A Guide to the Reference Literature* is wise, witty, original, and thorough—an ideal collaboration of the arts of journalism and librarianship.

Libraries and journalism are tied together in a lively and paradoxical history. Prior to the invention of the printing press and the newspaper, the most important records and documents of community life were kept on parchment. Libraries were the keepers of those manuscripts, and librarians were charged with preserving them against wear, loss, and destruction from the hazards of promiscuous use. Parchment was expensive, manuscripts few, the arts of copying tedious and time-consuming. As a result, parchment manuscripts were precious, even sacred. Parchment was durable, but manuscripts were so scarce that fire, vandalism, or the carnage of war could cause a cultural stroke: the loss of collective memory, of history, of the fundamental documents of community life. The library was, as a result, a fortress, a protection against loss, and the librarian a preserver against the forces of destruction and change.

Journalism, the printing press, and the newspaper changed all that. Journalism derives its name from the French word for *day*. Journalism is a diary, a daybook, a record of the significant happenings, occurrences, events, and sayings during a day in the life of a community. Journalism preserves not only the exotic, rare, and sacred but also the common, ordinary, and repetitive events of life. Printing on paper recommended itself because it overcame the rarity and fragility of parchment manuscripts. Paradoxically, placing writing on cheaper and flimsier material made the collective memory of the community more secure, and permitted the recording of the commonplace. Cheap and easy reproduction of material in large numbers guaranteed that nothing of significance would ever be lost again. Thomas Jefferson early recognized the great advantage of printing, and, in one of his letters, provided not only the basic justification of freedom of the press but underlined the central value of printing and the newspaper:

> Our experience has proved to us that a single copy, or a few, deposited ... in the public offices cannot be relied on for any great length of time. The ravages of fire and of ferocious enemies have had but too much part in producing the very loss we now deplore. How

many of the precious works of antiquity were lost while they existed only in manuscript? Has there ever been one lost since the art of printing has rendered it practicable to multiply and disperse copies? This leads us then to the only means of preserving those remains of our laws now under consideration, that is, a multiplication of printed copies.

Early newspapers were underwritten by government grants to print the laws and records of the community. This was more than patronage. Freedom of the press guaranteed the records of the community against loss, made them easily accessible for research, and assured that the basic documents of the community would not disappear through the errant habits of county clerks. Because printing and the newspaper preserved this record of the community against loss, documents could be safely circulated. As a result, the library changed its function and librarians their role. Rather than simply preserving records, libraries disseminated them and made them widely available. The librarian oversaw a circulation system rather than simply a preservation system. The newspaper, above all, became the "paper of record": the unofficial but indispensable transcript of the community. The library, in turn, became a central depository accessible not just to scholars but to every citizen of the community.

The amount of paper produced has grown to Everest-like proportions. As Walter Bagehot said over a century ago, "The newspaper is like the city: everything is there and everything is disconnected." The task of the library, through its reference section, is to connect the disconnected. Through bibliographies and bibliographic guides, directories, yearbooks, records of archives and collections and, in our day, databases and other computerized sources, the library references, integrates, and makes systematically available the holdings of the community. However, this record of the record—the materials that actually index what is out there and held—has never been itself, at least as concerns journalism, brought together in one convenient form. Until now, that is.

Jo Cates's *Journalism: A Guide to the Reference Literature* is an absolutely unique source and book. It is strictly a reference guide and it is strictly devoted to journalism—print and broadcasting. It is a thorough, exhaustive accumulation of over 700 sources in print and databases that collectively constitutes the records of journalism. Jo Cates is a first-class researcher rescuing obscure, often ephemeral, but always useful material from a thousand hidden niches in the archive and library.

She is ideally qualified to undertake this task. A superbly trained librarian, she has directed the library at The Poynter Institute for Media Studies for a number of years. There she serves students, faculty, and countless journalists and scholars who seek her advice and guidance to the literature and archive of journalism. Attuned to the needs of journalists and educators, sensitive to journalism as a craft and calling, she brings the polished skills of a librarian to very high-level detective work. This reference book makes widely available the generous advice and wide learning heretofore accessible only to the patrons of The Poynter Institute.

Also, and to one's immense pleasure, this is a reference book that is a delight to read. The annotated entries are mini-essays that are artfully crafted and critically acute. They are composed with grace and clarity, a steady and discerning intelligence, and great wit and good humor. The book disguises in its graceful effortlessness the immense and difficult work required to put it together.

Everything is here and everything is now connected. Journalism at last has a reference guide worthy of its calling. You have some happy reading herein and, even more, it will set you onto some happy hunting.

> James W. Carey
> Dean, College of Communications
> University of Illinois, Urbana-Champaign

Acknowledgments

I owe thanks to many people.

To the late Nelson Poynter, who offered a vision of excellence in journalism, I am indebted.

I thank Calder Pickett and the late William Price, who set the high standards in journalism bibliography.

Journalism and news librarians across the country contributed to this publication. Dolores Jenkins, reference librarian at the University of Florida, piled her car high with reference sources and drove down from Gainesville. Frances Wilhoit, head of the journalism library at Indiana University, opened her library to me and offered advice and support. Mary Allcorn of the University of Missouri, Eleanor Block of Ohio State University, Diane Carothers of the University of Illinois, Sammy Alzofon of the *St. Petersburg Times*, and Yvonne Egertson at the American Newspaper Publishers Association, by way of publications, collections, bibliographies, or advice, made valuable contributions. Thanks also to Eleanor Blum and *Basic Books in the Mass Media*. I eagerly await the third edition.

My colleagues at The Poynter Institute for Media Studies deserve more than my thanks. Bob Haiman, president and managing director, has been patient and supportive. He also promised a party as this book is published, and I shall hold him to that. Roy Peter Clark and Don Fry, associate directors, offered sage advice on writing and editing. Joyce Olson held my hand and proofread. The library staff deserves special recognition. Ken Kister, assistant librarian (who has also been called the Ralph Nader of encyclopedias and dictionaries) and friend, read many of these chapters and offered his expert opinions. Sandra Allen, library assistant, made numerous phone calls, proofread, and helped me get this out on time. David Shedden and Jane Kavanagh offered constant encouragement and read several chapters.

Series editor James R. Rettig has the good qualities I had hoped to find in an editor. Patient and intelligent, he gets to the heart of what the writer is trying to say, and never draws blood.

Kim Fisher, author of *On the Screen: A Film, Television, and Video Research Guide* (his award-winning book in this series published in 1986) gave good advice and lent an ear. Andy Countryman, *Detroit Free Press*, offered his view of journalism history and a comprehensive explanation of joint operating agreements. Marty Linsky, lecturer in public policy at Harvard University and keeper of the process approach, provided low-key cheerleading. Jim Carey, dean of the College of Communications, University of Illinois, offered wise words on journalism education. Art Caplan, director of the University of Minnesota's Center for Biomedical Ethics, made me laugh.

A. J. Anderson, professor of library science at Simmons College, mentor and friend, encouraged me to write again.

Thanks also to Gene Patterson, for his example, interest, and encouragement, and to Andy Barnes, Mike Foley, Chip Scanlan, and others at the *St. Petersburg Times* who offered advice (even when I didn't ask) and asked questions with journalistic zeal.

I am also indebted to Jon Lanham, associate librarian of Lamont Library at Harvard College, who offered me my first professional library job at the squeakiest library in Cambridge. He was always there and he always listened.

I thank Joe, who will be my husband when this book is finally published, my mother and father, Lindy, Iris, Jay, and Gandy.

Introduction

When I arrived at The Poynter Institute for Media Studies in the summer of 1985, I hadn't fully taken into account the job that lay ahead of me. My charge was to take a wall of books, a few scattered periodical and newspaper subscriptions, and some mildewed videotapes (the old building had a unique climate) and turn this odd assortment into a journalism reference and research center. My mission was to assemble a special collection of print and broadcast journalism materials which would answer the needs of The Poynter Institute, a nationally prominent school for the continuing education of professional journalists. The collection also had to lend itself to the hundreds of questions asked by editors, reporters, copy editors, teachers, and researchers who call and attend seminars here each year.

I needed this book. I remember sitting on a packing box in our new building, surveying the empty shelves, and wishing for just one volume that would lead me to current reference works on the subject. With Eleanor Blum's *Basic Books in the Mass Media* (University of Illinois Press, 1980) in hand, I began to build. I soon realized that Blum's book would not meet all my needs. Not only was it getting on in years (the second edition was published in 1980, the third edition is expected in 1990), it truly deals with the *mass* media and does not focus exclusively on reference works. The other giants in journalism bibliography, Warren C. Price's *The Literature of Journalism: An Annotated Bibliography* (University of Minnesota Press, 1959) and Price and Calder Pickett's *An Annotated Journalism Bibliography, 1958-1968* (University of Minnesota Press, 1970) are very helpful in listing both general and reference sources in print journalism — but only to 1968. Likewise, Carl L. Cannon's *Journalism: A Bibliography* (New York Public Library, 1924), based on the New York Public Library's journalism holdings, is very important for journalism titles published through the early 1920s. Roland E. Wolseley and Isabel Wolseley's eighth edition of *The Journalist's Bookshelf* (R. J. Berg, 1986) lists general sources in print journalism only and includes one chapter of reference sources.

So for those who find themselves in the same predicament as I was, for librarians in search of a reference collection development tool, students and others beginning research in journalism, and print and broadcast journalists who want to know more about their field, here is *Journalism: A Guide to the Reference Literature*. It is a selected, annotated bibliography and reference guide to the

English-language reference literature of print and broadcast journalism, and is part of the Libraries Unlimited series entitled Reference Sources in the Humanities. It covers sources published from the late 1960s through 1988, with a scattering of important 1989 sources squeezed in before final deadline in March. A small number of earlier classic sources also are included. More than 700 entries are numbered and arranged in chapters according to type of reference work. There are chapters on bibliographies and bibliographic guides; dictionaries; encyclopedias; indexes, abstracts, and databases; biographical sources; handbooks and manuals; dictionaries and yearbooks, stylebooks and books of English language usage; catalogs; and core periodicals, as well as chapters listing professional organizations and research centers.

Each entry includes author(s), title, place of publication, pagination, copyright date, annotation, and, when available, Library of Congress and ISSN or ISBN information.

Annotations are descriptive and evaluative. Most read like mini-reviews, aimed at librarians, educators, students, and anyone interested in beginning research in journalism. This book will also be useful in the newsroom and important to those writing about the media.

This book is *not* a reference guide to book publishing or advertising or telecommunications or public relations or film or television programming; books on these topics are not included here unless they specifically address journalism. For example, a bibliography on network television news would be included here. A guide to "The Andy Griffith Show" would not. (Actually, there is such a publication: *Mayberry, My Hometown* is an encyclopedic chronicle of the show.) This also is *not* a guide to general reference sources (Eugene P. Sheehy's *Guide to Reference Books*, Albert John Walford's *Guide to Reference Materials*, and others already serve this purpose), so users should remember that for every specialized who's who or other type of source, there probably is a general reference counterpart.

Titles were chosen for inclusion in this guide through consultation of bibliographic guides, catalogs, standard book review sources, and examination of special library collections.

Detailed subject and author/title indexes are provided so that no title gets buried in a chapter.

Until now, the reference literature of journalism has been, at best, scattered. It is evident, however, that the field of journalism is sadly lacking current reference sources in biography and photojournalism, as well as indexing sources and online databases. This field offers fertile ground for further reference works.

There are some hazards in writing a book of this sort—defining *reference* and defining *journalism*. As a librarian, I have no problem snapping a defining lid on reference works (but I admit to fudging a bit in the miscellaneous chapter). As a journalist, however, I am less inclined to offer a quick and dirty definition of journalism. When we serve up an idea for a new seminar or program for The Poynter Institute curriculum, we have learned to ask first, "Does it pass the journalism test?" Does it have to do with the gathering, evaluating, displaying or dissemination of news, opinion, or information?

Red Smith offered his view of the field in *No Cheering in the Press Box* (Holt, Rinehart and Winston, 1974), a collection of interviews with sportswriters: "The guy I admire most in the world is a good reporter. I respect a good reporter, and I'd like to be called that. I'd like to be considered good and honest and reasonably accurate. The reporter has one of the toughest jobs in the world—getting as near the truth as possible is a terribly tough job."

That too is journalism.

In journalism research and reference, there is no end to the queries and projects requiring mental power, creativity, and knowledge, not to mention lightning speed, accuracy, integrity of sources and, frequently, clairvoyance.

I hope this helps.

1
Bibliographies and Bibliographic Guides

1. Alkire, Leland G., Jr., comp. **The Writer's Adviser**. Detroit, MI: Gale, 1985. 452p. index. LC 84-24715. ISBN 0-8103-2093-2.

    More than 800 books and 3,000 articles are cited in this popular guide to writing. Although it is most useful to fiction writers, the journalist may find an item or two of value. The 34 chapters include Television, Radio, and Film, Realism, Book Reviewing (a surprisingly scanty section—only 15 entries), Style Manuals, General Advice and Inspiration, and Freelancing. This is not a scholarly work and we are reminded in the introduction that it is for working writers "seeking advice and direction." Entries for books contain critical annotations. Article entries are not annotated at all. Even though this is not a comprehensive guide, there are some surprising omissions. Two articles written by Donald Murray, a writing coach, English professor, and Pulitzer Prize winner, are included, but none of his well-read books on writing such as *Writing for Your Readers* (Globe Pequot Press, 1983) are listed. Numerous articles are culled from *The Writer* and *Writer's Digest*.

2. Anderson, Peter J. **Research Guide in Journalism**. Morristown, NJ: General Learning Press, 1974. 229p. index. LC 73-84662.

    Less of a journalism research guide than a dated guide for journalism students, "this guide, if used correctly, will direct the reader to source material, and it will explain how to organize and document a paper in a style that is guaranteed to satisfy either a professor or an editor." It includes an annotated list of general reference sources arranged by subject, then alphabetically by title. Chapters on "How to Write and Research a Topic in Journalism," "The Library Card System," and "Form of the Paper" are provided, as well as a section on "Journalistic Instructions" which lists "top" instructors and schools of journalism. There is a subject and title index.

3. **"Articles on Mass Communication in U.S. and Foreign Journals: A Selected Annotated Bibliography."** *JQ: Journalism Quarterly*. (A current bibliography of articles is included in every issue of *Journalism Quarterly*.)

    Currently edited by Joseph P. McKerns, Alfred N. Delahaye, and Ronald E. Ostman, this selected, international listing of current mass communication articles plays a dual role as a journalism index. Entries are arranged alphabetically by author within the following subject sections: advertising, broadcasting, communication theory, community journalism, courts and law, criticism and defense of the media, education, government and media, history and biography, international, magazine, management, minorities, public opinion, public relations, research methods, technology, visual communication, women and media, etc. Annotations are brief and descriptive. Articles are selected from such journals as *Columbia Journalism Review, Journal of Broadcasting and Electronic Media, Newspaper Research Journal, Public Opinion Quarterly, Journal of Communication,* and *Journal of Mass Media Ethics. Journalism Quarterly* articles are indexed separately. For further information on *Journalism Quarterly*, see entry 529.

4.   **Asian Mass Communication Bibliographies**. Singapore: Asian Mass Communication Research and Information Centre, 1976-1983.

Included in this series of mass media bibliographies are the following: *Mass Communication in Malaysia* (1975); *Mass Communication in India* (1976); *Mass Communication in Hong Kong and Macao* (1976); *Mass Communication in the Philippines* (1976); *Mass Communication in Taiwan* (1977); *Mass Communication in Nepal* (1977); *Mass Communication in Singapore* (1977); *Mass Communication in the Republic of Korea* (1977); *Mass Communication in Indonesia* (1978); *Mass Communication in Sri Lanka* (1978); *Mass Communication in Thailand* (1983). They range in length from 34 pages (Nepal) to 335 pages (Philippines).

5.   Barnhart, Thomas F. **The Weekly Newspaper: A Bibliography – 1925-1941**. Minneapolis, MN: Burgess, 1941. 107p. LC 41-13300.

This is useful now only as a historical guide to weeklies, but one written by an authority. Barnhart is also the author of *Weekly Newspaper Makeup and Typography* (University of Minnesota Press, 1949), *Weekly Newspaper Management* (Appleton-Century-Crofts, 1952), and *Weekly Newspaper Writing and Editing* (Dryden Press, 1949). Part of a Works Progress Administration Project (later the Works Projects Administration), this annotated bibliography lists 1,200 articles, theses, books, and pamphlets by subject. Apparently, most of the articles included here were read and annotated by WPA workers. There is no index.

6.   Bennett, James R. **Control of Information in the United States: An Annotated Bibliography**. Westport, CT: Meckler, 1987. 587p. index. (Meckler Corporation's Bibliographies on Communications and First Amendment Law, no. 1). LC 87-16475. ISBN 0-88736-082-3.

Bennett has good control of his information, although the general introduction is fuzzy in parts. He states that "the process of creating and sustaining a national consensus in the United States is the subject of this bibliography." Assembling this guide was an ambitious undertaking, and he admits that the "compilation offers the tip of the iceberg." Information control is a central theme in journalism, and many entries relate to that topic. There are almost 3,000 descriptively annotated book and periodical entries on censorship and "primary sources of power," most published after 1945. Included is a list of periodicals cited, and it is an impressive selection of some lesser-known but invaluable publications. Sections are labeled broadly (anticommunism and anti-Sovietism, corporations, government, the Pentagon, intelligence agencies and global control), but are further broken down into more accessible subjects. A section on "The Complex" is a strange mix of the military-industrial, government regulation, media, education, and "secrecy, censorship, disinformation and deceit." There are almost 200 entries in the media section, although the excellent subject index indicates that other entries on that subject are scattered throughout the book. There is also a contributor index.

7.   Blum, Eleanor. **Basic Books in the Mass Media**. 2d ed. Urbana, IL: University of Illinois Press, 1980. 426p. index. LC 80-11289. ISBN 0-252-00814-6.

If a journalism librarian could choose only one reference book to take to a desert island library, it might be *Basic Books in the Mass Media*. Blum was communications librarian at the University of Illinois when she published this second edition of her selected booklist of reference and general mass communications literature. It evolved from the first edition, entitled *Reference Books in the Mass Media*. Even though it is "selected," it contains 1,179 entries and is the most comprehensive and current bibliography available on mass communication. Chapters are broken down into general communications, books and book publishing, broadcasting, editorial journalism, film, magazines, and advertising and public relations. A chapter by Frances Wilhoit, head of the journalism library at Indiana University, is devoted to mass communication indexes. The author-title and subject indexes are complete and usable. Annotations are well-written and generally descriptive. The eagerly-awaited third edition will be published in late 1989 or 1990.

8. **Broadcasting Bibliography: A Guide to the Literature of Radio and Television**. 2d ed. Compiled by the NAB Library Staff. Washington, D.C.: National Association of Broadcasters, 1984. 66p.

A short, selective, and easy-to-follow listing of current basic books in broadcasting, this bibliography was compiled by people who ought to know. It includes an author-title index and a detailed table of contents, so lack of a subject index is not a problem. Chapters on fundamentals (mostly reference sources), business, law, and technology are arranged logically. A listing of almost 100 broadcasting periodicals, magazines, and newsletters is a bonus.

9. Brown, Charles H., comp. **Reader's Guide to the Literature of Journalism**. University Park, PA: Pennsylvania State University, School of Journalism, 1961. 87p. LC 62-09665.

This selected, annotated, but outdated bibliography, primarily on the historical and biographical literature of journalism, aims at the "general reader" and student. Though it is not a scholarly work, it is worth browsing through. Be prepared to skim, as there is no index. Entries are listed alphabetically by author in sections on history, major figures, special fields of journalism, women in journalism, government and the press, advertising, broadcasting, magazines, public opinion, etc.

10. Buteau, June D. **Nonprint Materials on Communication: An Annotated Directory of Select Films, Videotapes, Videocassettes, Simulations and Games**. Metuchen, NJ: Scarecrow Press, 1976. 444p. index. LC 76-21857. ISBN 0-8108-0973-7.

Communication is broadly defined in this dated listing of more than 1,400 audiovisual materials: "Communication is interpreted as a reflection of the process, primarily oral—the exchanges of messages, meaning, information. The written criticism and evaluation, however, plus the research preparation related thereto must of necessity be included." Chapters on films, videotapes and cassettes, simulations and games, and other sources are subdivided by subject into sections on educational technology, interview, language, persuasion, rhetorical topics, mass media, etc. Entries are numbered and include title, length and format, producer, distributor, sponsor, and a brief description. According to the author, most of these materials are aimed at college students. Annotations are not evaluative and many entries are undated.

A sample entry is as follows:

> He Couldn't Take It. Film-Maker's Cooperative, 1969. 11min. b/w. In this satire, Ted Baily attempts to live quietly without the interruptions of media (war news on the radio, music, commercials and stock market reports). Enticed out of his home, he becomes persuaded to race for a "bonus" of trading stamps. While accelerating, he loses his life. His desired serenity finally comes "without the interruption of more media."

The peculiar cross-category index lists all titles by subject and refers users to other subject categories of interest, but does not list entry or page numbers for individual titles.

The following sources might be useful as well: "Films About Newspapers," a booklet published by the American Newspaper Publishers Association; the "Films About Newspapers" section in the annual *Editor & Publisher International Yearbook* (entry 285); Michael D. Murray and Jack Colldeweih's "Source Catalog for Audio-Visual Material in Journalism" (ERIC, ED 159736, 1976) and "More Help for the Harried Professor: A Selected Program of Tapes in Print and Broadcast Journalism" (ERIC, ED 151805, 1976).

11. Buxton, Frank, and Bill Owen. **The Big Broadcast, 1920-1950**. New York: Viking, 1972. 301p. index. LC 73-149272. ISBN 670-16240-X.

Network radio programs are listed alphabetically and most entries include dates and characters. Cast lists and series histories are included for some listings. The section on networks, news, and newscasters could be useful. There is a name index only.

12.   Canadian Radio-Television Commission. **Bibliographie, Etudes Canadiennes sur les Mass Media: Bibliography, Some Writings on the Canadian Mass Media**. Ottawa: The Commission, 1975. 99p. index.

The journalism department at Université Laval, Quebec, and the Canadian Radio-Television Commission list in French and English more than 1,000 books, government documents, dissertations, and journal articles focusing on most aspects of mass media in Canada. Works are either written by Canadians or published by authors living in Canada. Also included are "works published by American firms with Canadian branches (on the advice of the National Library) if they were published in Canada as well as in the States." Items are numbered and arranged alphabetically by author. There are no annotations. An unusual subject index is divided into sections on references (bibliographies, biographies, statistics), media and society, areas of research, etc., and further subdivided.

13.   Cannon, Carl Leslie, comp. **Journalism: A Bibliography**. Detroit, MI: Gale, 1967 (Reprint of 1924 edition). 360p. LC 66-25646.

In the preface, Cannon states he has emphasized the present rather than the historical; thus, this list includes references useful to the "American newspaperman actively engaged in his profession or to the student of journalism." One of the first bibliographies of journalism, it is now an excellent historical study of the newspaper press in the United States and Great Britain from the 1800s to 1923. This partially annotated list contains the New York Public Library's journalism holdings as well as material outside that library, and includes books, magazine articles, pamphlets, and other materials. There are more than 30 topical chapters, including the Negro press, the morgue, paragraphing, sensational journalism, and the country press.

14.   Cassata, Mary, and Thomas Skill. **Television: A Guide to the Literature**. Phoenix, AZ: Oryx Press, 1985. 148p. index. LC 83-43236. ISBN 0-89774-140-4.

The three main parts of this book defy definition: Test Patterns, The Environment, and Directions. It is not a traditional guide, but a collection of bibliographic essays on various aspects of television and television research. A bibliography is included at the end of each chapter. This guide was originally published in three parts in *Choice* (January, February, April 1982), and was expanded in this guide to include more than 400 entries. "Test Patterns" includes chapters on the mass communication process, television history, and reference sources. "The Environment" covers television and children and contains good introductory essays on television news and television and politics. "Directions" gives an overview of the television industry, programming and policy, and skims sources in television criticism. An expanded section on ethics would be very helpful. There is no mention of online sources. There are author, title, and subject indexes.

15.   Caswell, Lucy Shelton. **Guide to Sources in American Journalism History**. Westport, CT: Greenwood Press, 1989. 319p. LC 89-11857. ISBN 0-313-26178-4. (Bibliographies and Indexes in Mass Media and Communications, no. 2).

The publication of Caswell's *Guide* was announced as *Journalism: A Guide to the Reference Literature* was going to press. Aiming at both scholars and students, this is a guide to archival and manuscript collections in journalism. Included are essays on the United States Newspaper Program, historical writing, research, and oral history. Jean Ward and Kathleen Hansen (authors of *Search Strategies in Mass Communication*, entry 371) contribute essays on bibliographies and databases.

16.   Chin, Felix. **Cable Television: A Comprehensive Bibliography**. New York: IFI/Plenum, 1978. 285p. index. LC 78-1526. ISBN 0-306-65172-6.

Chin says he has "attempted to provide the reader with all the best material ever published on any topic related to one of the most active areas of broadcasting, cable television." Annotations of 650 books, journal articles, and pamphlets are organized by subject. There is a subject and name index, as well as appendices on CATV systems, associations, and FCC rules. The "Chronology of Major Decisions and Actions Affecting Cable Television" through the mid-1970s might prove useful, even if the information is a little dated.

17.   Christians, Clifford, and Vernon Jensen. **Two Bibliographies on Ethics.** 2d ed. Minneapolis, MN: Silha Center for the Study of Media Ethics and Law, School of Journalism and Mass Communication, University of Minnesota, 1988. 49p. (No. 86093).
      Christians's "Books on Media Ethics" are arranged chronologically beginning with Nelson Crawford's *The Ethics of Journalism* (A. A. Knopf, 1924) in this nine-page bibliography. A brief introduction describes the scope of the publication and offers some background information on the author. Jensen's 36-page "Ethics in Speech Communication" is divided into sections on books and dissertations, chapters of books, journal articles, and bibliographic aids, and is arranged alphabetically by author. As would be expected, there is some overlap. Of 41 titles in the Christians list, 26 are included in Jensen's. Jensen, however, has not noted, as Christians does, later editions of at least four titles.

18.   Cooper, Thomas W., comp. **Television and Ethics: An Annotated Bibliography.** Boston, MA: G. K. Hall, 1988. 203p. index. LC 88-7206. ISBN 0-8161-8966-8.
      "Designed to assist readers and researchers interested in the relationships between television and ethics," this selectively annotated bibliography was compiled by Cooper, with the reference and research aid of other staffers at Emerson College (and inspired, no doubt, by Emerson's annual Television and Ethics Conference). It lists 1,170 titles, 473 of which are annotated. A lengthy introduction and methodology section prepare the user for what lies ahead. For example, when describing the book's audience, Cooper writes: "Hence, a balance among general, academic, professional, and trade publications has been sought. One finding, however, is that such a balance does not exist naturally within the field .... Consequently, the small proportion of titles from trade and industry journals represents an imbalance discovered during our searches."
      Fortunately, author and subject indexes allow relatively easy access to these important citations. Some introductory notes require second and third readings for clarity, such as the following:

> At the conclusion of each abstract, authorship and editing are ascribed in chronological order of the writing and adaptation of each abstract. For example, if the original abstract submitted by the author was ideal for his bibliography, the citation conclusion of the abstract reads <AU>, "author." If however, the Journal of Dissertation Abstracts in Journalism and Mass Communications (fictitious title) edited the author's abstract, which was rewritten by us for this bibliography, the final citation conclusion would read "author/ JODAJMC/editor," or in our abbreviated terms <AU/JOD/ED>.

The first section of the bibliography focuses on ethical contexts and contains chapters on classical ethics, professional ethics, communication and mass media ethics, journalism ethics, and teaching media ethics. Part 2, television and ethics, includes advertising, children and television, television news, entertainment, public and educational television, etc. Cooper offers a star-studded list of advisory editors (Clifford G. Christians, Eugene Goodwin, J. Michael Kittross, Donald L. McBride, Robert Roberts, and Christopher Sterling) and contributors (Christians, Goodwin, Kittross, McBride, Roberts, Sterling, Deni Elliott, Edmund B. Lambeth, John Merrill, Robert Picard, and Robert Schmuhl, to name a few). In addition, Peter Medaglia acted as managing editor, Robert Sullivan as research editor, and Christopher Weir as business editor.

19.   Danielson, Wayne A., and G. C. Wilhoit, Jr., comps. **A Computerized Bibliography of Mass Communication Research, 1944-1964**. New York: Magazine Publishers Association, Inc., 1967. 399p. index.

The Education Committee of the Magazine Publishers Association supported this study, and that may explain the emphasis on magazines in the 2,287 entries. It was published in the late 1960s, and the compilers and publisher were proud of their computer printout bibliography, as emphasized by the title. Its purpose is to "provide magazine executives and others with a comprehensive introduction to the social science journal literature on mass communication." Almost 50 social science journals were searched for mass communication-related articles published from 1944-1964, and this is the result. Numerous citations focus on broadcasting. Entries are arranged alphabetically by author, but the bibliography does not begin until page 192 because of a massive 191-page key-word index.

20.   De Mott, John, and Robert Roberts. **White Racism, Blacks, and Mass Communications: An Instruction Source Bibliography**. Paper presented at the Annual Meeting of the Association for Education in Journalism, Houston, TX, 5-8 August 1979. 35p. ERIC, ED 176 315.

Without table of contents, index, and annotations, how useful can this be? It all depends on the purpose of the guide, and the authors believe that this listing of about 500 books, periodical and magazine articles is sufficient "for the construction of not only a full complement of instructional units in a conventional program but also for creation of a comprehensive course in blacks and the media." Chapters include general listings on race relations, black history, and black mass media, but chapters most useful for the stated purpose of this bibliography are "Minorities and the Mass Media: Effects, Criticism, Portrayals" and "Employment of Blacks in the Mass Media." Entries are dated from the 1940s to the mid 1970s. If this bibliography is used in the classroom, it probably should be updated to include the last 10 years.

21.   Du Charme, Rita, comp. **Bibliography of Media Management and Economics**. 2d ed. Minneapolis, MN: Media Management and Economics Resource Center, University of Minnesota, 1988. 131p. ISBN 0-944866-01-8.

Approximately 400 books on media management are listed here. Unfortunately, it is not annotated, and the author admits that, "in an effort to be complete," all books listed have not necessarily been read. The subject categories are broad and include sections on broadcasting, cable, journalists, newspaper management, newspapers, etc. Books are arranged alphabetically by author within the subject areas. The 54-page index (authors only) includes the authors' indexed works, but no corresponding text page numbers. The compiler states that this bibliography will be issued annually (the first edition appeared in 1986). A form of this bibliography is included in John M. Lavine and Daniel B. Wackman's *Managing Media Organizations* (Longman, 1988).

22.   Dunn, M. Gilbert, and Douglas W. Cooper. **"A Guide to Mass Communications Sources."** *Journalism Monographs* 74, 1981. 42p.

Reference sources in mass communications are discussed in this handy bibliographic essay aimed at the social scientist. The authors say that "in the absence of any comprehensive guide to these data sources, many scholars are unaware of the available resources" and fail to mention Eleanor Blum's *Basic Books in the Mass Media* (entry 7) in the introductory comments. (Blum is, however, listed in the appendix, "A Selected List of Directories, Bibliographies and Indexes Useful in Mass Communications Research.") There are separate sections on print and electronic media, and each contains discussions of indexes, union lists, catalogs, archives, etc. Cable television, book publishing, and advertising are excluded.

23.   Einstein, Daniel. **Special Edition: A Guide to Network Television Documentary Series and Special News Reports, 1955-1979**. Metuchen, NJ: Scarecrow Press, 1987. 1,051p. index. LC 86-6599. ISBN 0-8108-1898-1.

More than 7,000 major network documentary programs, specials, and major series are listed and annotated. In the introduction, Einstein touches on the history and evolution of the documentary, and talks about television as a "tool for actuality reportage." By the mid-1980s, the magazine format and docudrama had all but snuffed out the long-form documentary. He relies on *TV Guide, Television Index*, and network and production company files for data. Part 1 consists of documentary series programming from 1955-1979. Part 2 includes documentaries produced by David L. Wolper, and part 3 lists television news specials and special reports. For the most part, Einstein excluded presidential press conferences, space-shot coverage, and nonfiction public television broadcasts. Entries are numbered and arranged by date of telecast. There are indexes to personalities and production/technical personnel. Title and subject indexes would make this a far more accessible source, but at least (and at last) the information is under one cover.

24.   Fejes, Fred. **Gays, Lesbians and the Media: A Selected Bibliography**. Boca Raton, FL: Department of Communication, Florida Atlantic University, 1987. 23p.

Media coverage of the gay and lesbian community makes for interesting and important bibliographical coverage, especially in the wake of extensive AIDS reporting. Fejes is concerned that most gay publications are not included in basic indexes he searched (*Business Periodicals Index, Communication Abstracts, Readers' Guide to Periodical Literature, Sociological Abstracts*, etc.), but fails to note that many of the journalism trade journals also are not indexed. It is in those journals and newsletters, most of which are not cited here, that a wealth of information can be found on this topic. This selected listing of more than 200 citations to newspaper and periodical articles, chapters in books, some dissertations, and books published primarily in the 1970s and 1980s is arranged alphabetically by author. There is no index, no table of contents, and no subject subdivision. A separate section on AIDS and the media would be most helpful. There is always a need for specialized bibliographies such as this, but annotations and indexes are usually advised. (For example, one must search out a 1981 issue of *Jump Cut* to find out what B. Zimmerman has to say about "Lesbian Vampires.") This list is a good starting point, but do not stop the search here.

25.   Fisher, Kim N. **On the Screen: A Film, Television, and Video Research Guide**. Littleton, CO: Libraries Unlimited, 1986. 209p. index. (Reference Sources in the Humanities Series). LC 86-20965. ISBN 0-87287-448-6.

Fisher has produced a timely, well-written, and nicely organized beginner's guide to the reference literature of television and motion pictures. It is included here because a substantial number of entries focuses on radio, television news, broadcast journalism, and other subjects relevant to journalism research. Annotations are both descriptive and evaluative, and the user has a definite sense as to the usefulness of each and every source. For example, it is good to know that some "browsing and digging is required," or that a particular source is "out of date but still respected," or that "a number of entries oddly conclude with a reference to the performer's sign in the zodiac." Most entries encompass the time period from the early 1960s through 1985, and focus on English-language works. Chapters are divided into broad categories based on type of reference work, and then further subdivided into film and television video sections. Entries are arranged alphabetically within chapters. Chapters on core periodicals, research centers, and societies and associations are included. The author/title and subject indexes are detailed.

26.   Ford, Edwin H. **History of Journalism in the United States: A Bibliography of Books and Annotated Articles**. Minneapolis, MN: Burgess, 1938. 42p.

According to Ford, "It is hoped that the references set down hereafter will serve to start students of the history of American journalism on a quest for precise and enlightening information." Of course, this is a dated source but an excellent listing of earlier works in American journalism history. Also included are brief sections on the British press. This bibliography is a Works Progress Administration project.

27.   Friedman, Leslie J. **Sex Role Stereotyping in the Mass Media: An Annotated Bibliography**. New York: Garland, 1977. 324p. index. (Reference Library of Social Science, vol. 47). LC 76-52685. ISBN 0-8240-9865-X.

Although in need of updating, Friedman's bibliography still offers a rich historical perspective. There are more than 1,000 references to books and book chapters, government documents, magazine and journal articles, theses, speeches, and other studies, and perhaps 200 of them touch on sex roles, stereotyping, and the news media, mass media, and print media. Articles from *Journalism Quarterly, Editor & Publisher, ASNE Bulletin, Columbia Journalism Review* and the defunct *Chicago Journalism Review* are included. Entries are numbered and arrangement is alphabetical by author within subject categories. Author and subject indexes are included.

28.   Gandy, Oscar H., Jr., Susan Miller, William J. Rivers, and Gail Ann Rivers. **Media and Government: An Annotated Bibliography**. Stanford, CA: Stanford University Institute for Communication Research, 1975. 93p. LC 80-456075.

According to the introduction, "this bibliography is ambitious." Books, book chapters, and journal articles (many from *Journalism Quarterly* and *Public Opinion Quarterly*) are included in this bibliography on government and the media, which "consists primarily of prototype studies which are, in the opinion of experts, outstanding or representative examples of research." Entries are arranged alphabetically by author and include bibliographic citation, methodology, and a description of findings or conclusions. Unfortunately, there is no table of contents or index, so those less familiar with names of experts will have to scan. It is divided into sections on the nature of news media, government information systems, impact of government on media, and the impact of media on government. Many familiar names turn up here: Altschull, Bagdikian, Argyris, Bogart, Wilhoit, Weaver, Polich, Nimmo, Guback, Emery, Schiller, Rivers, and Schramm, to name a few.

29.   Genther, Fred L., comp. **Guide to News and Information Sources for Journalists.** Rev. ed. San Luis Obispo, CA: California Polytechnic State University, 1981. 58p.

It is a little dated now, but Genther's guide can still serve as one skeletal introduction to the reference literature of journalism. Genther, who was a reference librarian at the Kennedy Library at California Polytechnic State University, selected about 100 sources he felt were most useful to journalism students and beginning reporters. Most entries are descriptively annotated, and parts of the guide center on holdings at the Cal Poly Library. Chapters are arranged according to subject matter or type of reference book. For example, there are sections on directories and dictionaries as well as chapters on marketing, advertising, and journalism law. There is no mention of online sources and there is no index. A journalism professor at the University writes in the introduction: "Familiarity with the GUIDE won't turn young reporters into amateur librarians. Nor will its use make more advanced news people able to solve all research problems without professional assistance." It is instead a "useful entente."

30.   Gillmor, Donald M., Theodore L. Glasser, and Victoria Smith. **"Mass Media Law: A Selected Bibliography."** Minneapolis, MN: Silha Center for the Study of Media Ethics and Law, University of Minnesota, School of Journalism and Mass Communication, 1987. 31p.

An unannotated listing of books and periodical articles on media law, this bibliography is arranged by subject, then author. There are sections on case books and general texts, the First Amendment, libel, privacy, courts, obscenity and pornography, broadcast and cable regulation, commercial speech, student press, and legal research. Gillmor also wrote (with Jerome A. Barron) *Mass Communication Law* (West, 1984).

31.   Gitter, A. George, and Robert Grunin, eds. **Communication: A Guide to Information Sources**. Detroit, MI: Gale, 1980. 157p. index. (Psychology Information Guide Series, vol. 3, Gale Information Guide Library). LC 79-26527. ISBN 0-8103-1443-6.

Almost half of the 723 references in this annotated guide are mass communications articles (many from *Journalism Quarterly*) or books, and they are divided into general subjects such as broadcasting, radio, television, and journalism. Most entries are from the

1970s, and are numbered and arranged alphabetically by author. As the editors indicate, they are "extending the work of previously published bibliographies in the areas that cover the literature through the late 1960s." As such, this source should be used in tandem with more comprehensive book bibliographies such as Blum's *Basic Books in the Mass Media* (entry 7). One chapter is devoted to reference works. Author, title, and subject indexes are included.

32.   Gordon, Thomas F., and Mary Ellen Verna, comps. **Mass Communication Effects and Processes: A Comprehensive Bibliography, 1950-1975**. Beverly Hills, CA: Sage, 1978. 227p. LC 77-26094. ISBN 0-8039-0903-9.

This comprehensive research bibliography lists references to psychological and social effects of the media from 1950-1975. The Literature Overview section is rather tedious, but a necessary evil in using this source. There are 2,704 entries with very few annotations, and the body of the bibliography is arranged alphabetically by author. The subject index is detailed and cross-referenced, but not designed for quick and easy access. Useful entries can be found indexed under magazines, newspapers, credibility, journalism, minorities, news, radio, and television. Gordon and Verna also wrote *Mass Media and Socialization: A Selected Bibliography* (Temple University, 1973).

33.   Gray, David B. **"A Bibliography for Newspaper Design, Graphics and Photos."** Providence, RI: The Providence Journal-Bulletin. Frequent updates.

Bibliographical information on newspaper and magazine design is, at best, scattered. Gray, managing editor of graphics at *The Providence Journal-Bulletin*, realizes this and publishes a short (usually 10-12 pages) and critically annotated bibliography of books, periodicals, magazine and journal articles, clip art, organizations, etc. A note at the end of the bibliography indicates this is updated "almost every month." It is a hodgepodge listing, with no index or table of contents. Citations for books include price and ISBN number, but no publication year. Listings appear under headings such as "How-To-Do Graphics," "Sources of Information for Graphics," "Graphics Services and Organizations," "Photo-journalism," "Newspaper Design," "Typography," "Mac Clip Art," "Tools for Pictures and Type," "Management: Appropriate or Helpful in Managing 'Creative' People," "Miscellaneous Publications," "Color," and "Computers/Electronics." Gray also indicates publications of interest to those working with Apple Macintosh equipment. He has pulled together much of the elusive literature in this pamphlet and has done designers a great service. Gray recommends Ed Henninger's "A Bibliography for Newspaper Designers" (entry 37), which is a listing of more than 200 books on design, graphics, and typography.

34.   Greenfield, Thomas Allen. **Radio: A Reference Guide**. Westport, CT: Greenwood Press, 1989. 185p. ISBN 0-313-22276-2.

The publication of *Radio: A Reference Guide* was announced as *Journalism: A Guide to the Reference Literature* was going to press. It is described as "an evaluative survey of bibliographical material on the history and development of radio and radio programming in America."

35.   Hansen, Donald A., and J. Herschel Parsons. **Mass Communication: A Research Bibliography**. Santa Barbara, CA: Glendessary Press, 1968. 144p.

The authors offer their opinions on existing mass communication research and say that numerous books and reports

> range in quality from the profound to the trivial, but—compared to at least some other fields—a disturbing majority must be categorized near the latter end of such a continuum. That disturbing majority has for the most part been omitted from this bibliography. This is not to say that each of the studies listed here is of unquestionable quality, but rather that the unquestionably valueless have been excluded.

Entries for nearly 3,000 scholarly journal articles, reports, and monographs from 1945 to the mid-1960s are divided into sections on bibliographies and reference materials, research and methods, social contexts of media, audience and diffusion, etc. Entries are further subdivided into such sections as general theory and content, and arranged alphabetically by author. There is, unfortunately, no subject index, nor are annotations provided. Scholarly research for the "social theorist" is emphasized, so users searching for *Editor & Publisher*-type citations are advised to look further.

36.   Hausman, Linda Weiner. **"Criticism of the Press in U.S. Periodicals: 1900-1939."** *Journalism Monographs*, no. 4, 1967. 49p. LC 68-06952. ISSN 0022-5525.

Hausman pulled some 500 articles on press criticism from the trusty *Readers' Guide to Periodical Literature* and concentrated on the time period starting at the turn of the century to the beginning of World War II. It is not the definitive listing, but a good starting point for students researching the time period.

37.   Henninger, Ed. **"A Bibliography for Newspaper Designers."** 2d ed. Dayton, OH: Dayton Daily News, 1988.

Henninger, assistant managing editor for graphics at the *Dayton Daily News*, offers a second edition of his unannotated bibliography for newspaper artists and designers. Arranged alphabetically by author, he lists more than 200 textbooks, catalogs, manuals, and other publications in graphic design, layout, color, and typography. Henninger has marked titles which "are strong on basics," so this guide will also be useful as a supplemental reading list for students. Entries include title and publisher, but, unfortunately, no date of publication. For another newspaper graphics editor's must-read list, see David Gray's "A Bibliography for Newspaper Design, Graphics and Photos" (entry 33).

38.   Higgens, Gavin, ed. **British Broadcasting 1922-1982: A Selected and Annotated Bibliography**. London: British Broadcasting Corporation Data Publications, 1983. 279p. ISBN 0-563-12137-8.

Annotated references to English-language books, periodical articles, and pamphlets from the 1920s to the early 1980s are listed in this bibliography of radio and television broadcasting. Brief and descriptive annotations emphasize the BBC.

39.   Hill, George H. **Black Media in America: A Resource Guide**. Boston, MA: G. K. Hall, 1984. 333p. index. (Reference Publication in Black Studies). LC 84-15672. ISBN 0-8161-8610-3.

In his preface, Hill, vice-president of a television production company and public relations firm, states that "this annotated bibliography seeks to be the most comprehensive and exhaustive bibliography ever compiled on black media." This partially annotated bibliography of books and periodical and magazine articles is not exhaustive. A "Communications/Media Works" section is divided into Books and Monographs, Dissertations and Theses. These are not arranged according to subject, and, unfortunately, the index is scanty. *JQ* is cited in both Journal References and the Newspaper and Magazine Articles section. Nowhere are *presstime, ASNE Bulletin*, or smaller journalism reviews mentioned. This is not a scholarly work, but because few reference sources have dealt with this topic, it should be consulted initially.

40.   Hill, George H., and Sylvia Saverson Hill. **Blacks on Television: A Selectively Annotated Bibliography**. Metuchen, NJ: Scarecrow Press, 1985. 223p. index. LC 84-23639. ISBN 0-8108-1774-8.

"Selectively annotated" is an understatement. The authors cover 45 years of black involvement in television and list more than 2,800 entries, but only books, dissertations, and theses (less than 60) are annotated. A surprisingly small section of journal article citations is taken from communications periodicals, and a search in *Social Sciences Index*, for example, reveals that relevant entries are absent. More than 2,600 popular magazine article entries are divided into 40 sections, but the table of contents and subject/author index do not show it. Because of its limitations, this bibliography is best used as a source for popular literature on blacks in broadcasting, religious broadcasting, broadcast management and ownership, news, and news/talk programs.

41. Hoerder, Dirk, ed. (Christine Harzig, ass't. ed.) **The Immigrant Labor Press in North America, 1840s-1970s: An Annotated Bibliography.** Westport, CT: Greenwood Press, 1987. index. (Bibliographies and Indexes in American History, no. 4, 7-8). LC 87-168. **Volume 1: Migrants from Northern Europe.** 278p. ISBN 0-313-24638-6. **Volume 2: Labor Migrants from Eastern and Southeastern Europe.** 725p. ISBN 0-313-26077-X. **Volume 3: Migrants from Southern and Western Europe.** 583p. ISBN 0-313-26078-8.
 According to the editors,

> the idea of compiling this bibliography was born when it became obvious that the detailed studies of the role of individual ethnic groups in the North American working classes already available needed to be supplemented by a broad comparative approach taking into account the cultures of origin, migration processes, and specific forms of acculturation in the United States or Canada.

Each volume provides a lengthy introduction and user's guide, a discussion of the immigrant labor (not union) press, and descriptions of individual newspapers and periodicals. Volume 1 focuses on Northern Europe; volume 2, Eastern and Southeastern Europe; volume 3, Southern and Western Europe. From Lithuanians to Dutch-Speaking Peoples, chapters are arranged primarily by language group, are written by experts, and include an introduction, bibliography, and title, place, and chronological indexes. Entries include translated titles, editors, publishers, dates, and depositories. These three volumes grew out of a 1978 symposium, "American Labor and Immigration History, 1877-1920s: Recent European Research," held at the University of Bremen, Federal Republic of Germany, where a project entitled "Bibliography and Archival Presentation of Non-English Language Labor and Radical Newspapers and Periodicals in North America, 1840s-1970s" was proposed. Other useful sources on the ethnic press include Sally Miller's *The Ethnic Press in the United States* (entry 475) and Lubomyr R. Wynar's *Encyclopedic Directory of Ethnic Newspapers and Periodicals in the United States* (entry 322).

42. Hoffman, Frederick J., Charles Allen, and Carolyn F. Ulrich. **The Little Magazine: A History and Bibliography.** 2d ed. Princeton, NJ: Princeton University Press, 1947. 450p.
 The little magazine is an "important source of information about twentieth century writing," according to the authors. The first half of the book defines *little magazines* and places them in historical perspective. The second half is a chronological listing of magazines by year, then alphabetically. Most magazines listed began after 1910. Publication history and editorial information are provided and the length of the annotation is a good indication of the magazine's overall importance. There also is a supplementary list of about 100 magazines which influenced the little magazine movement.

43. Howell, John Bruce. **Style Manuals of the English-Speaking World: A Guide.** Phoenix, AZ: Oryx Press, 1983. 138p. index. LC 82-42916. ISBN 0-89774-089-0.
 Manuals from the United States, Canada, and Great Britain are included, as well as a sampling of style manuals from the "English language publishing communities" of Australia, India, New Zealand, Nigeria, etc. Most of the manuals are current (published between 1970-1983) or "classic." To be included, the manual must be at least five pages long and in English. The "General Manual" section contains 124 entries arranged alphabetically and further subdivided into commercial publishers, government printing, term papers and theses, and university presses. Notes on bibliographic style are included. More than 100 entries are arranged alphabetically by compiler in the "Subject Manual" section. Subjects range from agriculture to zoology. Most of the stylebooks under the "News and News Magazines" heading are included in chapter 8 of this text. An appendix describes three handbooks on nonsexist language. The index includes compilers, titles, and general subjects.

44.   Jackson, Fleda Brown, Wm. David Sloan, and James R. Bennett. **"Journalism as Art: A Selective Annotated Bibliography."** *Style* 16 (1982): 466-487.

This small and selective journalism bibliography is included here because its topic is widely discussed in the classroom and the newsroom. What is the difference between journalism and literature? Is there a difference? Should there be? Books, journal articles, masters' theses, and other sources are examined, and the bibliography is divided into three parts. The first section includes historical studies of journalism and studies of individual writers. Part 2 is entitled "Journalism as Literary Art," and the last section concerns journalistic prose style. Entries are arranged alphabetically within the three sections. The authors surveyed basic journalism bibliographies and 30 communications, mass communications, and journalism magazines and periodicals. This is a broad overview of an even broader subject, but it works. It is a useful starting point.

45.   **Journalism Bibliography**. Julian Adams, ed. Blue Springs, MO: Journalism Education Association, Inc., 1984. 16p.

This excellent bibliography of scholastic journalism is packed with several hundred book citations with brief annotations. Entries are arranged alphabetically by author within sections on high school journalism textbooks, advising school publications, yearbooks, history, freedom of the press, radio and television, style, editorial and opinion writing, photojournalism, careers, etc. Most entries were published from 1975 through 1983.

46.   Kaid, Lynda Lee, Keith R. Sanders, and Robert O. Hirsch. **Political Campaign Communication: A Bibliography and Guide to the Literature**. Metuchen, NJ: Scarecrow Press, 1974. 206p. index. LC 73-22492. ISBN 0-8108-0704-1.

More than 1,500 books, pamphlets, journal articles, public documents, theses, and dissertations on political campaign communication in the United States from 1950-1972 are included in this bibliography. The authors carefully explain scope and methodology, and indicate that "its major purpose is to offer suggestions as to how the user may stay abreast of this burgeoning literature, using the bibliographic entries provided here as a point of departure." Included is an annotated list of 50 books "we believe to be seminal to the study of political campaign communication" and a list in German and French of books and periodical articles with foreign perspectives. Entries are numbered and arranged alphabetically by author. There are no annotations. See also *Political Campaign Communication: A Bibliography and Guide to the Literature 1973-1982* (entry 47).

47.   Kaid, Lynda Lee, and Anne Johnston Wadsworth. **Political Campaign Communication: A Bibliography and Guide to the Literature 1973-1982**. Metuchen, NJ: Scarecrow Press, 1985. 217p. LC 84-23508. ISBN 0-8108-1764-0.

Political communication embraces many fields and disciplines, and researching this general subject can sometimes be an overwhelming task. The authors are to be congratulated for this update of *Political Campaign Communication: A Bibliography and Guide to the Literature* (entry 46). This bibliography lists 2,461 English-language books, pamphlets, journal articles, dissertations, and theses. Popular magazine and newspaper articles, unpublished papers, and government documents are not included; neither do the authors mention in the introduction whether they conducted online searches of the literature. Publications on the role and effects of the communications media, credibility of the mass media, and media use in political campaigns are covered, in addition to general works on political campaigns. One must rely on the subject index to gain entry to the bibliography. Citations are in alphabetical order and numbered consecutively. This guide is the starting point for most scholarly research on this subject.

48.   Kittross, John M., comp. **A Bibliography of Theses and Dissertations in Broadcasting: 1920-1973**. Washington, D.C.: Broadcast Education Association, 1978. 238p.

Kittross reminds the user that "much of what we know about mass communication was the product of graduate-level research." He continues, "Often, a thesis or dissertation affects more people than any other single piece of work in a person's career." On that note, more than 4,300 dissertations and theses from American universities are highlighted. All aspects of broadcasting are covered. In a section entitled "How This Project Came About," Kittross offers details on other bibliographies upon which this publication is built: "Doctoral Dissertations in Radio and Television, 1920-1957," and "Graduate Theses and Dissertations in Broadcasting: A Topical Index," both of which appeared in the *Journal of Broadcasting* in the late 1950s. Some statistical analyses are included, as well as subject, key-word, and chronological indexes. A table of contents refers the user to page numbers, but the pages are not numbered. The numbered entries are arranged alphabetically by author and include title of thesis or dissertation, college or university, year degree awarded and, when available, last name of thesis adviser.

49.   Kowalski, Rosemary Ribich. **Women and Film: A Bibliography**. Metuchen, NJ: Scarecrow Press, 1976. 278p. index. LC 76-25051. ISBN 0-8108-0974-5.

A chapter on women columnists and critics containing more than 150 entries is the selling point of this bibliography. There are more than 2,000 book and article references with brief descriptive annotations, usually one sentence, arranged alphabetically by author within chapters. There is a name and subject index. As one might guess, there are numerous references to Pauline Kael.

50.   La Brie, Henry G. III. **The Black Press: A Bibliography**. Kennebunkport, ME: Mercer Press, 1973. 39p.

A simple one-page preface introduces 400 entries on the black press, subdivided into sections on books, periodicals and monographs, unpublished theses and papers, and newspaper articles. Entries range from I. Garland Penn's *The Afro-American Press and Its Editors* (Ayer, 1969, reprint of 1891 ed.) to Lawrence D. Reddick's unpublished dissertation "The Negro and the New Orleans Press, 1850-1860." There is no index.

51.   Lasswell, Harold D., Ralph D. Casey, and Bruce Lannes Smith. **Propaganda and Promotional Activities: An Annotated Bibliography**. Chicago, IL: University of Chicago Press (c1935), 1969. 450p. LC 75-77979.

McCoy does not include a great deal about propaganda in his *Freedom of the Press: An Annotated Bibliography* (entry 61), but suggests that those searching for studies of propaganda turn to this Lasswell and Smith volume. That is fine advice. This volume was more than 30 years old when it was reissued, and it is still valid today. (It was updated by Smith, Lasswell, and Casey in 1946 in *Propaganda Communication, and Public Opinion: A Comprehensive Reference Guide* [entry 91].) The authors indicate that this is a "research tool for use of specialists in the social sciences, as well as for a more general public." Descriptive annotations are, according to the authors, "terse." Divided into several subject sections, the most useful ones might be the channels of propaganda, and censorship and propaganda. Author and subject indexes are included, as well as cross references.

52.   Lent, John A. **Asian Mass Communications: A Comprehensive Bibliography**. Philadelphia, PA: Temple University School of Communications and Theater,1975. 708p. LC 76-621167. Supplement, 1978. 619p.

This massive bibliography embraces all aspects of mass communications in Asia, and there are thousands of entries. Subjects include advertising, public relations, film, freedom of the press, government information, history, news agencies, printed media, radio, and television. The supplement alone includes more than 8,000 entries found since 1974 and new material on Mongolia, Nepal, etc. Journal, periodical, and newspaper articles, as well as books, speeches, theses, dissertations, and conference proceedings, are listed but not annotated. Arrangement is by region (Asia, East Asia, Southeast Asia, and South Asia), country, then subject. It is unfortunate to find a volume of this size and scope with no index.

53.   Lent, John A. **Caribbean Mass Communications: A Comprehensive Bibliography**. Waltham, MA: Crossroads Press, 1981. 152p. (Archival and Bibliographical Series). ISBN 0-918456-39-8.

Even though many of the 2,653 entries are not in English, this is important as an overview of and a historical and bibliographical reference point to the mass communication literature of the Caribbean. Books, journal articles, and working papers are included. Chapters are divided by region and country, and then arranged alphabetically within subject sections such as general mass communications, freedom of the press, history, print media, broadcasting, advertising. There is a section on the U.S. Caribbean. With the addendum, the bibliography includes mass communication literature from the eighteenth century up to mid-1980. Unfortunately, only a few items are annotated. The author index is adequate, but a subject index would be very helpful.

54.   Lent, John A. **Comic Art: An International Bibliography**. Drexel Hill, PA: published by author, 1986. 156p. index.

Almost 2,000 books and periodical articles are included in this selected international bibliography focusing on political and editorial cartoons, comic strips, and comic books. There are no annotations. Entries are arranged geographically by continent, then country, and range from a *Journalism History* article entitled "Museum of Cartoon Art Offers Possibilities for Research" to "Exposure to Comics-Magazines and Knowledge/Attitude Toward Family Planning of Rural Residents," AB Thesis, University of Philippines. The contents of *Target* magazine from Spring 1982 to 1986 are included in a general section. Subject, author, title, and cartoonist indexes also are provided. Randall W. Scott's *Comic Books and Strips: An Information Sourcebook* (Phoenix, AZ: Oryx Press, 1988) might also be useful.

55.   Lent, John A. **Global Guide to Media and Communications**. Munich, NY: K. G. Saur, 1987. 145p. ISBN 3-598-10746-3.

This "global guide" does not include the United States, but nowhere does Lent indicate why. Eleven compilers (including Jim Richstad, Robert Roberts, and Hamid Mowlana) contributed to this uneven and occasionally annotated collection of books, dissertations and theses, monographs, serials, and periodical articles published through 1984. Entries are arranged geographically and focus on media systems and communications. There is no index.

56.   Lichty, Lawrence W., comp. **World and International Broadcasting: A Bibliography**. Washington, D.C.: Association for Professional Broadcasting Education, 1971. Various pagings.

This bibliography has a table of contents made in the twilight zone. Sure enough, there is a number for each entry, but it refers to number of pages in the chapter. In addition, Lichty writes, "For the most part I have depended on other bibliographies, indices, and listings. If these contained mistakes, I am repeating them; as well as adding my own mistakes." He began work on this nearly 10 years before it was finally published, but apparently did not consider verification important. He intended to compile a "rough, working bibliography" of radio and television broadcasting. In that he succeeds. Entries are divided by geographic area and arranged chronologically by year. The United States, Canada, and Great Britain are not included.

57.   Linton, David, and Ray Boston, eds. **The Newspaper Press in Britain: An Annotated Bibliography**. London: Mansell Publishing Ltd., 1987. 361p. index. LC 86-23837. ISBN 0-7201-1792-5.

The 2,909 briefly annotated entries chronicle British newspaper history. The periodical press is excluded. The index provides the only subject access point. All periodical, book, and thesis citations are arranged alphabetically by author and numbered consecutively. Fortunately, the subject index is detailed and provides adequate subject access to the bibliography. Unfortunately, titles are not indexed. The introduction provides a fine overview of the history of newspapering in the United Kingdom, but ends with a curious thought:

It was no accident that the first newspaper revolution in modern times—the linotype machine—in itself did nothing for journalism. It was not intended to do so. Will the same be said of the second revolution—computerization? We think that it will; and would simply add this warning: those who today live by the market must expect also to die by the market.

58. Madden, Lionel, and Diana Dixon. **The Nineteenth-Century Periodical Press in Britain: A Bibliography of Modern Studies, 1901-1971**. New York: Garland, 1976. 280p. index. (Garland Reference Library of the Humanities, vol. 53). LC 76-21872. ISBN 0-8240-9945-1.

Focusing on general studies and studies of individual periodicals and newspapers, this annotated bibliography of the British press in the nineteenth century covers books, pamphlets, periodical articles, and theses published from 1901-1971. Entries are numbered and arranged by date of publication under general sections. An alphabetical listing of individual periodicals and newspapers is included. Sullivan's multivolume *British Literary Magazines* (entry 486) would be a useful additional source.

59. **Marxism and the Mass Media: Toward a Basic Bibliography**. New York: International General, 1972- .

An unusual, irregular series, this bibliography is devoted to compiling a "global, multilingual annotated bibliography of Marxist studies covering all aspects of communications." This is no small task. It is international in scope and in the No. 1-2-3 revised edition (Nov. 1978), citations date from the mid-1800s to 1974. English, French, and Italian languages are all represented. Citations are numbered, and there are subject, author, and country indexes.

60. McCavitt, William E., comp. **Radio and Television: A Selected, Annotated Bibliography**. Metuchen, NJ: Scarecrow Press, 1978. 229p. LC 77-28665. ISBN 0-8108-1113-8. **Supplement One, 1977-1981**. 1982. 155p. LC 82-5743. ISBN 0-8108-1556-7. **Supplement Two, 1982-1986**. 1989. ISBN 0-8108-2158-3. (Compiled by Peter Pringle and Helen Clinton).

If the purpose of the first volume is, as the author indicates, to provide a guide for purchasing broadcasting books and to indicate what is still needed by showing what exists now, why did he not give us a subject index? It would have been immensely helpful. Fortunately, the table of contents is useful in searching the 1,100 selected and descriptively annotated listings of books and other publications covering 1920-1976. Topics such as history, public broadcasting, research, surveys, and criticism are further subdivided. The programming section, for example, is broken down into news, public affairs, documentaries, etc. In the supplement of 566 entries, the stated purpose is still the same, as is bibliographical arrangement, but coverage has been expanded to include video, videotext, and satellites. The second supplement covering 1982-1986 was published as this volume went to press.

61. McCoy, Ralph E. **Freedom of the Press: An Annotated Bibliography**. Carbondale, IL: Southern Illinois University Press, 1968. 576p. index. LC 76-10032. ISBN 0-8093-0335-3.

Press freedom and free expression in English-speaking countries is bibliographically chronicled, and any student of the topic will want to read this cover to cover. *Press* is defined broadly to include books, periodicals and newspapers, films, records, radio, and television, and all time periods since the beginning of printing are covered. This bibliography contains more than 8,000 citations to books, pamphlets, journal articles, and films. Newspaper, news magazine articles, and texts of laws are not included. The subject and title index is detailed and there are major subject headings for blasphemy, libel, censorship, First Amendment, fair trial, obscenity, broadcasting, sedition laws, and even library book selection policies. For further information on propaganda, McCoy refers to Lasswell, Casey, and Smith's contributions (entries 51 and 91). Annotations are primarily descriptive and concise. Entries are arranged alphabetically by author. Also of interest might be Frank Hoffman's *Intellectual Freedom and Censorship: An Annotated Bibliography*, to be published by Scarecrow Press in 1989.

62. McCoy, Ralph E. **Freedom of the Press: A Bibliocyclopedia**. 10-year supplement, 1967-1977. Carbondale, IL: Southern Illinois University Press, 1979. 544p. index. LC 78-16573. ISBN 0-8093-0844-4.

More than 6,000 books, pamphlets, journal articles, dissertations, films, and other items are included in this annotated supplement, as well as some pre-1967 titles not in the earlier bibliography. There are far fewer entries for heresy, blasphemy, and sedition, McCoy notes, but more for government and the media and free press/fair trial.

63. McGoings, Michael C. **Newsmen's Privilege, 1970-1974**. Washington, D.C.: Library of Congress, Law Library, 1976. 19p. LC 77-601676.

McGoings focused on the early 1970s because that was the "period which may be considered the height of the newsmen's privilege controversy." Books, periodical articles, and U.S. Congressional Hearings are listed in this annotated bibliography; entries range from Dale R. Spencer's *Law for the Newsman* (Lucas Brothers, 1973) to "Reporters and Their Sources: The Constitutional Right to a Confidential Relationship" in a 1970 issue of *Yale Law Review*. Lisa Epstein's "Newsman's Privilege, An Annotated Bibliography, 1967-1973" (California State Library, Law Library, 1973) also might provide some useful references.

64. McKerns, Joseph P. **News Media and Public Policy: An Annotated Bibliography**. New York: Garland, 1985. 171p. (Public Affairs and Administration, vol. 11; Garland Reference Library of Social Science, vol. 219). LC 83-049290. ISBN 0-8240-9004-7.

Pity the scholar who is trying to grasp, document, or dissect the relationship between the news media and the United States government. However, that is precisely the audience McKerns aims for, and he has done a superb job with this selective, annotated bibliography. He dismisses most of the literature of the popular press as superficial, and therefore focuses on books, monographs, theses, and dissertations published since the late 1960s-1984. His criteria for selection is rigid: subjects must deal with at least one aspect of news media and public policy, the publication must follow "commonly accepted standards of research," and the work must be "significant beyond its time of publication." The bibliography is divided into chapters such as newsmaking and the conventions of journalism (which includes an important section on ethics and values), the executive branch of government, legislative, judicial, and their bureaucracies. The 731 entries are consecutively numbered and arranged alphabetically by author within chapters. The subject index is spare and somewhat difficult to use. Since much has been written on this topic since 1984, a supplement would be desirable.

65. Middleton, Karen P., and Meheroo Jussawalla. **The Economics of Communication: A Selected Bibliography with Abstracts**. New York: Pergamon Press, 1981. 249p. LC 80-20505. ISBN 0-08-026325-9.

Most of the 386 entries here have been published since 1970, and include books, periodical articles, and reports. Although this bibliography does not address journalism exclusively, there are some worthwhile listings for television and newspapers. The indexes are adequate but confusing. Entries are numbered consecutively, yet the indexes refer the user to the page number. Abstracts are lengthy, some at least 300 words. Other possible sources are Bruce M. Owen and David Waterman's *A Selected Bibliography in the Economics of the Mass Media* (Stanford University, Center for Research in Economic Growth, 1970) and *Mass Communication: A Bibliography* (1973).

66. Miles, William, comp. **The People's Voice: An Annotated Bibliography of American Campaign Newspapers, 1828-1984**. Westport, CT: Greenwood Press, 1987. 210p. index. (Bibliographies and Indexes in American History, no. 6). LC 87-11969. ISBN 0-313-23976-2.

Most presidential campaign newspapers are issued only during the campaign to promote the party and ticket, and then die a natural death. Miles has resurrected 733 of them, dating from 1828 to 1984, including Jesse Jackson's *Rainbow News*. Fewer than 100 newspapers can be counted after 1900. Excluded are general party-supported and partisan sheets, press releases, and mimeographed newsletters. The lengthy introduction gives a historical overview of campaign literature and political parties. The bibliography is arranged chronologically according to campaign. Within each campaign, the successful candidate and papers are listed first, then the defeated candidate, official third-party candidates, and would-be candidates. Listings are numbered and include title, dates of publication, place, and (when available) editor, slogan, biographies, and library holdings. Indexing is ample, with an editor, publisher, and candidate index, and separate title and geographical indexes.

67. Mowlana, Hamid, ed. **International Flow of News: An Annotated Bibliography.** Paris: UNESCO, 1985. 272p. index.

International news and foreign correspondents are themes in this selected bibliography of 1,500 references. Part 1 defines *news flow* and offers an overview of research trends. Part 2 is a section on theories, methods, and policies, with entries arranged alphabetically by author. Part 3 focuses on the regional and national flow of news, and is subdivided into sections on Africa, Arab states, Asia, Eastern Europe, Western Europe, North America, and South and Central America. Entries range from "The Flow of International Events, July-Dec. 1969," a World Event/Interaction Survey Interim Technical Report, to "The Perception of Foreign News" in a 1971 issue of the *Journal of Peace Research*. Mowlana also is the author of *International Communication: A Selected Bibliography* (Kendall/ Hunt, 1971). Jim Richstad and Jackie Bowen's *International Communication Policy and Flow: A Selected, Annotated Bibliography* (East-West Center, 1976) might also provide some useful references.

68. Nafziger, Ralph O., comp. **International News and the Press: Communications, Organization of News Gathering, International Affairs, and the Foreign Press—An Annotated Bibliography.** New York: Ayer (c1940), 1972. 223p. LC 72-04675. ISBN 0-405-04759-2.

A meticulous and well-organized source, this international bibliography has withstood the ravages of time. It now serves as a useful historical guide to international news from the early 1900s to the beginning of World War II. Documents, books, pamphlets, magazine articles, and studies are included in sections labeled either International News or Foreign Press, and then arranged in chapters such as Washington Correspondence, Foreign Correspondence, Censorship, Press Law, News Gathering Organizations, and Press and Public Opinion. Descriptively annotated entries are listed alphabetically by author. Foreign press entries are arranged geographically by continent, then country. There is only an author index, so it is fortunate that the table of contents is detailed.

69. Nancarrow, Paula Reed, et al., comps. **Word Processors and the Writing Process: An Annotated Bibliography.** Westport, CT: Greenwood Press, 1984. 146p. index. LC 83-22749. ISBN 0-313-23995-9.

Mention of the art of journalism eventually leads to discussion of the technology. This should have been a useful guide to the effects of word processors on the art and science of writing. Instead, it is a mishmashed listing of about 600 periodical articles, books, dissertations, and unpublished papers. The authors claim that this is a "comprehensive listing of the major resources" and list items published mostly in the early 1980s. "Old" citations (1975 or earlier) are included for their historical value. The subject index is sketchy. Not all entries are annotated, and of the 46 relevant journals listed, fewer than half are annotated. Even the authors apologize for their annotations: "If our criticisms reflect our ignorance of the most recent computer technologies or computer science theories, we beg indulgence because we are writing teachers first and computer specialists only in an applied way." They wax amazed at the wonders of word processing and indicate that in some cases "we have retained citations that are clearly unrelated to our questions," apparently to show that "an appealing title was misleading." Consult William Zinsser's *Writing with a Word Processor* instead; it is not a reference book, but is far more useful.

70. Nelson, Marlan. **Free Press—Fair Trial: An Annotated Bibliography**. Logan, UT: Utah State University, 1971. 89p.

An exhaustive bibliography for its time, this listing of 600 books, periodical articles, theses, and dissertations needs an update. Still, it is useful as a historical resource, covering 1950-1969. Material was culled from legal and scholarly journals and trade and popular periodicals.

71. Noyes, Dan, ed. **Reporter's Reference Guide**. Beverly Hills, CA: Urban Policy Research Institute, 1976. 42p.

Noyes is straightforward in his introduction:

> This guide is incomplete. It represents only a first step in compiling a thorough guide to reference materials for reporters and researchers. Some of the information included here is now outdated and should be replaced by more contemporary sources. Some annotations are too brief and deserve greater detail. Information on the cost and method of obtaining many of these sources is missing.

This is all true, especially years after the original publication date. For example, the National Faculty Directory is listed, but the ERIC indexes (entries 162 and 182) are omitted. The 190 annotated entries are arranged alphabetically by author within the following categories: business, consumer affairs, education, foundations, general, individuals, government/politics, health, law, labor, media, military, and real estate. The beginning reporter is better served by *The Reporter's Handbook* (entry 370).

72. Paine, Fred K., and Nancy E. Paine. **Magazines: A Bibliography for Their Analysis, with Annotations and Study Guide**. Metuchen, NJ: Scarecrow Press, 1987. 690p. index. LC 86-29825. ISBN 0-8108-1975-9.

As the title plainly states, this is a guide for locating sources on magazines. It takes up where J. A. Schacht, in his *A Bibliography for the Study of Magazines* (entry 84), left off in 1978. In fact, the authors say they intentionally excluded most material in the Schacht book. They also say they examined more than 15,000 items and included a very selected list of 2,200 of those books, dissertations, and magazine, journal, and newspaper articles focusing mainly on journalistic and business aspects of the industry. Annotations are descriptive and short, sometimes just a sentence or two. Part 1 is a study guide listing journals, magazines, and newsletters that publish articles pertaining to the magazine industry in the United States. Also included is a chapter on reference books. Part 2 is a selected bibliography divided into 31 broad subject categories such as editing, audience, writing, production and design, history, business, advertising, and ethics. Indexing is sparse, limited to part 2, with no author index.

In the preface, the authors attempt to define *magazine* and distinguish the differences between magazines and newspapers. Some readers may, however, disagree with statements such as "Helping readers understand rather than simply presenting a 'laundry list of facts' is more important than magazines."

73. Palmegiano, E. M. **The British Empire in the Victorian Press, 1832-1867: A Bibliography**. New York: Garland, 1987. 234p. index. (Themes in European Expansion, vol. 8; Garland Reference Library of Social Science, vol. 389). LC 86-29624. ISBN 0-8240-9802-1.

A painstaking work, the introduction alone takes up 56 pages, and offers a rich historical overview of the British empire, the British people, and the writings of the press. Almost 3,000 articles from a sampling of 50 London-based magazines are listed. There are no annotations, but very short notes are included for articles that are not self-explanatory. The checklist is arranged alphabetically by magazine title, with article entries listed by date and numbered consecutively. Titles such as *Blackwood's Edinburgh Magazine, Chamber's Journal,* and *Household Words* are included. The first section lists 37 magazines dealing specifically with the empire, and gives publication history as well as location information.

Most titles can be found in the British Library, but it is interesting to note that *The Anti-Slavery Reporter* can be found at the Newark Public Library. The preface states that "journals have been determined on the basis of their historical significance," and that those in the *Wellesley Index to Victorian Periodicals* and 16 in *Poole's Index* are included. There is an author index, but the subject index is a travesty. It is primarily geographical in nature and contains vast listings under Australia, Canada, China, India, etc. William S. Ward's *British Periodicals and Newspapers, 1789-1832: A Bibliography of Secondary Sources* (University Press of Kentucky, 1972) addresses the time period immediately before this and may be of some use.

74. Parker, Elliott S., and Emelia M. Parker. **Asian Journalism: A Selected Bibliography of Sources on Journalism in China and Southeast Asia**. Metuchen, NJ: Scarecrow Press, 1979. 472p. index. LC 79-022785. ISBN 0-8108-1269-X.

The authors tell us that this volume was entirely computer processed, "a fact of little importance except to demonstrate the comparative ease with which a general purpose computer can be used to print a bibliography." It may have been easy to print, but it is difficult to use and read. More than 2,000 books, articles, essays, and theses on the "communication process" in China and Southeast Asia are listed in this printout. (No items on Korea can be found.) Most are English-language sources, published before 1960 and dealing with print journalism. Radio and television receive less attention. Parker and Parker say that Lent's *Asian Mass Communications* (entry 52), among other sources, should be consulted first.

75. Picard, Robert G., and James P. Winter, comps. **Press Concentration and Monopoly: A Bibliography**. Columbia, SC: Association for Education in Journalism and Mass Communication, Mass Communication and Society Division, 1985. 23p.

More than 300 publications focusing on chain ownership, joint operating agreements, and local monopolies in North America are listed in this Press Council and Monopoly Research Project. Divided into sections on books, articles, government reports, and unpublished materials, entries are arranged alphabetically by author and focus on topics such as the effects of concentration and monopoly on news coverage, diversity of opinion, labor relations and management activities, and economic behavior. There are no annotations or indexes. While not comprehensive, "the bibliography contains the most important literature in the field and is intended to provide researchers starting points at which to carry out further research in the areas in which they are most interested."

76. Picard Robert G., and Rhonda S. Sheets, comps. **Terrorism and the News Media Research Bibliography**. Columbia, SC: Association for Education in Journalism and Mass Communication, Mass Communication and Society Division, 1986. 33p.

A part of the Terrorism and the News Media Research Project, this selective bibliography contains more than 450 entries arranged in sections on books, articles and book chapters, government reports and documents, and unpublished material.

77. Pitts, Michael R. **Radio Soundtracks: A Reference Guide**. 2d ed. Metuchen, NJ: Scarecrow Press, 1986. 337p. index. LC 85-30409. ISBN 0-8108-1875-2.

The dedication page reads "For Rudy Vallee." This second edition is more than twice the size of the first, published in 1976, since many old shows have become available since then. Material from the late 1920s to the 1960s (the golden age of radio) is covered, and all entries are numbered consecutively. Part 1 consists of an alphabetical listing of radio programs available on tape; part 2 is a sample listing of radio specials on tape; part 3 contains radio programs available on LP records (no 45 rpm or 78 rpm recordings listed); part 4 is performers' radio appearances on LP records; compilation record albums not included in parts 3 or 4 make up part 5. An appendix lists tape and record sources. Performers and shows are listed in the index. While Pitts indicates that this is not a "complete guide to all the radio programs ever broadcast or a listing of every performer's radio appearances," it is a very useful, well-constructed, and entertaining guide.

78. Price, Warren C. **The Literature of Journalism: An Annotated Bibliography**. Minneapolis, MN: University of Minnesota Press, 1959. 489p. LC 59-013522. ISBN 0-317-10434-9.

An objective, comprehensive, and well-organized jewel of an annotated bibliography. Price's definition of *journalism* is broad, and he lists 3,147 English-language books on newspapers, magazines, ethics, education, management, radio, television, and public opinion published through 1957. Annotations are mostly descriptive, though some are evaluative. There are 52 subject categories and perhaps the only ones he intentionally skips are fiction and high school journalism. Historical and biographical works are emphasized. The "Bibliographies and Directories" is especially useful for those who seek early twentieth century bibliographies on the press. The subject index has some nice features such as an entry for textbooks, subdivided by subject area. More than 200 bibliographies and directories are included, and should be of particular interest to the serious researcher. Price writes that "relatively few efforts have been made in journalistic research toward compiling general and descriptive bibliographies of the press as a whole." This book is his answer and triumph.

79. Price, Warren C., and Calder M. Pickett. **An Annotated Journalism Bibliography, 1958-1968**. Minneapolis, MN: University of Minnesota Press, 1970. 278p. index. LC 70-120810. ISBN 0-8166-0578-5.

When Warren Price died in 1967, Calder Pickett carried on and produced this supplement to *The Literature of Journalism* (entry 78). The 2,172 entries are numbered, arranged alphabetically by author, and cover the history of journalism, biography, narratives, anthologies, appraisals of the press, ethics, law, techniques of journalism, journalism education, magazines, periodicals, management, public opinion and propaganda, public relations, radio and television, foreign press, and bibliographies and directories. Fortunately, there is a detailed subject index. Annotations are brief and descriptive. Pickett says, "Worthy or not, here it is, this supplement, a volume almost as comprehensive as its predecessor, a fact that may seem strange but that somehow seems apt, for this is mainly a supplement of mass media titles of the busy 1960s." He also thanks Price and says, "Often I have wished for his help, knowing he would have been able to answer questions. I hope he would feel I have not done him a disservice in assembling a work that was so important to him." Price and Pickett's volumes constitute the very best of journalism bibliography. Pickett also compiled an anthology of articles entitled *Voices of the Past: Key Documents in the History of American Journalism* (Macmillan, 1977).

80. Pride, Armistead S. **The Black Press: A Bibliography**. Jefferson City, MO: Chauma Department of Journalism, Lincoln University, 1968. ["The Black Press to 1968: A Bibliography." *Journalism History* 4 (Winter 1977-1978): 148-53.]

This represents a first effort in documenting the history of the black press. Pride gathered these 386 references to books and magazine and journal articles in 1968 for what was then the Association for Education in Journalism. Contents include advertising and marketing, analysis and criticism, biography and history, competition, coverage of the black community by nonblack media, employment, magazines, radio, and television. Entries are numbered and arranged alphabetically by author within chapters. There are no annotations. Lenwood Davis's *A History of Journalism in the Black Community: Preliminary Survey* (Council of Planning Librarians, 1975) might also provide some useful references.

81. Richstad, Jim, and Michael McMillan, comps. **Mass Communication and Journalism in the Pacific Islands: A Bibliography**. Honolulu, HI: published for the East-West Center by the University of Hawaii Press, 1978. 333p. index. LC 77-020795. ISBN 0-8248-0497-X.

The editors point out that little attention has been paid to mass communication in most Pacific islands, and their research proves them correct. There is one citation each for Easter Island and Midway Island. Hawaii has almost 2,000. This Center for Cultural and

Technical Interchange Between East and West bibliography contains 3,332 books, periodicals, articles, documents, pamphlets, etc., and covers 1854-1975, with some entries from 1976. Topics include the press, newspapers, freedom of the press, broadcasting, news agencies, organizations, radio broadcasting, cinema, and television in the Pacific Islands. It is arranged alphabetically by more than 20 island groupings, and broken down into specific subject areas. Entries are numbered and arranged chronologically within those subjects. Richstad also produced *The Pacific Islands Press: A Directory* (East-West Communication Institute, 1973).

82. Rivers, William. **Finding Facts: A Research Manual for Journalists**. New York: Magazine Publishers Association, 1966. 65p.

A basic and dated research guide, this contains chapters on general reference sources and specialized sources in the humanities, biological sciences, physical sciences, and social sciences. There also are entries for sources in communication, broadcasting, film, newspapers, and magazines. Each entry offers general bibliographic information and a description of the source. As the title suggests, this is more useful as a beginning reference guide for journalists than as a beginning reference source in journalism.

83. Rose, Oscar, ed. **Radio Broadcasting and Television: An Annotated Bibliography**. New York: H. W. Wilson, 1947. 120p. LC 47-3360.

This source is old, but not yet dead. Books and pamphlets primarily on radio until 1945 are descriptively annotated. This work attempts to be comprehensive, and it probably was in its time. Technical studies are not included. The index contains titles and authors.

84. Schacht, John A. **A Bibliography for the Study of Magazines**. 4th ed. Urbana, IL: College of Journalism and Communications, University of Illinois, 1979. 95p.

The fourth edition (earlier editions were published in 1966, 1968, and 1972) contains 600 new listings and includes a section on foreign magazines and publishers. This selected and annotated bibliography of journal articles, reports, conference papers, and proceedings is divided into sections on bibliographies, directories, general sources, history, audiences, editorial research, magazine content, law, magazine advertising, circulation, editors and editing, and layout and production. Appendices selectively list periodicals and indexes covering magazine journalism. See *Magazines: A Bibliography for Their Analysis, with Annotations and Study Guide* (entry 72) for materials on magazines published after 1978.

85. Schreibman, Fay C., comp. **Broadcast Television: A Research Guide**. Frederick, MD: University Publications of America, 1983. 62p. (American Film Institute Factfile 15). index. ISBN 0-89093-571-8.

In a mere 62 pages, Schreibman, co-editor of *Television Network News: Issues in Content Research* (George Washington University, 1978) and compiler of *Television News Resources: A Guide to Collections* (entry 86), gives a clear picture of domestic television broadcasting reference sources. This descriptively annotated, selected "factfile" is divided into three sections. Part 1 consists of general reference works, historical sources, programming information, and economic and technological aspects of the field. Particularly useful is the short section on research, which is further subdivided into studies from academic sources, research methods, yearbooks, and rating services. Lists of television-related periodicals and indexes, catalogs of television archive collections, and news transcript and script sources are contained in part 2. Part 3 identifies special libraries and academic and network archives. Biographies, memoirs, and material on general mass communications are not included. There are author and title indexes, but no subject index. Schreibman should get a "thumbs up" from every librarian in the field for including a useful section on "How to Approach a Special Library or Archive."

86. Schreibman, Fay C., comp., **Television News Resources: A Guide to Collections**. Washington, D.C.: Television News Study Center, George Washington University, 1981. 27p. LC 82-146621.

Schreibman lists useful sources for the novice television researcher and includes information on news documentaries, network television news archives, and local stations' news archives. This is a guide to American television news sources in 20 collections in the United States. It is not a "how to" guide, but a very brief listing of what is available. There is no index.

87. Schwarzlose, Richard A. **Newspapers: A Reference Guide**. Westport, CT: Greenwood Press, 1987. 417p. index. (American Popular Culture). LC 87-246. ISBN 0-313-23613-5.

Although the author, an associate professor of journalism at Northwestern's Medill School of Journalism, seems more knowledgeable when discussing the history of newspapering than when critiquing the profession, he has written a thoughtful and well-organized selective guide to the literature of American newspapers. This ambitious work refers to more than 1,700 books, and covers newspaper history, business, freedom of the press, technology, design, ethics, reporters, and reporting through the mid-1980s. Each chapter is an essay, and includes complete bibliographical references at the end. It does not replace Blum (entry 7) or Price (entries 78 and 79), but the author says this guide "offers a selective update of Price and Price-Pickett." This is debatable because Schwarzlose does not focus on radio or television broadcasting. Major research collections are discussed in an appendix. The chapter on references and periodicals about newspapers is concise and well-done.

88. Shearer, Benjamin F., and Marilyn Huxford, comps. **Communications and Society: A Bibliography on Communications Technologies and Their Social Impact**. Westport, CT: Greenwood Press, 1983. 242p. LC 83-12657. ISBN 0-313-23713-1.

Chapter headings which may be useful in journalism include "Mass Media as Creators and Reflectors of Public Opinion," "Politics and the Mass Media," and "Shaping of Mass Media Content." Most chapters are subdivided into sections on print media, radio, and television. The 2,732 selected and unannotated entries are numbered and arranged alphabetically by author within subject sections. The authors indicate that they did much of their initial research at the University of Illinois Communications Library.

89. Signorielli, Nancy, and George Gerbner, comps. **Violence and Terror in the Mass Media: An Annotated Bibliography**. Westport, CT: Greenwood Press, 1988. 264p. index. (Bibliographies and Indexes in Sociology, no. 13). LC 87-29556. ISBN 0-313-26120-2.

Scholarly articles and books on violence and terror in the mass media comprise the bulk of this bibliography. The 784 entries are numbered, divided into sections on mass media content, mass media effects, pornography, and terrorism, then arranged alphabetically by author. Content and effects chapters are by far the largest, with 673 entries and 184 pages. Annotations are descriptive. The introduction lists several other useful bibliographic studies of terrorism and violence, including Richard L. Moreland and Michael L. Berbaum's "Terrorism and the Mass Media: A Researcher's Bibliography" in Abraham H. Miller's (ed.) *Terrorism: The Media and the Law* (Transnational, 1982) and *Violence and the Media: A Bibliography* (Toronto: The Royal Commission, 1977). This publication started as a UNESCO project in 1984 and includes, according to the compilers, most relevant publications through early 1987. Most works included were published in the United States, although "an effort was made to obtain and include studies from all countries where relevant research has been conducted. Communications research in general and media violence studies in particular have had the widest reach in the United States." Author and subject indexes are provided.

90. Sloan, Wm. David, comp. **American Journalism History: An Annotated Bibliography**. Westport, CT: Greenwood Press, 1989. 359p. ISBN 0-313-26350-7. (Bibliographies and Indexes in Mass Media and Communications, no. 1).

The publication of *American Journalism History* was announced as *Journalism: A Guide to the Reference Literature* was going to press. According to prepublication literature, this bibliography of periodical articles and books published from 1810-1988 is arranged by historical period and general theme. Annotations are brief and descriptive.

91. Smith, Bruce Lannes, Harold D. Lasswell, and Ralph D. Casey, comps. **Propaganda, Communication, and Public Opinion: A Comprehensive Reference Guide**. Princeton, NJ: Princeton University Press (c1946), 1966. index. 435p.

An update of Lasswell, Casey, and Smith's *Propaganda and Promotional Activities: An Annotated Bibliography* (entry 51), this volume lists books and periodical articles published from 1934 through early 1946.

92. Smith, Bruce Lannes, and Chitra M. Smith, comps. **International Communication and Political Opinion: A Guide to the Literature**. Westport, CT: Greenwood Press (c1956), 1972. 325p. index. LC 72-01108. ISBN 0-8371-007-3.

Though it purports to be a further update to *Propaganda and Promotional Activities: An Annotated Bibliography* (entry 51) and *Propaganda, Communication, and Public Opinion: A Comprehensive Reference Guide,* (entry 91) this selected bibliography focuses more on international issues. The 2,563 entries are divided into sections on theoretical and general writings, political persuasion and propaganda, specialists in political persuasion, channels of international communication (from radio and television to rumor), audience characteristics, research methods, and bibliographies.

93. Smith, Myron J., Jr., comp. **U.S. Television Network News: A Guide to Sources in English**. Jefferson, NC: McFarland, 1984. 233p. LC 82-42885. ISBN 0-89950-080-3.

John Chancellor says in the foreword that "I find it ironic, but not totally surprising, that the best record of this immensely influential medium of television will be found in the printed word." This may not be the best record, but it is the first of its kind. This is a selected bibliography of English-language sources (mostly United States) listing 3,215 numbered citations to books, papers, periodical articles, government documents, dissertations, and theses published from the 1940s-1982. Unfortunately, there is no mention of online sources or databases. Chapters are broadly labeled and further subdivided. Arrangement is alphabetical within chapters. Subjects include reference works, histories, networks and programming, network news and collections, domestic and foreign affairs, and biography. Book titles and a few periodical entries are descriptively annotated, mostly in a sentence or two. There are subject and author indexes, but a title index would help. This is a useful but ugly guide, with entries crammed on pages single-spaced. Smith also compiled *Watergate: An Annotated Bibliography of Sources in English, 1972-1982* (Scarecrow Press, 1983).

94. Snorgrass, J. William, and Gloria T. Woody, eds. **Blacks and Media: A Selected, Annotated Bibliography, 1962-1982**. Tallahassee, FL: Florida A&M University Press, 1985. 150p. LC 84-15296. ISBN 0-8130-0810-7.

The relationship between blacks and the media, especially coverage of the explosive civil rights years, is explored in listings of 743 books, chapters, and magazine and journal articles. Chapters on print media, broadcast media, advertising and public relations, film, and theater contain numbered entries arranged alphabetically by title, not author. Annotations are short and evaluative. Though Snorgrass and Woody limit themselves to a fairly short historical period, they do include books and other materials that were reprinted between 1962-1982. Indexing is curious: titles of books and magazine articles are listed, but there is no subject index. This source would benefit from some further subject arrangement. For example, in the magazine articles portion of broadcast media, an article entitled "Is Network News Slighting the Minorities?" is preceded by "Is Kunta Kinte the New Fonzie?" Numerous selected articles from *The Quill, Columbia Journalism Review, Journalism Quarterly*, and *Journal of Broadcasting* are mentioned. Snorgrass, past president of the American Journalism Historians Association, died in 1987.

95.   Sotiron, Minko, ed. **An Annotated Bibliography of Works on Daily Newspapers in Canada 1914-1983. Une Bibliographie Annotée des Ouvrages Portant sur les Quotidiens Canadiens**. Montreal: Inkstain Publications, 1987. 288p. index. ISBN 0-9693102-0-X.

In addition to "works on daily newspapers," and the Canadian press, this annotated bibliography of 3,766 books, periodical articles, dissertations, and other materials also covers advertising and ethics. General works on Canada are listed first and other entries are arranged geographically by province. The 545 French entries, however, are grouped in a separate section, have a separate index, and are listed and annotated only in French.

96.   Sterling, Christopher H., comp. **Communication Booknotes**. Columbus, OH: Center for Advanced Study of Telecommunications, The Ohio State University. (Formerly Mass Media Booknotes 1969-1982). 1969- , (6 issues/year). ISSN 0045-3188.

This bimonthly annotated booklist is an excellent collection development tool for librarians as well as an up-to-date guide to current communications, telecommunications, and media publications. The booknotes include listings under telecommunications, broadcasting, international communication, foreign communication, general communications, and popular culture. Regional contributors offer listings from Australia, Great Britain, Canada, France, Germany, etc. Two annual special issues focus on United States government documents and the cinema. Now published at the Center for Advanced Study of Telecommunications, *Communication Booknotes* has been spruced up considerably and is no longer printed on pink or green paper. Sterling also has created other useful bibliographies such as "Broadcasting and Mass Communications: A Survey Bibliography" (11th ed., 1986), "Telecommunications Policy: A Survey Bibliography" (5th ed., 1986), and "Foreign and International Communications Systems: A Survey Bibliography" (3d ed., 1986), all published by the Telecommunications Policy Program, George Washington University.

97.   Swindler, William F. **A Bibliography of Law on Journalism**. New York: Columbia University Press, 1947. 191p.

Swindler says that "the researcher needs a catalogue to all that has gone before, which would seem to be of lasting value, as well as a guide to the selection of current and future materials. This has been the twofold aim of this bibliography." In this he succeeds. The listing includes more than 1,100 books, monographs, and periodical articles published from 1844 to the 1940s focusing on journalism law, although popular and ephemeral materials are excluded. A 20-page bibliographic essay precedes the bibliography and offers a historical overview of the subject. Entries are numbered and arranged alphabetically by author within the following sections: texts and general works, history, press freedom, censorship, public records, libel, privacy, contempt, confidences, copyright, advertising, communications, radio, etc. A separate section on international and foreign law also is subdivided by subject. Author and subject indexes are provided. Consult this classic work when researching any aspect of journalism and the law. Swindler also is the author of *Problems of Law in Journalism* (Macmillan, 1955).

98.   Wall, Celia Jo, comp. **Newspaper Libraries: A Bibliography, 1933-1985**. Washington, D.C.: Special Libraries Association, 1986. 126p. index. LC 86-14604. ISBN 0-87111-319-8.

The literature of news libraries extends far beyond the standard library journals, and this is an attempt to gather a comprehensive listing of books, chapters, professional and trade journal articles, unpublished papers, and pamphlets on the subject. English-language material from 1933-1985 is numbered and arranged alphabetically in chapters such as history, organization and administration, reference materials in the newspaper library, newspaper indexing, automation, and newspaper librarianship. Articles from *Editor & Publisher, presstime*, and *Journalism Quarterly* are included. Since there are few published volumes on news libraries and the like, this is a valuable source. Annotations, lists of journals consulted, and a separate chapter for full-text online newspaper databases would make it even better.

99.   Watts, Elizabeth A. **"Annotated Bibliography on Media Coverage of AIDS, Cancer, Swine Flu and Related Topics."** Athens, OH: Ohio University, E. W. Scripps School of Journalism, 11p.

Media coverage of AIDS and other topics is the subject of this descriptively annotated bibliography of books, magazine and periodical articles, and dissertations. Entries are arranged alphabetically by author in sections on AIDS, cancer, swine flu, birth control pills, word usage, science coverage, etc. Jo Cates's *Covering AIDS: A Selected Bibliography* (The Poynter Institute for Media Studies, 1988) might also provide some useful references.

100.   Wedell, George, Georg-Michael Luyken, and Rosemary Leonard, eds. **Mass Communications in Western Europe: An Annotated Bibliography.** Manchester, England: European Institute for the Media, 1985. 327p. index. (Media Monograph, no. 6). ISBN 0-948195-04-5.

Mass Communications includes press, radio, television, film, publishing, telecommunications, and informatics and information technology, in this international, selected bibliography. More than 750 documents and books and some periodical articles are organized by country, then arranged alphabetically by author. According to the editors, "it is the intention of this work to give references to the most recent developments in the Western European communications scene, including legislation and official documents, as well as of scholarly and policy-oriented texts." The following countries are included: Austria, Belgium, Switzerland, Cyprus, Federal Republic of Germany, Denmark, Spain, France, United Kingdom, Greece, Italy, Republic of Ireland, Iceland, Luxembourg, Norway, Netherlands, Portugal, Sweden, Finland, and Turkey. There are subject and author indexes.

101.   Wilhoit, Frances Goins, and D. Craig Mitchell, comps. **Mass Media Periodicals: An Annotated Bibliography.** Bloomington, IN: Indiana University, Center for New Communications of the School of Journalism, Ernie Pyle Hall, 1978. 33p.

Even though this listing is more than 10 years old, it wears its age well. Some journals have since been renamed and others are no longer published (*MORE*, for example). Wilhoit, head of the journalism library at Indiana University and currently conducting feasibility studies on a journalism index, has put together a selected and annotated listing of mass media journals, indexes, and yearbooks. Entries are English-language sources, and focus on print and broadcast journalism. Entries are arranged alphabetically. Wilhoit also is the bibliographer of Indiana University Journalism Library's monthly "New Book List," an excellent collection development tool.

102.   Wolseley, Roland E., and Isabel Wolseley. **The Journalist's Bookshelf: An Annotated and Selected Bibliography of United States Print Journalism.** 8th ed. Indianapolis, IN: R. J. Berg, 1986. 400p. index. LC 84-070769. ISBN 0-89730-139-0.

This annotated booklist of print journalism in the United States has once again been updated and includes more than 2,000 entries (the 7th edition published in 1961 had 1,324 entries). Unfortunately, it still contains some very dated material. There is little cross-referencing because the authors say it "would swell the size of the book too much"; thus, users are invited to "scan" other categories. There is no subject index, so scanning will indeed be necessary. The authors include an interesting section on "Journalism Fiction," but it has been reduced because "few if any of these books are of interest to scholars." Though their definition of *journalism* is narrow (broadcast journalism is not included), the authors do have sections on ethics, minority press, college journalism, and high school journalism. *The Journalist's Bookshelf* is more useful as a journalism history source than as a current bibliography of journalism.

2
Encyclopedias

103.   Brown, Les. **Les Brown's Encyclopedia of Television**. New York: New York Zoetrope, 1982. 496p. bibliog. LC 82-007867. ISBN 0-918432-28-6. (Formerly titled **The New York Times Encyclopedia of Television**, 1977).

Brown, former editor-in-chief of *Channels of Communications*, now entitled *Channels: The Business of Communication* (entry 508), and author of books such as *Television: The Business Behind the Box*, (Harcourt Brace Jovanovich, 1971), has made his mark in television research. Brown calls the time period between editions "Television II," and many of the 400 new entries and other rewritten and updated articles reflect changes in technology, deregulation, and programming. The scope is broad. On one page, for example, there are entries for RCA SATCOM, Ronald Reagan, "The Real McCoys," "The Real West," and Harry Reasoner. Arrangement is alphabetical and includes terminology, programs, and biographical entries. There is solid information on the networks, and a smattering of entries on documentaries, broadcast personalities, correspondents, and anchors. This might be used in conjunction with *Halliwell's Television Companion* (entry 105).

104.   Graham, Irvin. **Encyclopedia of Advertising**. 2d ed. New York: Fairchild Publications, 1969. 494p. LC 68-14544.

Although this is an advertising encyclopedia, it holds an impressive number of entries relating to journalism, graphic arts, layout, photography, radio, television, and typography. In a pinch, it could prove useful. More than 1,000 entries are arranged alphabetically. Laurence Urdang's *The Dictionary of Advertising Terms* (Tatham-Laird & Kudner, 1977), which contains more than 4,000 entries, might be consulted as well. However, since Urdang's is first an advertising dictionary, the definition for *newspaper* begins, "a publication, usually a periodical accepting advertising...."

105.   Halliwell, Leslie, and Philip Purser. **Halliwell's Television Companion**. 2d ed. New York, London: Granada, 1982. 713p. ISBN 0-246-11714-1.

Written with a British slant, of course, Halliwell has fattened up his *Teleguide* (Granada, 1979) and fashioned it into a useful companion volume to *Les Brown's Encyclopedia of Television* (entry 103). Similar in style to his *Filmgoer's Companion* (Scribner's, 1984), this is an alphabetical guide to programming, television terminology, and television personalities.

106.   Horn, Maurice, ed. **The World Encyclopedia of Comics**. New York: Chelsea House, 1976. 785p. LC 75-22322. ISBN 0-87754-030-6.

Joseph Pulitzer recognized the importance of comic art when he first printed Richard Outcault's "Yellow Kid" in a 1896 issue of *The World*. That is the sort of information available in this valuable guide and "browser" for both comics scholars and buffs. More than 1,200 cross-referenced entries cover 80 years and offer a world picture of the comics through 1975. Entries written by 15 contributors include themes, plots, character lists, adaptations into other media, artists, and writers. There also are separate biographical entries for artists, writers, and editors. A glossary is included, as well as articles on the world history of comics and a history of newspaper syndication.

107.   Hudson, Robert V. **Mass Media: A Chronological Encyclopedia of Television, Radio, Motion Pictures, Magazines, Newspapers, and Books in the United States.** New York: Garland, 1987. 435p. bibliog. index. (Garland Reference Library of Social Science, vol. 310). LC 85-45153. ISBN 0-8240-8695-3.

"Information in a Hurry" could be the subtitle. A useful source for students and those searching for a fact or two, this chronological list of mass-media events in the United States through 1985 is not a scholarly tool. Chapters such as "The Great Depression, 1930-1941" and "The American Revolution, 1765-1783" are subdivided into sections on books and pamphlets, newspapers, and magazines. (Motion picture, radio and television categories are included from 1878 on.) Entries are arranged chronologically within these subdivisions. There is a name and subject index. There also are factual errors and some surprising omissions: for example, the Janet Cooke scandal in 1981 was a major media event, but neither she nor the Pulitzer Prize she forfeited is mentioned. In fact, the only Pulitzers mentioned are the prizes awarded in literature.

108.   Ingelhart, Louis E. **Press Freedoms: A Descriptive Calendar of Concepts, Interpretations, Events, and Court Actions, from 4000 B.C. to the Present.** New York: Greenwood Press, 1987. 430p. bibliog. index. LC 86-31834. ISBN 0-313-25636-5.

No mere calendar, this encyclopedic chronology of freedom of the press covers all time periods from prehistory to the present. Though the arrangement is strictly chronological, with chapters such as "Printing in a World of Irreverence, 1500 through 1599," a detailed subject and name index makes it fully accessible. Brief descriptive entries include events which occurred and court decisions issued in North America, South America, Europe, Asia, Africa, and Australia. There also is a selected bibliography of about 200 important books on press freedom. Aimed at teachers and students, this volume is a valuable ready reference source and highlights other areas ripe for research. See also McCoy's *Freedom of the Press: An Annotated Bibliography* (entry 61) and *Freedom of the Press: A Bibliocyclopedia* (entry 62). Ingelhart also authored *Freedom for the College Student Press* (Greenwood Press, 1985) and *Press Law and Press Freedom for High School Publications* (Greenwood Press, 1986).

109.   **International Center of Photography Encyclopedia of Photography.** Cornell Capa, Jerry Mason, and William L. Broeker, eds. New York: Crown Publishers, 1984. 607p. illus. bibliog. LC 84-1856. ISBN 0-517-55271-X.

The ICP, director Capa, Broeker, and Mason have created one of the most handsome and high-toned one-volume reference sources in print today. Capa states that "all concerned sought to produce a volume light enough to hold in hand, beautiful to look at, and inexpensive enough for wide public use, one that would cover the range from the aesthetic and historical to the technical and practical aspects of the medium." It succeeds (except, weighing in at more than five pounds, it is more than a handful). More than 1,300 entries are arranged alphabetically and describe, according to the introduction, the aesthetic, communicative, scientific, technical, and commercial applications of photography. Of special interest are entries for documentary and social documentary photography, photojournalism, and satire in photography. More than 250 biographical entries for inventors and photographers born between 1840 and 1940 and examples of their photography, as well as a biographical supplement of more than 2,000 photographers, are included. An excellent subject bibliography is the final feature. Photography receives some scholarly treatment here, but both the general reader and professional photographer will find their own particular uses for this rich source.

110.   **International Encyclopedia of Communications**. Erik Barnouw, editor-in-chief, et al. New York: Oxford University Press (published jointly by Oxford and The Annenberg School of Communications, University of Pennsylvania), 1989. 4 vols. illus. bibliog. index. LC 88-18132. ISBN 0-19-504994-2 (set).

In spite of its youth, this is one of the most important publications in the field of communications, and it is the first of its kind. It addresses a broad range of topics in communications with numerous references to subjects in journalism and mass communication. More than 450 scholars and professionals contributed to this four-volume collection of signed articles on animal communication, arts, communications research, computers, education, folklore, government regulation, international communication, journalism, language and linguistics, literature, media, motion pictures, music, nonverbal communication, photography, political communication, print media, radio, religion, speech, television, communication theories and theorists, etc. There are more than 550 alphabetically arranged articles, a comprehensive index, a topical guide, cross-references, and illustrations. Each entry also contains a brief bibliography, listing basic bibliographic information but, unfortunately, no publishers. (Place of publication, however, is included.) In all, 9 editorial board members, 25 section editors, and 170 editorial advisers were involved in this project.

111.   Jaspert, W. Pincus, W. Turner Berry, and A. F. Johnson. **The Encyclopaedia of Type Faces**. 4th ed. Poole, Dorset, England: Blandford Press (distributed in the U.S. by Sterling), 1983. 416p. bibliog. index. LC 84-106555. ISBN 0-7137-1347-X.

Jaspert warns in his fourth edition reprint note that he is "well aware of inconsistencies in the book." Apparently, this fourth edition reprint was the first to be offset, and a few type specimens were juggled inadvertently. Other problems also are noted. More than 1,200 specimens of typefaces are arranged alphabetically within three main sections— Romans, Lineales, and Scripts. This edition holds 400 new or revived typefaces. It will be used primarily by designers and artists, and students will no doubt consult it for design and typography projects. Each entry lists designer and date, describes the typeface, and displays examples of the type. Separate indexes to designers and typefaces make this a handy and accessible guide. This is not to be confused with *The TypEncyclopedia* (entry 116), which is an illustrated encyclopedia of typographic terms containing a limited specimen section. *The ITC Typeface Collection* (entry 468) is useful for a straight alphabetical collection of numerous typefaces. Also of possible interest is Michael L. Kleper's *The Illustrated Dictionary of Typographic Communication* (Graphic Dimensions, 1983).

112.   Kurian, George Thomas, ed. **World Press Encyclopedia**. 2 vols. New York: Facts on File, 1982. bibliog. index. LC 80-25120. ISBN 0-87196-621-2.

According to Kurian, "In both scope and size, it is the most comprehensive survey of the world's press *ever* attempted." He is undoubtedly correct. In two volumes and 1,202 pages, he and his 46 contributors have surveyed the press in 180 countries through the late 1970s. The first section contains six articles on the world press such as "International Information Politics" and "Press Councils of the World." Section 2 chronicles the world's 82 developed press systems and discusses press history, economics, censorship, education and training, etc. Profiles range in length from four pages (Bolivia and Albania) to 76 pages (United States). A chronology of important events and a selected bibliography conclude each entry. Section 3 contains 33 short profiles on smaller and developing press systems. The minimal and underdeveloped press in 65 countries is presented in tabular format in secton 4. All country profiles are arranged alphabetically within sections. Appendices include a listing of news agencies, press associations, and media rankings. Rankings are taken from Kurian's *The Book of World Rankings* (Facts on File, 1979), but his *New Book of World Rankings* (Facts on File, 1984) contains updated information. See also the *International Encyclopedia of Communications* (entry 110).

113.   Paneth, Donald. **The Encyclopedia of American Journalism**. New York: Facts on File, 1983. 548p. index. LC 81-12575. ISBN 0-87196-427-9.

This encyclopedia of newspapers, magazines, radio, television, photography, newsreels, and documentaries lists more than 1,000 entries, some dictionary-length, some essays. The most influential educators, columnists, editors, black journalists, reporters, women journalists, and foreign correspondents also are surveyed. Also included are the "Legendary Figures" of which, according to Paneth's subject index, there are only 13. (Legendary names range from A. J. Liebling to the fictional Hildy Johnson, star reporter in "The Front Page.") Legal cases, broadcasting and broadcasting networks, news agencies, journalism periodicals, and military terms exemplify subjects covered in this well-designed and crisply written reference source. Entries are alphabetical and cover the field of journalism through 1982. Major entries provide bibliographical references. Journalism students will use this as a source for research topics, journalism librarians may bolt it to the reference desk, and newsrooms might get some use out of it also.

114.   Pinkard, Bruce. **The Photographer's Bible: An Encyclopedic Reference Manual**. New York: Arco, 1982. 352p. illus. LC 82-20658. ISBN 0-668-05781-5.

The editor, photojournalist, or photojournalism student who seeks a solid one-volume source focused on aspects of photography from aesthetics to mechanics ought to examine this book. Unusual terminology may make it difficult to locate some entries. For example, the author calls beginning photography "photography for the first time." There are numerous cross-references. Alphabetical entries range from a sentence or two to several pages. More than 250 black-and-white photographs and several pages of color photographs further enhance this work. The appendix is a little handbook in its own right, listing associations and organizations, publishers, museums and exhibitions, and various manufacturers. Also recommended is the *International Center of Photography Encyclopedia of Photography* (entry 109), which is richer in biographical entries.

115.   Polking, Kirk, Joan Bloss, and Colleen Cannon, eds. **Writer's Encyclopedia**. Cincinnati, OH: Writer's Digest, 1983. 532p. bibliog. LC 83-1058. ISBN 0-89879-103-0.

The editors say "this book was created to respond to those anguished cries from writers who have hunted through hundreds of sources for scattered and specialized information and then written or phoned us and said, 'I wish there were just one book I could use to find out things like this!' " (preface). Those "things like this" are some 1,200 terms, expressions, organization names, etc., used primarily in publishing. Some television and radio terms are included. Aimed at the professional writer, this does not masquerade as a reader's encyclopedia. Entries are arranged alphabetically and contain general information, references, and sources of additional information. This additional information can be found, not surprisingly, in other Writer's Digest books. The appendix offers some useful entries, such as "50 Common Errors in Writing" prepared by the Associated Press Writing and Editing Committee, and magazine and newspaper organizational charts.

116. Romano, Frank J. **The TypEncyclopedia: A User's Guide to Better Typography**. New York: Bowker, 1984. 188p. illus. index. LC 84-16783. ISBN 0-8352-1925-9.

Dedicated to J. Ben Lieberman, author of *Type and Typefaces* (Myriade Press, 1977) and designed by Rolf Rehe, author of *Typography and Design for Newspapers* (Design Research International, 1985) and *Typography: How to Make It Most Legible* (Design Research Publications, 1974), this guide has been in good designing hands. This practical, alphabetical, and heavily illustrated source covers more than 100 important terms. The most current in type and typography terminology, ranging from alignment and ideograph to optical spacing and trap, is represented. Thre is an index. The type cross-reference section from *Ligature* covers basic typeface designs and matches them with their various commercial names. A skimpy six-page type specimen section lists ITC and AM Varityper names only. For type selection, use a real specimen book such as the *ITC Typeface Collection* (entry 468) or *The Encyclopaedia of Type Faces* (entry 111) among others.

117. Rovin, Jeff. **The Encyclopedia of Superheroes**. New York: Facts on File, 1985. 443p. illus. index. LC 85-10329. ISBN 0-8160-1168-0.

The superheroes chronicled in this well-executed book are not of the Woodward-Bernstein variety. What we have here are more than 1,300 crimefighting characters from comic strips, television, movies, radio, literature, comic books and other magazines, and even video games. Each alphabetical entry describes the character, alter egos, occupation, costume, tools, weapons, and personal history. Though the flawed hero index does not include alter ego names, the book is a triumph. Any student or scholar of popular culture or comic art will find this valuable.

118. Stevenson, George A. **Graphic Arts Encyclopedia**. 2d ed. New York: McGraw Hill, 1979. 483p. bibliog. index. LC 78-7298. ISBN 0-07-061288-9.

In need of some revision, especially in the wake of current trends in newspaper graphics and design, this is still a useful and fairly detailed alphabetical listing of graphic arts terms and techniques. It is not, however, aimed specifically at newspaper and magazine graphics and design. There are numerous illustrations and charts, a bibliography, various tables, and separate indexes for products, manufacturers, and subjects. The author suggests that it be used either as a ready reference source or as a textbook. Adequate for brief overviews and descriptions, it has limited use as a textbook.

119. Terrace, Vincent. **Encyclopedia of Television: Series, Pilots and Specials, 1937-1973**. New York: New York Zoetrope, 1986. 480p. LC 85-043428. ISBN 0-918432-69-3. **Encyclopedia of Television: Series, Pilots and Specials, 1974-1984**. New York: New York Zoetrope, 1985. 458p. LC 84-061786. ISBN 0-918432-61-8. **Encyclopedia of Television: Series, Pilots and Specials, The Index: Who's Who in Television, 1937-1984**. New York: New York Zoetrope, 1986. 662p. LC 86-43211. ISBN ᴖ ᴠ432-71-5.

This three-volume set is a limited source for journalistic endeavors. Terrace sets us up for disappointment with this statement from volume 1: "many obscure feature films, as well as live coverage of sporting and news events, were broadcast on an experimental basis to the few television sets existing at the time." He then tells us that news and sports are not within this encyclopedia's range. Entertainment programming is the focus, but talk shows and documentaries are covered. Entries are numbered and arranged alphabetically in volumes 1 and 2. Volume 1, covering 1937-1973, describes 4,982 programs, including cast lists and credits. Volume 2 encompasses 1974-1984 and contains 2,878 programs. The index, volume 3, is divided into four sections: performers, producers, directors, and writers. Names are arranged alphabetically within those sections, and refer the user to volume and entry number. Terrace says it contains the names of more than 18,000 performers, 5,000 producers, 5,000 writers, and 3,500 directors.

120. Terrace, Vincent. **Radio's Golden Years: The Encyclopedia of Radio Programs 1930-1960**. San Diego, CA: A. S. Barnes, 1981. 308p. index. LC 79-87791. ISBN 0-498-02393-1.

This browsing tool chronicles old-time radio, listing alphabetically about 1,500 nationally broadcast network shows and syndicated entertainment programs from 1930-1960. A few new programs from the 1970s also are included. (John Dunning's *Tune In Yesterday: The Ultimate Encyclopedia of Old-Time Radio, 1925-1976* [Prentice-Hall, 1976] might also be consulted, but its use is limited as it excludes news and documentaries.) Documentaries and talk-interview shows are covered here. Information is spotty in parts, but entries usually include a story line, cast lists, and some credits. Buxton's *The Big Broadcast, 1920-1950* (entry 11) obviously overlaps this material, but he includes names you wish Terrace had—writers and directors. The entry for "Hear It Now" tells us that Edward R. Murrow narrated this documentary-type program, that "this series replayed famous events previously heard on the air," and this hour-long show was first broadcast on CBS in 1950. Unfortunately, not even a sampling of these famous events is offered, but we do learn that Alfredo Antonini conducted the orchestra.

121. **World Communications: A 200 Country Survey of Press, Radio, Television, and Film**. 5th ed. New York: Unipub, 1975. 533p. bibliog.

Though the information obviously is dated, it still represents an enormous amount of important statistical data from the *UNESCO Statistical Yearbook*. This is a survey of press, radio, television, and film in every country, arranged by type of media. A more current and detailed source for statistics on the world press is the *World Press Encyclopedia* (entry 112), but this still has its uses.

3
Dictionaries

122.   Armstrong, Brian. **The Glossary of TV Terms**. London: Barrie and Jenkins, 1976. 94p. LC 77-360018. ISBN 0-214-20212-7.

All in all, this is a disappointing volume of mostly nontechnical terms used in television in Great Britain. Use this in a pinch, but only if other sources such as *The Complete Dictionary of Television and Film* (entry 131) or the *Dictionary of Film and Television Terms* (entry 141) are not readily available.

123.   Blake, Reed H., and Edwin O. Haroldsen. **A Taxonomy of Concepts in Communication**. New York: Hastings House, 1975. 158p. bibliog. index. (Humanistic Studies in the Communication Arts, Communication Art Books).

Only the most well-known and general terms used in communication, and some in mass communication, are included in this glossary. It aims at the student or layperson seeking an overview of the vocabulary. Terms are arranged alphabetically within broad subject categories. There are author and subject indexes. Consult *The Communication Handbook: A Dictionary* (entry 128) or *A Dictionary of Communication and Media Studies* (entry 147) for more in-depth treatment.

124.   Brown, Bruce. **Brown's Index to Photocomposition Typography: A Compendium of Terminologies, Procedures and Constraints for the Guidance of Designers, Editors and Publishers**. S. W. Greenwood, ed. Minehead, Somerset, England: Greenwood Publishing, 1983. 320p. bibliog.

Brown has kept his users in mind, reminding us that he designed this little book, measuring approximately 16 centimeters in length, to be used at the drawing board. Part 1 of this comprehensive guide to photocomposition typography delivers more than 100 pages of terminology. Part 2 focuses on spacing, and part 3 on photocomposition systems. The fourth part considers typeface tables, alternate names, and manufacturers. Parts 5 and 6 examine typefactors and copyfitting.

125.   Brown, Timothy G. **International Communications Glossary**. Washington, D.C.: Media Institute, 1984. 97p. index. LC 84-62298. ISBN 0-937790-27-3.

It appears the author intended this to be far more than a dictionary of international communications. It turns out to be a Media Institute indictment in glossary format of UNESCO and the New World Information Order. According to the introduction, "the glossary explores how the advocates of a New World Information Order use language to mask their real intentions." Keeping this in mind, this can be a useful additional reference source. Almost 50 terms and phrases are arranged alphabetically in chapter 1 and some entries are more than a page long. Included are alternative media, censorship, correct and factual information, national communications policies, and (a personal favorite) progressive incorporation of communications technology. Some definitions deserve more detailed treatment, as in the case of *propaganda*: "This is not an easy one. According to the West, propaganda is what most of the Second and Third World governments and governmentrun news services put out. According to those entities, propaganda is what Western governments and news services put out. It all depends whose ox is being gored." Chapter 2 describes more than 40 organizations involved in international communications. Appendices include a short bibliography, a chronological description of "Government Actions and Press Freedom 1981-82," and an explanation of the United States International Communications Policy. See the *Glossary for International Communications: Communications in a Changing World* (entry 144) for similar treatment.

126.   Brown, William P., and Kathryn Sederberg. **The Complete Dictionary of Media Terms**. Chicago, IL: Commerce Communications, 1986. 151p. LC 86-70712. ISBN 0-913247-01-4.
       Advertising media terms are emphasized, but this dictionary is useful in defining some broadcasting terms. According to the authors,

> In the media world, a bad break isn't poor luck but awkward typesetting; a band isn't necessarily a musical group but a range of broadcast frequencies; and carts aren't used for transportation but as video tape containers. Dummies are suggested magazine layouts. Gutters become inside margins in magazines. *The Complete Dictionary of Media Terms* is intended to help you through this word maze.

The Newspaper Advertising Bureau published *Jargon: A Compendium of Terms in Use By Newspapers and Their Clients*, which might also be useful.

127.   Conners, Tracy Daniel. **Longman Dictionary of Mass Media and Communication**. New York: Longman, 1982. 255p. (Longman series in public communication). LC 82-92. ISBN 0-582-28337-X.
       This dictionary was designed to bridge the communication gap between communicators in advertising, television and radio broadcasting, film, graphic arts, journalism, photography, and publishing. Several thousand entries are arranged alphabetically and name the field of communication in which the term or phrase is used. There are some surprising omissions; for example, a journalism "lead" is defined here as a news tip or inside information. While that is not incorrect, the *lead* is more commonly defined as the first paragraph in or the main idea of a story. Still, it is an ambitious and well-organized sourcebook. Fourteen contributing editors selected and compiled terms. *Webster's New World Dictionary of Media and Communications*, to be published by Prentice-Hall in 1990, might also be useful.

128.   Devito, Joseph A. **The Communication Handbook: A Dictionary**. New York: Harper & Row, 1986. 337p. LC 85-17547. ISBN 0-06-041638-6.
       Essay-length entries aim at nonexperts — students, professionals, and researchers in search of definitions to the basic vocabulary used in communication. Entries are arranged alphabetically and may serve as a starting point for further research. Theoretical and practical terms are included in the areas of literature, art, television, speech, and science. This is not an adequate substitute for a good journalism dictionary, and it is not designed to be.

129.   Diamant, Lincoln, ed. **The Broadcast Communications Dictionary**. 3d rev. ed. New York: Greenwood Press, 1989. 266p. ISBN 0-313-26502-X.
       The publication of this dictionary was announced as *Journalism: A Guide to the Reference Literature* was going to press. The second edition was published in 1978, so the third edition is a welcome update. Technical, nontechnical, and slang terms used in radio, television, film, video, and audio are arranged alphabetically. Terms in programming, production, network, and station operations are addressed, along with engineering terms.

130.   Ellmore, R. Terry. **The Illustrated Dictionary of Broadcast-CATV-Telecommuni-cations**. Blue Ridge Summit, PA: TAB Books, 1977. 396p. LC 77-008529. ISBN 0-8306-7950-2.

A broad source for the beginner, this book stresses theoretical and technical termi-nology used by the broadcast and cable professional. Several thousand brief entries are arranged alphabetically. In spite of its age, this dictionary is still a recommended source.

131.   Ensign, Lynne Naylor, and Robyn Eileen Knapton. **The Complete Dictionary of Television and Film**. Briarcliff Manor, NY: Stein and Day, 1985. 256p. LC 83-42634. ISBN 0-8128-2922-0.

It may not be the first book "to compile, define, and standardize the language of tele-vision and film," but it probably is the most thorough. More than 2,500 terms and phrases, including jargon and slang, from the early silent picture days to the present, are included. Most important, common definitions as well as other meanings are given. Alphabetically arranged and easy to use, it should appeal to both the professional and the student.

132.   Hubbard, Stuart W. **The Computer Graphics Glossary**. Phoenix, AZ: Oryx Press, 1983. 94p. LC 82-42918. ISBN 0-89774-072-6.

A time-saving source for the artist, designer, or editor beginning to survey computer graphics language, this lists and defines technical and business terms. Product names also are included among approximately 750 terms, arranged alphabetically.

133.   Hurwitz, Leon. **Historical Dictionary of Censorship in the United States**. Westport, CT: Greenwood Press, 1985. 584p. bibliog. index. LC 84-15796. ISBN 0-313-23878-2.

Why are they called the Pentagon Papers? What were the issues in Cox Broadcasting Corporation v. Cohn? This dictionary is designed to answer such questions, but the criteria for selection and inclusion of items is unclear. Though only a portion covers constitutional censorship and First Amendment rights, "it attempts to present an overview of the types of speech and press that have been subjected to censorship, repression, and punishment" (preface). The lengthy introduction identifies four categories of governmental censorship: political, community, constitutional, and moral. Entries are arranged alphabetically and cross-referenced. The index includes subjects and titles. The list of almost 500 legal cases may be the strongest feature. Appendices include a chronology of events from 1644-1984, a table of cases, and a selected bibliography. Also of interest might be Jonathon Green's *Encyclopedia of Censorship*, which will be published by Facts on File in 1989.

134.   Jacobson, Howard B., ed. **Mass Communications Dictionary**. New York: Philo-sophical Library, 1961. 393p. LC 60-053157. ISBN 0-8022-0785-5.

As a source for current terminology in mass communications, this is obviously a very dated book. However, it proves useful as a historical study of common terminologies by the press and in printing, broadcasting, film, advertising, and communication research in the late 1950s and early 1960s. Arrangement is alphabetical, and many definitions, even those that are one sentence, are signed.

135.   Kent, Ruth Kimball. **The Language of Journalism**. Kent, OH: Kent State University Press, 1970. 186p. bibliog. LC 71-100624. ISBN 0-87338-091-6.

In her introduction, Kent writes, "Does the world of journalism need the up-to-date glossary of terms here presented? The answer is yes, for there is not a comparable book readily available to the journalism student." The answer is still yes because, as useful as this was and is, it is in dire need of updating. Also, it is out of print. *The Longman Dictionary of Mass Media and Communication* (entry 127) and *The Encyclopedia of American Jour-nalism* (entry 113) should be consulted as well. Alphabetically arranged entries focus on print journalism, and include jargon, technical terms, and selected terms in graphic arts, photography, book production, and the electronic press. Computer terms are excluded.

136.   Maggio, Rosalie. **The Nonsexist Word Finder: A Dictionary of Gender-Free Usage**. Phoenix, AZ: Oryx Press, 1987. 210p. bibliog. LC 87-17788. ISBN 0-89774-449-7.

Though not aimed specifically at the journalist, this book certainly addresses a basic problem with press language. For example, instead of "spokesman," the author suggests the following: speaker, representative, advocate, etc. Avoid "spokesperson," she says. "It is awkward and contrived, and it is generally used only for women." She also suggests that the term "ogre" be used in place of "ogress." Sexist and ambiguous terms and phrases are arranged alphabetically in this well-written and often entertaining word finder. Writing guidelines and selected readings make up the appendices. See also Casey Miller and Kate Swift's *Handbook of Nonsexist Writing* (Harper & Row, 1988).

137.   McDonald, James R. **The Broadcaster's Dictionary**. Rev. ed. Denver, CO: Wind River Books, 1987. 198p. LC 86-9215. ISBN 0-938023-04-7.

Broadcasting terms, many dealing with broadcast electronics, are listed alphabetically. The author writes, "It is hoped that this book will prove useful in training entry-level personnel in all station departments to speak and understand the same language." Appendices include lists of associations, organizations, and societies, preventive maintenance routines, and problem-solvers such as "A Painless Filter Tutorial" and "Cooling Your Equipment." Definitions are short and to the point.

138.   Mintz, Patricia Barnes. **Dictionary of Graphic Arts Terms, a Communication Tool for People who Buy Type and Printing**. New York: Van Nostrand Reinhold, 1981. 318p. bibliog. LC 80-25236. ISBN 0-442-26711-8.

The terminology of the graphic arts industry, with emphasis on newspapers and commercial printers, is presented alphabetically. Included are printing, typography, binding, publishing, papermaking, and design terms and techniques. It aims at editors and production supervisors, and should be particularly useful to the student.

139.   Murray, John. **The Media Law Dictionary**. Washington, D.C.: University Press of America, 1978. 139p. LC 78-63257. ISBN 0-8191-0616-X.

Murray is stingy with prefatory and introductory material, leaving users to their own resources. More than 400 standard and mass media law terms and phrases are defined, some in great detail, with references to cases and historical background. Definitions are, on the whole, very well-written and easy to understand. A table of cases and a table of cases with terms, as well as a short bibliography, comprise the appendices. Murray suggests that his dictionary is appropriate for students and "news handlers and editorialists." Never chatty, he offers the "news handler" just enough information with which to engage in intelligent conversation on neutral reportage, a lively debate on access to information, or an argument over fighting words.

140.   National Association of Broadcasters, **Standard Definitions of Broadcast Research Terms**. James E. Fletcher, ed. 3d ed. Washington, D.C.: National Association of Broadcasters, 1988. 75p. index. ISBN 0-89324-039-7.

Terminology used in broadcast audience measurement is offered in great detail, considering the size of the book. Sections focus on terminology and jargon, statistical measures, sampling, and survey methods. This is useful for the scholar in search of standard definitions to more than 100 terms.

141.   Oakey, Virginia. **Dictionary of Film and Television Terms**. New York: Barnes and Noble, 1982. 206p. LC 82-48254. ISBN 0-06-463566-X.

A typical entry reads: "Announcement. A commercial. 'We'll be back after the following announcement.' " It is comforting to see some terms used in a complete sentence. More than 3,000 briefly defined words and phrases are listed alphabetically and address the technical and nontechnical, informal, business, and artistic aspects of film and television. There are cross-references, and terms capitalized within a definition have separate entries. Oakey has compiled a serviceable reference for industry professionals and students.

142. Penney, Edmund. **A Dictionary of Media Terms**. New York: Putnam, 1984. 158p. LC 83-27051. ISBN 0-399-12958-8.

Ray Bradbury provides an appropriate commentary in the introduction: "Well, enough of kicking the dead horse alive. Here is the talk, here are the words that encompass the ideas that lubricate an Industry to help make of it an Art. Jump in. But be careful not to trip over the clapper board, the Green-Man, or the Release Negative." This listing of the "workaday vocabulary," more than 1,000 terms, phrases, jargon, and slang used in television, radio, and film, is an adequate source for the beginner, but others are urged to look elsewhere for more thorough definitions. *The Complete Dictionary of Television and Film* (entry 131) offers more terms, more details, and less superficiality.

143. Stone, Bernard. **The Graphic Artists' Illustrated Glossary**. Englewood Cliffs, NJ: Prentice-Hall, 1987. 117p. illus. LC 86-22536. ISBN 0-13-363052-8.

The vocabulary of the working graphic artist is presented here, and Stone says he has "attempted to present the mutually agreed-upon meanings of words and phrases as they relate to art, design, and copy preparation." Printing and production terms are excluded. Nearly 600 terms and phrases include numerous photographs and drawings, illustrating what crop marks look like and the difference between ragged-right and ragged-left type columns. Alphabetically arranged entries range from "greeking" (nonreadable type-like characters to simulate the size and position of type in a layout or dummy) to "reducing glass" (a looking glass for viewing images in reduced dimensions).

144. Sussman, Leonard R. **Glossary for International Communications: Communications in a Changing World**. Volume III. Washington, D.C.: Media Institute, 1983. unpaged. LC 83-62432. ISBN 0-937790-18-4.

In his introduction, Sussman mentions George Orwell and Newspeak, and talks at length about UNESCO and its relationship with the press. Finally, he addresses the glossary: "This glossary seeks to demonstrate the varied uses of a single word or term in the decade-long debates." Included are 50 terms and phrases in communications, each with four definitions: first world, second world (or Marxist), third world, and UNESCO. Entries include equitable news flow, freedom of the press, journalistic code, New World Information Order, right to communicate, source of information, and human rights. Sussman says this is aimed at students, reporters, lawyers, and public policymakers in international discussion. "It will be possible to understand the aims of the participants and the intent of the drafters." See also the *International Communications Glossary* (entry 125).

145. Thompson, Philip, and Peter Davenport. **The Dictionary of Graphic Images**. New York: St. Martin's Press, 1980. 258p. LC 80-28163. ISBN 0-312-20108-7.

Imaginative use of the visual cliché is the theme of this unusual source. Entries are arranged alphabetically, and, of course, there are numerous black and white photographs and illustrations. Entries range from atomic cloud to ZZZZZ, and include graphic art forms in books, newspapers, magazines, and television. There also are examples of record sleeves, posters, and advertisements of all kinds. When the creativity level is down, pick this up.

146. Vince, John. **Dictionary of Computer Graphics**. White Plains, NY: Knowledge Industry Publications, 1984. 132p. bibliog. LC 84-17178. ISBN 0-86729-134-6.

Designed with the computer layperson in mind, this dictionary contains almost 200 terms, some quite technical. However, it might prove useful for newspaper or television graphic artists, especially those involved in pagination and informational graphics. Color plates and line drawings and figures are included.

147. Watson, James, and Anne Hill. **A Dictionary of Communication and Media Studies**. London: Edward Arnold, 1984. 183p. ISBN 0-7131-6410-7.

A dictionary with a British slant, terms and phrases are listed alphabetically, defined in great detail, and cross-referenced. This is a scholarly source for students of communication. Entries on broadcasting, architecture, art, film, language, the press, radio, media technology, and communication theories are included.

148.   Weik, Martin H. **Communications Standard Dictionary**. New York: Van Nostrand Reinhold,1983. 1045p. LC 81-021842. ISBN 0-442-21933-4.

Communications is defined as the "branch of science and technology concerned with the process of representing, transferring, and interpreting the meaning assigned to data by and among persons, places, or machines." If you can make sense of that, this might be the dictionary for you. Technical terminology in communications and communications systems is arranged alphabetically and cross-referenced.

4
Indexes, Abstracts, and Databases

Indexes and Abstracts

The following indexes, abstracts, and databases are sources focusing on various aspects of journalism. Unfortunately, only a few indexes are devoted solely to journalism and none is comprehensive. For the most part, indexes to individual newspapers are not included. (University Microfilms International's annual *Serials in Microform* lists numerous newspaper indexes, and Milner's *Newspaper Indexes* [entry 425] provides a union list.) For updates on indexes available on compact disk, users are advised to check the latest edition of *CD-ROMs in Print* (Meckler). Addresses of database vendors and suppliers are listed in the Appendix.

149. **ABC News Index**. Woodbridge, CT: Research Publications, 1969- . 4 issues/year.
   "Nightline," "ABC News Closeup," "ABC News Special," "Business World," "20/20," "This Week with David Brinkley," "World News Tonight," and "Viewpoint" are included in this index which provides access to the complete transcripts on microfiche (entry 490). It is issued quarterly and cumulated annually. A 1970-1985 cumulative index is available. Users can search the index for subject, program title, or names of personalities. A brief abstract, date, and fiche number accompany each entry. See also the *Television News Index and Abstracts* (entry 185).

150. **Abstracts of Popular Culture**. Bowling Green, OH: Bowling Green University Popular Press, 1976-1982. 4 issues/year. LC 77-647685. ISSN 0147-2615.
   Citations and abstracts to periodical articles and conference papers focus on popular culture or "the New Humanities," but abstracts are not organized by subject. Citations are arranged by broad and general subject headings such as "Television," and refer only to accession number. Even though *JQ: Journalism Quarterly, Broadcasting,* and *Columbia Journalism Review* are included, their contents are more accessible in the Wilson indexes (entries 156, 165, 181, and 184).

151. **Alternative Press Index**. Baltimore, MD: Alternative Press Center, 1969- . Quarterly. LC 76-24027. ISSN 0002-662X.
   Clearly a by-product of the sixties, this index pays tribute to the more "radical" and lesser-known journals of the alternative press. Periodicals ranging from the *Journal of Palestine Studies* to *Phoenix Rising* (an "anti-psychiatry" journal) are indexed along with other alternative, ethnic, Marxist, feminist, and gay publications. Even the *St. Louis*

Journalism Review (entry 546) has found a home here. It is a physically unattractive source, with computer-generated type crammed on pages. It also is slow with indexing, and it may take a year or two for an article to appear. Nevertheless, this is very important in journalism research. Obviously, it is a useful guide for identifying and delving into the alternative press publications, but it also is a vehicle by which one can study how the alternative press covers the press. Subject headings such as "Journalism," "Television Reporters and Reporting," "Newspaper Reporters and Reporting," "Photojournalism," "Newspapers and Politics," and even "Alternative Press" make this possible.

152. **Art Index.** New York: H. W. Wilson, 1929- . Quarterly. LC 31-7513. ISSN 0004-3222.
    Although there are a few citations under "Newspaper Layout and Photography," "Journalism," and "Editing," this index excels in coverage of photojournalism and photography. Articles appear under the headings "Photography, Journalistic," "Television Programs-News," "Photography, Documentary," "War Photography," and "Photography of Sports." Entries to the periodical literature of art, architecture, fine and graphic arts, design, and photography are arranged alphabetically by subject and author. References to yearbooks and museum bulletins are scattered. It is also available online on Wilsonline.

153. **Arts and Humanities Citation Index.** Philadelphia, PA: Institute for Scientific Research, 1977- . 3 issues/year. LC 79-642953. ISSN 0162-8445.
    More than 1,400 journals are fully indexed and 4,700 are selectively indexed to provide citation indexing to a full range of humanities and arts journals, from the *Journal of Country Music* to the *Journal of Ecclesiastical History*. This citation index provides access to an article, and then lists authors or researchers who have cited it. It is issued in five parts: citation index, source index, corporate index, permuterm subject index, and guide and journal lists. For example, the source index offers a bibliographic description of all items cited in footnotes or bibliography for each entry.
    Warning: This is not *Readers' Guide*. A little time and patience must be invested in learning to massage this source for the information you seek. It is also available online (entry 195). Selectively covered are *JQ: Journalism Quarterly, Communication Research, Communication Education, Public Opinion Quarterly, Written Communication,* and the *Journal of Popular Culture.* Of similar limited use might be the *Social Sciences Citation Index,* also produced by the Institute for Scientific Research.

154. Blassingame, John W., and Mae G. Henderson, eds. **Antislavery Newspapers and Periodicals.** 5 vols. Boston, MA: G. K. Hall, 1980. LC 79-20230. ISBN 0-8161-8163-2 (v. 1), -8434-8 (v. 2), -8558-1 (v. 3), -8559-X (v. 4), and -8560-3 (v. 5).
    Only letters are indexed in this multivolume annotated index of various nineteenth-century abolitionist and reform newspapers, but the editors chose to list letters "because we felt they contained more of the personal details of history than did editorials, signed articles, book reviews, advertisements, and the like." Annotations are arranged chronologically in each journal. Volume 1 includes the *Philanthropist* (Mount Pleasant, OH), *Emancipator* (Jonesborough, Tennessee), *Abolition Intelligencer* (Shelbyville, KY), *Genius of Universal Emancipation, African Observer,* and the first 15 years of the *Liberator* (Boston). Volume 2 contains the second part of the *Liberator, Anti-Slavery Record* (New York), *Human Rights* (New York), and the *Observer* (Alton, IL). Volume 3 holds the *Friend of Man* (Utica, NY), *Pennsylvania Freeman, Advocate of Freedom* (Hallowell, ME), and the *American & Foreign Anti-Slavery Reporter* (New York). Volume 4 contains the first 20 years of the *National Anti-Slavery Standard*, and volume 5 the last 11 years. This is an unusual collection, and provides another avenue in the study of black and southern history, editors and editing, and publishing practices.

155. **British Humanities Index.** London: Library Association, 1962- . Quarterly. ISBN 0-85365-668-1.
    This source is essential in searching, for example, periodical literature on newspapering in Great Britain, and indexes articles in the humanities as well as the social

sciences. Entries are arranged alphabetically by subject, and focus on all aspects of the humanities, including journalism, political journalism, newspapers and editors, television news, and television documentaries in the United Kingdom. Consult the *Subject Index to Periodicals* for articles published prior to 1961.

156. **Business Periodicals Index**. New York: H. W. Wilson, 1958- . Monthly.
     Journalism is a business, and this index is easy to overlook if one forgets that. *Business Periodicals Index*, a subject index to all aspects of business and management, is brimming with subject headings relevant to journalism and media management: "Journalism Awards," "Journalistic Ethics," "Interns," "Minorities in Journalism," "Journalism as a Profession," "Newspaper Editors," and "Television Broadcasting-News." In addition, *Editor & Publisher* and *Broadcasting* are indexed. This also is available online (entry 201) and on compact disk.

157. **Canadian Periodical Index. Index de Periodiques Canadiens**. Ottawa: Canadian Library Association, 1938- . Monthly. LC 49-2133. ISSN 0008-4719.
     Almost 100 Canadian and some American magazines are included in this index of general-interest periodicals. Citations are arranged alphabetically by author and subject. Subject headings are in English, although there are French cross-references. Business, the arts, social sciences, education, science, and technology are all covered. In addition, numerous subject headings such as "College and School Journalism," "Radio Broadcasting -News," "Television Broadcasting-News," "Freedom of the Press," "Crime and the Press," "Ethnic Press," and "Reporters and Reporting," make this a valuable source to be used in addition to the *Readers' Guide to Periodical Literature* (entry 181). See also the *Canadian News Index* (Micromedia).

158. **CBS News Index**. Ann Arbor, MI: University Microfilms International Research Collections, 1975- . Quarterly. LC 76-648172. ISSN 0362-3238.
     CBS News broadcasts from 1975 to the present are indexed in this quarterly source with annual cumulations. Full-text transcripts of the broadcasts are available on microfiche (entry 492). It is arranged alphabetically by subject and name. See also the *Television News Index and Abstracts* (entry 185).

159. **Communication Abstracts**. Beverly Hills, CA: Sage Publications, 1978- . 4 issues/ year. LC 78-645162. ISSN 0162-2811.
     The major communication abstracting source, *Communication Abstracts* also touches on numerous mass communications and journalism-related items. Abstracts are numbered and subdivided into sections of articles, then books and book chapters. Each issue contains approximately 300 abstracts from nearly 100 journals and 30-40 books. A complete list of periodicals abstracted in *Communication Abstracts* (around 200 titles) is published in the third issue of each volume. Subject indexes in random issues have included media ownership, media stereotypes, First Amendment, freedom of the press, government and the media, journalism history, libel, news selection, news gathering, and television news. Subject and author indexes cumulate annually. *Communication* is broadly defined, and this source should not be overlooked. The *International Index to Television Periodicals* (International Federation of Film Archives) on microfiche might also provide useful references.

160. **Comprehensive Dissertation Index, 1861-1972**. Ann Arbor, MI: University Micro- films International, 1973. 37 vols. LC 73-89046. **Supplement, 1973-1982**. 1984. Annual, with multiyear cumulations.
     With 37 volumes in the original index, 38 volumes in the supplement, and no abstracts, this can be an unwieldy, and sometimes frustrating, source to use. There is an author index, and sections are arranged by subject in sciences, social sciences, and humanities (where mass communications dissertations appear). If you have the money, search *Dissertation Abstracts Online*, which not only retrieves abstracts (since 1980), but

also accesses *Comprehensive Dissertation Index, American Doctoral Dissertations, Dissertation Abstracts International,* and even *Masters Abstracts.* If you want to keep the search simple, consult *Journalism Abstracts* (entry 171), which abstracts doctoral dissertations and masters' theses from 1963 to the present.

161. **The Cumulated Magazine Subject Index, 1907-1949.** Boston, MA: G. K. Hall, 1964. 2 vols. LC 65-98.

Of great historical value, this index complements the *Readers' Guide to Periodical Literature* (entry 181) and offers subject and author access to the general periodical literature of its time. Regional magazines receive emphasis. Subject headings such as "Army Newspapers," "Negro Newspapers," and "Reporters and Reporting," allow access to articles entitled "Newspapers – How They Annihilate Time" in *Munsey's Magazine* and "Ethics of Newsboys" in the *Westminster Review.* Consult *Pooles' Index* or *Nineteenth Century Readers' Guide to Periodical Literature* for pre-1907 writings.

162. **Current Index to Journals in Education (CIJE).** Educational Resources Information Center. Phoenix, AZ: Oryx Press, 1969- . Monthly, with semiannual cumulations.

In addition to serving as an index to almost 800 education periodicals, *CIJE* also allows easy access to the journalism education-related literature in periodicals we would normally overlook. For example, a recent issue of *Omega: The Journal of Death and Dying* contains "Death As a Measure of Life: A Research Note on the Kastenbaum-Spilka Strategy of Obituary Analyses." *CIJE*'s sibling, *Resources in Education* (entry 182), indexes and abstracts the unpublished material, documents, etc., in education. Both are part of the ERIC family and are available online (entry 208) and on compact disk. This is a source not to be overlooked, as it indexes *Critical Studies in Mass Communication, English Journal, Journalism Educator, C: JET, Quill & Scroll,* and *JQ: Journalism Quarterly. Education Index,* available in printed indexes and online (entry 207) might also be useful, but it relies heavily on *Journalism Educator.*

163. **Essay and General Literature Index.** New York: H. W. Wilson, 1900- . Semiannual, with annual cumulation. LC 34-14581. ISSN 0014-083X.

A newspaper editor called recently and wanted to find an essay that Henry J. Smith, managing editor of the *Chicago Daily News,* wrote more than 50 years ago. *Essay and General Literature Index,* which allows author, title, and subject access to collections of essays, provided the missing pieces – the title and the collection in which the essay was located. Sometimes overlooked, this dependable old standby presents the researcher with an alternative to periodical literature. Fruitful subject headings include "Government and the Press," "Newspaper Publishing," "Freedom of the Press," "Television Broadcasting of News," and "Press and Politics." This also is available on compact disk.

164. **Graphic Arts Literature Abstracts.** Rochester, NY: Rochester Institute of Technology, Technical and Education Center of the Graphic Arts, 1954- . Monthly. ISSN 0090-8207.

Selected articles from *Graphic Arts Monthly, American Printer, Editor & Publisher, IFRA Newspaper Techniques,* and other graphic arts publications are numbered, abstracted, and arranged by subject in this monthly source. There are author and key-word indexes and a detailed table of contents. Business and financial subjects are covered, as well as articles on science, research, technology, marketing, graphic design, copy preparation, and education. In one recent issue listing nearly 200 citations, articles ranged from "The Importance of Satellite Technology for Newspaper Page Facsimile" to "Many Hazards Endanger Graphic Communications Workers."

165. **Humanities Index.** New York: H. W. Wilson, June 1974- . Quarterly. LC 75-648836. ISSN 0095-5981.

This index to the arts, history, language, and literature includes a wide range of English-language print and broadcast journalism-oriented periodicals. For pre-1974 articles, use the *Social Sciences and Humanities Index* (1965-1974) and the *International Index* (1907-1965). See also the *Social Sciences Index* (entry 184), its sibling. *Columbia Journalism Review, Communication Quarterly, Journal of Broadcasting, Journal of Popular Culture, JQ: Journalism Quarterly, Journalism History,* and even *The Quill* are indexed. Consult this index for articles on current research trends as well as news and views on journalism. Especially useful are subject headings labeled "Newspaper Reading," "Newspaper Layout and Photography," "Journalistic Ethics," and "Broadcast Journalism." It is indispensable, and available online (entry 212) and on compact disk. See also the *American Humanities Index* (Whitson Press).

166. **Index to Black Newspapers**. Ann Arbor, MI: University Microfilms International Research Collections. Quarterly.

This quarterly index provides access to the Black Newspaper Collection (entry 491), and indexes the following newspapers: *Afro-American* (Maryland), *AM Journal* (Chicago), *Amsterdam News* (New York), *Argus* (St. Louis), *Call & Post* (Cleveland), *Chicago Defender, Michigan Chronicle* (Detroit), *Los Angeles Sentinel, New Pittsburgh Courier*, and *Norfolk Journal & Guide*. There are personal-name and subject sections.

167. **Index to Journalism Periodicals**. London, Ontario: University of Western Ontario Journalism School, 1986- . Available on microfiche. 2 updates/year.

More than 40 journalism periodicals are selectively indexed in this microfiche source. Entries are arranged by broad subject (censorship, reporting, women and media, etc.) in either the "Old Journals" section, containing citations more than 10 years old, or the "Current Journals" section, which lists citations to articles published during the last 10 years. It is updated twice a year and entries are cumulative. Entries list title, volume, month, and year, but do not include authors or page numbers. There is a subject headings list. Journals selectively indexed include the following: *ASNE Bulletin, APME News, Columbia Journalism Review, Content, Grassroots Editor, IPI Report, Nieman Reports, Journalism History, Journalism Quarterly, Masthead, Newspaper Research Journal, Quill, presstime*, and *Washington Journalism Review*. Although this index is not comprehensive and can be cumbersome to use, the University of Western Ontario is to be commended for being a pioneer in journalism periodical indexing. See also the *Canadian Journalism Data Base* (entry 204).

168. **Index to Legal Periodicals**. New York: H. W. Wilson, 1908- . Monthly. LC 41-21689. ISSN 0019-4077.

For articles such as "The Installation Commander Versus an Aggressive News Media in an On-Post Terrorist Incident: Avoiding the Constitutional Collision," in *Army Law*, reach for this index. Legal periodicals, yearbooks, reviews, etc. published in the United States, Canada, Great Britain, Ireland, Australia, and New Zealand are indexed. This is one of the best sources for searching communications law, and subject headings such as "Freedom of the Press," "Censorship," and "Libel and Slander" provide easy access. This also is available online. See also *Legal Resource Index* (entry 216), an online database offering abstracts of legal periodicals, and *Media Law Reporter* (entry 533).

169. Jacobs, Donald M., ed. **Antebellum Black Newspapers**. Westport, CT: Greenwood Press, 1976. 587p. index. LC 76-002119. ISBN 0-8371-8824-5.

Freedom's Journal, The Rights of All, The Weekly Advocate, and the *Colored American* are indexed separately in this index of pre-Civil War black newspapers. Entries are arranged chronologically under alphabetically arranged subject headings. Biographical material for editors is included, along with newspaper background and publishing information. This is a valuable source on newspaper publishing history and black journalism. The entire contents are indexed, unlike *Antislavery Newspapers and Periodicals* (entry 154), which indexes letters only.

170. Jodziewicz, Thomas W. **Birth of America: The Year in Review, 1763-1783; A Chronological Guide and Index to the Contemporary and Colonial Press**. Glen Rock, NJ: Microfilming Corporation of America. 152p. LC 76-50542. ISBN 0-667-00288-X.

This selected index of 52 colonial and revolutionary newspapers on microfilm is arranged chronologically and provides a year-by-year account of the colonial press. According to the introduction, "during the era of the American Revolution, the colonial press served to convey patriot and, for a time, non-patriot sentiments within the colonies from New Hampshire to Georgia, as well as to instruct colonists in how to dress and what to buy." Descriptive and topical chronologies for each year, as well as citations to newspaper articles "that are consciously selected to illustrate the chronological text" are included. Newspapers range from the *Boston Evening Post* to the *Gazette of the State of Georgia*. There is a subject index.

171. **Journalism Abstracts**. Columbia, SC: Association for Education in Journalism and Mass Communication. 1963- . Annual. ISSN 0075-4412.

Doctoral dissertations and masters' theses in journalism and mass communications from 50 universities in the United States and Canada are indexed and abstracted. A detailed subject index and separate author and institution indexes allow thorough access to this important source. Research subjects range from the alternative press to the Associated Press. Students write their own abstracts, so the quality, style, and readability vary. An average of 250-300 abstracts appears in each annual issue.

172. **The Magazine Index**. Belmont, CA: Information Access, 1977- . Monthly. LC 85-10113.

Magazine Index would be even more popular if it were available in print, but it is a microform source. It is widely accessed online (entry 217). This index to general periodicals is similar to *Readers' Guide to Periodical Literature* (entry 181), as it covers similar publications. General articles on most aspects of print journalism and television broadcasting are included.

173. Matlon, Ronald J., ed. **Index to Journals in Communication Studies Through 1985**. Annandale, VA: Speech Communication Association, 1987. 645p. LC 87-061400.

In this index, "communication studies" is a mix of communication, mass communication, journalism, and speech. Part 1 includes tables of contents through 1985 of the following journals: *Quarterly Journal of Speech* (1915-), *Communication Monographs* (1934-), *Communication Education* (1952-), *Critical Studies in Mass Communication* (1984-), *Southern Speech Communication Journal* (1935-), *Western Journal of Speech Communication* (1937-), *Central States Speech Journal* (1949-), *Communication Quarterly* (1953-), *Association for Communication Administration Bulletin* (1972-), *Philosophy and Rhetoric* (1968-), *Journal of Communication* (1951-), *Human Communication Research* (1974-), *Journal of Broadcasting and Electronic Media* (1956-), *Journal of the American Forensic Association* (1964-), and *JQ: Journalism Quarterly* (1924-). All entries are numbered.

Part 2 is an index of contributors, and part 3 is loaded with indexes: the coded classification of subjects in communication studies, subject index, and key-word index. Relevant material is indexed under the umbrella headings of journalism, print media, radio, and television, which are further divided and subdivided. There is no introductory or explanatory material except for a terse explanation of coded classifications. Most of these journals are indexed elsewhere; however, the convenience of having the entire contents of these 15 journals reproduced and indexed in one volume may well outweigh the inconvenience of having to deal with coded classifications.

174. Modern Language Association. **MLA International Bibliography of Books and Articles on the Modern Languages and Literatures**. New York: Modern Language Association, 1921- . Annual. LC 64-20773. ISSN 0024-8215.

While its use in journalistic research is limited and specialized, the *MLA Bibliography* is worth mentioning. Now that it has a subject index, the topics of "American Journalism" and "New Journalism" can be searched to unveil gems such as this: "American Literature. Prose. 1900-1999. Wolfe, Thomas Kennerly, Jr. *The Right Stuff*. Role of JOURNALISM compared to Mailer, Norman: *The Executioner's Song*; Capote, Truman: *Handcarved Coffins*. 1:9393." International articles focusing on modern languages, literature, folklore, and linguistics are included. It is available online for users who still find the Classified and Subject sections impossible to use.

175. **The National Newspaper Index**. Belmont, CA: Information Access, 1979- . Monthly. LC 83-9488.

The New York Times, Christian Science Monitor, Wall Street Journal, Chicago Tribune, and the *Los Angeles Times* are indexed and available on microfilm. This is also available online (entry 219). The *Canadian News Index* (Micromedia) indexes Canadian newspapers such as the *Toronto Star* and *Vancouver Sun.*

176. **NewsBank Index**. New Canaan, CT: NewsBank, 1975- . Monthly. ISSN 0737-3813.

Selected articles from more than 450 newspapers across the country are indexed monthly and made available in full text on microfiche in this news reference service. The paper indexes cumulate quarterly and annually. Its timeliness, wide range of newspapers indexed, general subject indexing, and guaranteed availability of articles make this a perfect source for those who require instant gratification. NewsBank is useful as a general survey of the press and in searching journalistic topics such as "Printing and Publishing Industries-Newspapers," "Television Broadcasting," "Mass Media and Politics," "Religions-Television Ministries," and even "Traffic-Traffic Reporters." Articles on film, television, and fine arts are included in *NewsBank: Review of the Arts: Film and Television.* All *NewsBank* indexes are available on compact disk.

177. **The New York Times Film Reviews, 1913-1968**. New York: The New York Times and Arno Press, 1970. 6 vols. LC 70-112777. ISSN 0362-3688. **Supplement**, 1969/70- . Every two years.

The reference literature of film is well covered in other sources, but these collections of reviews are included here because of their "newspaper of record" status. Reviews are reproduced exactly as they appear in *The New York Times*, so each volume takes on the appearance of a well-kept clipping scrapbook. More than 18,000 reviews are reprinted in the original volumes, and biennial volumes have been published since 1971. There are title, name, and corporate-name indexes. This is one of the best sources available for examples of good critical writing. Film critics and journalism students should give this the most wear and tear.

178. **The New York Times Index**. New York: The New York Times Co., **First Series**, 15 volumes, 1851-1912; **Second Series**, 68 volumes, 1913-1929; **Third Series**, 1930- . Semimonthly. LC 13-13458. ISSN 0147-538X.

This is one of only a few printed newspaper indexes to earn a separate entry because, as the subtitle modestly informs us, it is "a book of record." *The New York Times Index* is an amazing subject, geographical-name, and personal-name reference source, as it "can be used by itself for a basic chronological overview of the news, or it can be used as a guide to the location of the full articles in the original newspapers." Abstracts of all significant news articles, features, and editorials are included. It cumulates annually. Also available is a *Guide to the Incomparable New York Times Index* (entry 358), a 71-page treatise complete with index. Consult Milner's *Newspaper Indexes: A Location and Subject Guide for Researchers* (entry 425) for other printed newspaper indexes. *The New York Times* is indexed in numerous online sources and is available in full text on NEXIS (entry 226). The New York Times also publishes *The New York Times Obituaries Index* (vol. 1, 1858-1968; vol. 2, 1969-1978).

179. **The Official Washington Post Index**. Woodbridge, CT: Research Publications, 1979- . Monthly, with annual cumulations. ISSN 0193-9580.

If *The New York Times Index* is "a book of record," then the *Washington Post Index* is a record of government. This subject and name index contains abstracts of all news and feature stories, editorials, reviews, obituaries, cartoons, photographs, maps, and even advertisements with information of "permanent value" that appeared in the final edition and regional weeklies in D.C., Maryland, and Virginia. It is available in full text on Vu/Text, DataTimes, and DIALOG.

180. **PAIS Bulletin**. New York: Public Affairs Information Service, 1914- . Monthly. LC 16-920. ISSN 0731-0110.

Periodical articles, books, government documents, and reports focusing on all aspects of contemporary public issues or public policy are listed in this subject index. Numerous sources in German, French, Italian, Portuguese, and Spanish are utilized as well as those in English. Articles such as "El Salvador: A Comparative Study of Canadian and American Press Reporting, 1981-1983" from the *Canadian Journal of Latin American and Caribbean Studies* are found here. Numerous citations appear under general broadcasting, journalism, radio, television, and press headings. *JQ: Journalism Quarterly* is indexed. The *PAIS Bulletin* also is available online (entry 227).

181. **Readers' Guide to Periodical Literature**. New York: H. W. Wilson, 1900- . Monthly. LC 05-14769. ISSN 0034-0464.

Readers' Guide, the deity of popular periodical indexes, offers a wealth of information to anyone willing to dig a little. Certainly, in searching the literature of journalism, one will run into the " 'Don Johnson Made Me Cry (Almost)' and Other Confessions of a Celebrity Reporter" articles. There also are articles such as "The $19,000 Press Pass: A Former Journalism School Dean Asks 'Is It Worth It'?" from *The Washington Monthly*. All major news and current affairs magazines are included in this author and subject index. Subject headings such as "Black Journalists," "Terrorism and the Press," "Police-Press Relations," "Journalistic Ethics," and "Television Broadcasting-News" can yield useful articles. *Readers' Guide* also can be used to trace the popular historical trail with articles from "Is the Newspaper Office the Place for a Girl?" (1901) to "Women: The New Majority in Journalism School" (1986). It is available online (entry 229) and on compact disk. Also of use is *Nineteenth Century Readers' Guide to Periodical Literature* and *Access: The Supplementary Index to Periodicals* (John Gordon Burke, publisher), another general-interest index, which makes it a point not to duplicate any periodicals indexed in the *Readers' Guide*. See also *Readers' Guide Abstracts* (entry 228).

182. **Resources in Education (RIE)**. Bethesda, MD: Educational Resources Information Center, 1966- . Monthly, with annual cumulation. (Subscriptions to Superintendent of Documents, U.S. Government Printing Office, Washington, D.C.). ISSN 0197-9973.

Part of the ERIC family of publications, this monthly subject and author abstracting service attempts to harness the reports, documents, papers, and other materials which so easily get buried and lost. Among these are the Association for Education in Journalism and Mass Communication (AEJMC) papers presented at annual meetings. *Journalism Monographs* (entry 525) is also included. Subject headings such as "Journalism History," "Television News," "Press Opinion," and "News Sources" provide numerous entry points and make this a fairly painless abstracting source to use. Publications are available on microfiche, arranged according to ERIC document number. Paper copies also are available from ERIC Document Reproduction Service. *RIE* can be searched online in the ERIC database (entry 208), which includes *RIE*'s sister publication *Current Index to Journals in Education* (CIJE, entry 162).

183. Satin, Allan D. **A Doonesbury Index: An Index to the Syndicated Daily Newspaper Strip "Doonesbury" by G. B. Trudeau, 1970-1983**. Metuchen, NJ: Scarecrow Press, 1985. 269p. LC 85-2037. ISBN 0-8108-1800-0.

This index of "Doonesbury" is included because of the strip's impact on cartoon art and editorial statement. "Doonesbury" has affected journalism mainly by raising issues related to censorship, obscenity, credibility, and sensationalism. Names of public figures, subjects, events, issues, fictional characters, and phrases are indexed in great detail and cross-referenced. All strips published in major newspapers from October 26, 1970 (when the first strip appeared in *The Washington Post*) to January 2, 1983 (when Gary Trudeau went on sabbatical) are indexed in exhaustive detail.

184. **Social Sciences Index**. New York: H. W. Wilson, June 1974- . Quarterly. LC 78-1032. ISSN 0094-4920.

More than 350 social sciences periodicals focusing on political science, psychology, economics, law, geography, etc. are indexed, but useful articles on print and broadcast journalism can still be found. Articles on journalism and politics, freedom of the press, news agencies, reporters and reporting, and news programs on television are located in English-language periodicals ranging from the *Journal of Adolescence* to the *Far Eastern Economic Review*. This is a subject and author index. It also is available online (entry 235). For pre-1974 articles, use the *Social Sciences and Humanities Index* (1965-1974) or the *International Index* (1907-1965). See also the humanities counterpart, *Humanities Index* (entry 165).

185. **Television News Index and Abstracts: A Guide to the Videotape Collection of the Network Evening News Programs in the Vanderbilt Television News Archives**. Nashville, TN: Vanderbilt Television News Archives, 1968- . Monthly. LC 74-646462. ISSN 0085-7157.

Network news from mid-1968 to the present is thoroughly abstracted in this detailed index to ABC, CBS, and NBC evening news reports. (Reports are available on videotape in the Vanderbilt Television News Archives [entry 723], along with videotapes of special newscasts not included in this index). Abstracts for each day's news are arranged according to network, date, and time, and include reporters' names, time code information, and commercials. The index is arranged alphabetically according to name and subject, and there is a separate index to reporters. There is usually a three- or four-month time lag, which is not surprising considering the detail involved. An excerpt from the December 1987 index (December 7) reads:

-5:42:40 WT. HSE. CHRISTMAS TREE/NANCY RAISA RELS.
(S: DR) Scenes shown of Nancy Reagan receiving Wt. Hse. Christmas tree.
Raisa Gorbachev noted needed reminding of Nancy Reagan's coffee invitation [Nancy Reagan- explains situation.]
(S: DR) Nancy Reagan quoted regarding Raisa Gorbachev.
5:43:30 (COMMERCIAL: Pam; FTD; Mercedes-Benz; Maalox Whip.)

This is one of the most important resources available in researching the growth and development, rise and fall of television news.

186. **The Times Index**. Reading, England: Newspaper Archive Developments, 1973- . Monthly.

See also the following: *Index to the Times* (1906-1972, Times), *Palmer's Index to the Times Newspaper* (1790-June 1941, Palmer), and *The Times Index* (1785-1790, Newspaper Archive Developments).

The Times, as well as *The Sunday Times, The Times Literary Supplement, The Times Educational Supplement,* and *The Times Higher Education Supplement* are now indexed. One of its best uses is as a book of record. There are annual cumulations beginning in 1977.

187. **Topicator: Classified Article Guide to the Advertising/Communications/Marketing Periodical Press**. Florissant, CO: Topicator, 1965- . Bimonthly. LC 82-2479. ISSN 0040-9340.

Topicator has a lot going against it: it only indexes about 20 periodicals, it is not particularly timely, and access is via subject only. Emphasis is on marketing and advertising, so its use is limited, but it indexes titles such as *TV Guide, Marketing & Media Decisions,* and *Television/Radio Age*.

188. **TV Guide 25-Year Index by Author and Subject**. Catherine Johnson, ed., Joyce Post, indexer. Radnor, PA: Triangle Publications, 1979. 506p. LC 79-67725. ISBN 0-9603684-0-X. **Cumulative Supplement**, 1978-1982. Catherine Johnson, ed. 1983. 176p. LC 83-51316. ISBN 0-9603684-3-4. Annual supplements.

More than 14,000 articles published from 1953-1977 in the metropolitan New York edition of *TV Guide* are indexed. It contains more than 42,000 subject, author, and show entries, and is a good source for historical material on network television news and programming. Various supplements are available: 1978-1980 Supplement, 1978-1982 Cumulative Supplement, and annual supplements. Though the only complete sets of *TV Guide* are located in the Library of Congress and at *TV Guide*'s headquarters, *TV Guide* is available on microfilm.

189. **The Wall Street Journal Index**. New York: Dow Jones, 1957- . Monthly. LC 59-35162. ISSN 0083-7075.

The Wall Street Journal, also available online, is more than a newspaper of business and finance. In fact, the latest circulation figures indicate that the *Journal* outsells *USA Today, The New York Daily News,* and *The New York Times*, as it has for years. The index is divided into two parts, Corporate News and General News. It contains short abstracts, and provides as much ready reference material as it does indexing information.

190. Weinberg, Steve, and Jan Colbert, eds. **The Investigative Journalist's Morgue**. Columbia, MO: Investigative Reporters and Editors, 1986. 188p.

The IRE story is described as follows:

> Investigative Reporters and Editors, Inc. was established by journalists who were weary of starting at ground zero every time they began an investigation. The founders knew that sharing ideas and information was the cornerstone of IRE. They began compiling stories that had been done by investigative journalists around the country, and envisioned a resource center with easy access for all members.

This shared information assumes the form of an index of investigative newspaper articles, published from the late 1970s to the mid-1980s, in newspapers such as the *Pensacola News-Journal* and *The Wall Street Journal*. Entries are arranged alphabetically by subject and contain an identification number, name of newspaper, brief description of the article or series, and date(s) of publication. Headlines and page numbers are excluded, but that is not a problem if you order the piece directly from IRE (there is a fee). Subjects cover the usual muckraking range—AIDS, handguns, nursing homes, toxic waste, etc. The editors promise annual updates of this unique morgue, one of the most promising sources available for solid examples of researching, interviewing, reporting, and writing.

Databases

Addresses of database service suppliers and vendors are listed in the Appendix.

191. **ABI/Inform**. Producer: UMI/Data Courier, Inc. Printed version: None. Coverage from: August 1971. Update frequency: Weekly. Abstracts: Yes.

Database service/vendor: American Library Association, BRS, BRS After Dark, BRS/Colleague, Data-Star, Dialcom (coverage from 1978), Dialog, Executive Telecom System, ESA-IRS, Knowledge Index, Mead Data Central, Orbit, Tech Data.

Contents: Summaries of principal business and management articles in more than 650 journals. Newspaper, magazine, and broadcast management are covered. Management Contents, available through BRS, BRS After Dark, BRS Colleague, Data-Star, DIALOG, and Orbit, might also be useful.

192. **Access Reports/Freedom of Information Newsletter**. Producer: Washington Monitor, Inc. Printed version: *Access Reports/Freedom of Information*. Coverage from: September 1983. Update frequency: Biweekly. Abstracts: No.

Database service/vendor: NewsNet.

Contents: Full text of newsletter reporting freedom of information developments, including legal decisions and regulatory changes.

193. **AGORA**. Producer: Agence France Presse. Printed version: AFP dispatches. Coverage from: July 1983 (selected stories from 1958 to the present). Update frequency: Daily. Abstracts: No; full text.

Database service/vendor: G.Cam, Telesystemes-Questel.

Contents: Full text of French and international news stories published by Agence France Presse. French and English.

194. **America: History and Life**. Producer: ABC-CLIO. Printed version: *America: History and Life, Part A: Article Abstracts and Citations; Part B: Index to Book Reviews; Part C: American History Bibliography*. Coverage from: 1964. Update frequency: 3 times/year. Abstracts: Yes.

Database service/vendor: Dialog, Knowledge Index.

Contents: Abstracts of articles from approximately 2,000 international journals in the humanities and social sciences. Focus is United States and Canadian history. *JQ: Journalism Quarterly* and *Journalism History* are indexed. For world history, see *Historical Abstracts* (entry 211).

195. **Arts and Humanities Search**. Producer: Institute for Scientific Information. Printed version: *Arts and Humanities Citation Index* (entry 153). Coverage from: 1980. Update frequency: Biweekly. Abstracts: No.

Database service/vendor: BRS, BRS After Dark, BRS/Colleague, Dialog.

Contents: Indexes approximately 1,300 humanities journals focusing on film, television, radio, history, literature, philosophy, etc. Excerpts from books also included.

196. **The Associated Press News**. Producer: Associated Press. Printed version: None. Coverage from: (see below). Update frequency: Daily, usually available 24 hours after publication. Abstracts: No.

Database service/vendor: DataTimes and Vu/Text (1985-), Dialog (July 1984-), Mead Data Central (1977-), NewsNet (most recent two weeks), PROFILE Information (September 9, 1983-), U.S. Telecom (current).

Contents: Full text of national and international news and feature stories, business, sports, Washington, D.C. newswire. Excluded are state and regional news reports. AP staff consists of 1,600 journalists in 136 U.S. bureaus and 83 foreign bureaus, and is one of the most important suppliers of news to the media.

197. **Associated Press Political File**. Producer: Associated Press. Printed version: None. Coverage from: (see below). Update frequency: Daily for campaign stories. Abstracts: No.

Database service/vendor: DataTimes (December 1985-), Vu/Text (1980-).

Contents: Full text of local, state, and national political news and statistics in three categories of Biography (updated as needed), Campaign Story, and Summary Documents (updated after primaries and elections).

198. **Audit Bureau of Circulations On-Line Service**. Producer: Audit Bureau of Circulation. Printed version: ABC Circulation Reports. Coverage from: Current. Update frequency: Monthly. Abstracts: No.

Database service/vendor: Interactive Market Systems, Market Science Associates, Telmar Group.

Contents: Circulation data (statistical and demographic) for 1,900 newspapers, 200 magazines, and farm publications. Subscription and membership in ABC required.

199. **BBC Summary of World Broadcasts**. Producer: British Broadcasting Corporation Monitoring Service. Printed version: None. Coverage from: (see below). Update frequency: Within 2 days. Abstracts: No; full text.

Database service/vendor: Mead Data Central (1979-), DataTimes and PROFILE Information (1982-).

Contents: Full-text translations of television and radio news broadcasts from more than 100 countries. Also available on microform (entry 502).

200. **Biography Index**. Producer: H. W. Wilson Company. Printed version: *Biography Index*. Coverage from: July 1984. Update frequency: Twice weekly. Abstracts: No.

Database service/vendor: Wilsonline.

Contents: Citations to biographical material in English-language periodicals and books. Obituaries, interviews, and bibliographies included. All fields and historical periods covered. Also available on compact disk. See also *Biography Master Index*, available on DIALOG.

201. **Business Periodicals Index**. Producer: H. W. Wilson Company. Printed version: *Business Periodicals Index* (entry 156). Coverage from: June 1982. Update frequency: Twice weekly. Abstracts: No.

Database service/vendor: Wilsonline.

Contents: Index of more than 300 English-language business, management, and economic periodicals. Scope is international. Subjects covered include communications, and printing and publishing. Also available on compact disk.

202. **Bylines**. Producer: United Media Enterprises. Printed version: None. Coverage from: Current only. Update frequency: Daily. Abstracts: No; full text.

Database service/vendor: The SOURCE.

Contents: Full text of more than 60 United Features Syndicate newspaper feature columns.

203. **Canadian Business and Current Affairs**. Producer: Micromedia Limited. Printed version: (see below). Coverage from: (see below). Update frequency: Monthly. Abstracts: No.

Database service/vendor: Dialog (1980-), CISTI and IST-Informatheque, Inc. (1982-), QL Systems (1975-).

Contents: Index to articles in more than 170 Canadian business periodicals, 300 popular magazines, and 10 newspapers. *The Canadian Business Index, Canadian News Index,* and *Canadian Magazine Index* are merged here along with the *Bibliography of Works on Canadian Foreign Relations* and corporate filings with the Ontario Securities Commission. Good source for Canadian business and industry information as well as current affairs.

204. **Canadian Journalism Data Base**. Producer: University of Western Ontario, Graduate School of Journalism, Center for Mass Media Studies. Printed version: None. Coverage from: 1965. Update frequency: Monthly. Abstracts: No; full text.

Database service/vendor: QL Systems.

Contents: Full text of research papers and press council decisions, and journalism bibliography. Also includes directory of professional journalists and a job bank. Focuses primarily on Canadian journalism and journalists. See also the *Index to Journalism Periodicals* (entry 167).

205. **Canadian Press Newstex**. Producer: The Canadian Press. Printed version: None. Coverage from: (see below). Update frequency: Daily (Infomart updates continuously). Abstracts: No; full text.

Database service/vendor: Infomart Online (1988-), QL Systems (1981-).

Contents: Full text of local, national, and international English-language news reports from the Canadian Press wire service. The Associated Press, Reuters, Agence France Presse, and Broadcast News Limited (a Canadian news service for private radio and television stations) also contribute to Newstex.

206. **DataTimes**. Producer: DataTimes Corp. Printed version: None. Coverage from: Varies. Update frequency: Varies. Abstracts: No; full text.

Contents: The DataTimes service contains full text articles, reports, and statistics from newspapers, magazines, and wire services. Business sources such as *The Wall Street Journal* are provided through a gateway to Dow Jones News/Retrieval. Newspapers currently available full text on DataTimes are: *Arkansas Gazette, Austin American-Statesman, The Baton Rouge State-Times/Morning Advocate, The Bergen Record, Chicago Newspaper Index, Chicago Sun-Times, Chicago Tribune, Colorado Springs Gazette Telegraph, The Courier-Journal* (Louisville), *The Daily Oklahoman, The Daily Texan, The Dallas Morning News, The Harrisburg Patriot/Evening News, Houston Chronicle, The Journal Record, Newsday, The Orange County Register, Reading Times/Reading Eagle, The Sacramento Bee, The San Diego Union-Tribune, San Francisco Chronicle, The Seattle Times, St. Petersburg Times, Star-Tribune* (Minneapolis-St. Paul), *USA Today,* and *The Washington Post.* The Australian Newspaper Network (also called Queensland Newspaper Information Service), which includes the *Courier-Mail, Telegraph,* and the *Sunday Mail* (Brisbane) is available on DataTimes. Canadian papers available include *The Gazette* (Montreal), *The Ottawa Citizen, The Toronto Star, The Vancouver Sun,* and *The Windsor Star.*

207. **Education Index**. Producer: H. W. Wilson Company. Printed version: *Education Index.* Coverage from: December 1983. Update frequency: Twice weekly. Abstracts: No.

Database service/vendor: Wilsonline.

Contents: Index to articles in more than 350 education-related journals. Secondary and college journalism education covered. See also ERIC (entry 208). Available on compact disk.

208. **ERIC** (Educational Resources Information Center). Producer: U.S. Department of Education, Office of Educational Research and Improvement. Printed version: *Current Index to Journals in Education* (CIJE, entry 162); *Resources in Education* (RIE, entry 182). Coverage from: 1966, RIE; 1969, CIJE. Update frequency: Monthly. Abstracts: Yes.

Database service/vendor: BRS, BRS After Dark, BRS/Colleague, Dialog, Knowledge Index, Orbit.

Contents: The *Resources in Education* subfile consists of documents, technical reports, conference papers, open papers, bibliographies, proceedings, etc., which can be located by ERIC document number on microfiche. The *Current Index to Journals in Education* contains citations to more than 750 education-related journals and serial publications. Useful for information on journalism education. An important source. Also available on compact disk.

209. **Facts on File World News Digest**. Producer: Facts on File, Inc. Printed version: *Facts on File* (entry 461). Coverage from: (see below). Update frequency: Weekly. Abstracts: No.

Database service/vendor: Dialog (1982-), Mead Data Central (1975-), Vu/Text (1982-). Contents: Full text of summaries of national and international weekly news events. Excludes printed index of the *World News Digest* and "In This Issue" column appearing in printed version. Summaries compiled from stories in major newspapers and from news services. Also available on compact disk.

210. **Gannett News Service**. Producer: Gannett News Media Services. Printed version: None. Coverage from: April 4, 1987. Update frequency: Daily. Abstracts: No; full text.

Database service/vendor: DataTimes.

Contents: Full text of national and international news features, state and regional stories, articles by Gannett reporters and nonsyndicated freelancers. Excluded are sports and business digests.

211. **Historical Abstracts**. Producer: ABC-CLIO. Printed version: *Historical Abstracts: Part A, Modern History Abstracts (1450-1914), Part B: Twentieth Century Abstracts (1914 to the Present)*. Coverage from: 1973. Update frequency: Quarterly. Abstracts: Yes.

Database service/vendor: Dialog, Knowledge Index.

Contents: Abstracts of articles from 2,000 social science and humanities journals covering world history (United States and Canada excluded). Dissertations and books included since 1980. For American history, see *America: History and Life* (entry 194).

212. **Humanities Index**. Producer: H. W. Wilson Company. Printed version: *Humanities Index* (entry 165). Coverage from: February 1984. Update frequency: Twice weekly. Abstracts: No.

Database service/vendor: Wilsonline.

Contents: Citations to articles, book reviews, obituaries, bibliographies, interviews, and reviews in almost 300 English-language humanities periodicals. Subjects covered include journalism, art, film, communications, philosophy, photography, and world literature. An important source. Also available on compact disk.

213. **The Information Bank Abstracts**. Producer: The New York Times Company. Printed version: None. Coverage from: 1969, The New York Times; 1972, other publications. Update frequency: Daily. Abstracts: Yes.

Database service/vendor: Mead Data Central.

Contents: Abstracts of articles from newspapers such as *The New York Times, Christian Science Monitor, Los Angeles Times, The Chicago Tribune,* etc., and approximately 40 general-interest magazines.

214. **IPS-USA/Global Information Network**. Producer: IPS-USA/Global Information Network. Printed version: None. Coverage from: (see below). Update frequency: Within 2 days. Abstracts: No; full text.

Database service/vendor: American Library Association and Dialcom (most recent 2-3 months), Mead Data Central (April 1984-).

Contents: Inter Press Service (Rome) is a news wire service covering foreign events and developing countries in Asia, Latin America, Africa, and Europe. Stories selected from daily IPS newscasts.

215. **Knight-News-Tribune News Wire**. Producer: Knight-News-Tribune (KNT) Newswire. Printed version: None. Coverage from: 1986. Update frequency: Daily. Abstracts: No; full text.

Database service/vendor: Vu/Text.

Contents: Full text of selected articles from Knight-Ridder newspapers, Tribune newspapers, *The Boston Globe*, and *Dallas Morning News*.

216. **Legal Resource Index**. Producer: Information Access Company. Printed version: *Legal Resource Index*, available on microfilm; *Current Law Index* (for law journals). Coverage from: 1980. Update frequency: Monthly. Abstracts: Yes.

Database service/vendor: BRS, Dialog, Mead Data Central, West Publishing Company (Westlaw).

Contents: Abstracts of articles appearing in more than 700 law journals, law reviews, bar association journals, and legal newspapers. Subject, author, case name, and statute access. Good source in searching legal aspects of print and broadcast journalism such as libel and slander, newspaper publishing and litigation, headlines, television broadcasting of news, ethical aspects of television politics, radio journalism, free press and fair trial, and newspaper court reporting. Updated daily on *Newsearch* (entry 222). For full-text court decisions, statutes, and regulations, access LEXIS or Westlaw.

217. **Magazine Index** and **Magazine ASAP**. Producer: Information Access Company. Printed version: *Magazine Index*, available on microform (see entry 172). Coverage from: 1959-March 1970, 1973 (*Magazine Index*), 1983 (*Magazine ASAP*). Update frequency: Monthly. Abstracts: No.

Database service/vendor: BRS, BRS After Dark, BRS/Colleague, Dialog, Knowledge Index.

Contents: Indexes articles in more than 400 general-interest magazines on business, current affairs, regional news, arts, and literature. Also covers print and broadcast journalism. *Magazine Index* indexes all magazines covered in *Readers' Guide to Periodical Literature* and provides, as does *Magazine ASAP*, full text of articles in more than 100 magazines. It is updated daily on *Newsearch* (entry 222). The InfoTrac Database on optical disk also indexes articles in business, technical, and general-interest periodicals. The *Popular Magazine Review Online*, available on BRS, provides citations to nearly 200 popular periodicals from 1984 to the present. *Academic Index*, now available on DIALOG, is a new social sciences and humanities database.

218. **NADbank**. Producer: Newspaper Marketing Bureau, Inc. Printed version: None. Coverage from: Current. Update frequency: NA. Abstracts: No.

Database service/vendor: Harris Media Systems, Interactive Market Systems, Market Science Associates, Telmar Group.

Contents: Formerly Newspaper Audience Data Bank. Data on newspaper readership in Canada. For data on Canadian magazine readership, see PMB (Print Measurement Bureau), available from same vendors as NADbank.

219. **National Newspaper Index**. Producer: Information Access Company. Printed version: *National Newspaper Index*, available on microfilm. Coverage from: (see below). Update frequency: Monthly, daily on *Newsearch* (entry 222). Abstracts: No.

Database service/vendor: BRS, BRS After Dark, BRS/Colleague, Dialog, Knowledge Index.

Contents: Index of *Christian Science Monitor, The New York Times, The Wall Street Journal* (1979-), *The Los Angeles Times,* and *The Washington Post* (1982-). News stories, editorials, letters, features, and obituaries included. Excluded are weather charts, stock market tables, puzzles, and horoscopes.

220. **National Readership Survey**. Producer: Joint Industry Committee of National Readership Surveys. Printed version: None. Coverage from: 1968. Update frequency: Quarterly. Abstracts: No.

Database service/vendor: Donovan Data Systems, Interactive Market Systems, Telmar Group.

Contents: Audience measurements, statistical, and demographic data for weekly, monthly, and bimonthly newspapers and magazines in the United Kingdom. Permission of supplier required for use of this database.

221. **NCOM** (Nordic Documentation Center for Mass Communication Research). Producer: NORDICOM. Printed version: The NORDICOM Bibliography. Coverage from: 1975. Update frequency: Quarterly. Abstracts: Yes.

Database service/vendor: Datacentralen.

Contents: Abstracts of journal articles, books, dissertations, reports, and conference papers on Scandinavian mass communications. Countries covered are Denmark, Finland, Iceland, Norway, and Sweden. Some English-language documents.

222. **Newsearch**. Producer: Information Access Company. Printed version: None. Coverage from: Current month. Update frequency: Daily. Abstracts: No.

Database service/vendor: BRS, BRS After Dark, BRS/Colleague, Dialog, Knowledge Index.

Contents: Daily bibliographic update for *Computer Database, Magazine Index, Management Contents, Legal Resource Index, National Newspaper Index,* and *Trade and Industry Index.* Entire contents of magazines, newspapers, trade journals, and other publications indexed. Advertisements excluded.

223. **Newsline**. Producer: Finsbury Data Services. Printed version: None. Coverage from: One week. Update frequency: Daily. Abstracts: No.

Database service/vendor: Finsbury Data Services (a Reuter Company), ESA-IRS.

Contents: English-language headline file of stories in approximately 40 United Kingdom and major European papers. Available at 9 a.m. (United Kingdom time) on day of publication. Items available in abstract form on Textline, also supplied by Finsbury, after one week.

224. **Newspaper Abstracts**. Producer: University Microfilms International. Printed version: *Newspaper Abstracts,* available on microfilm. Coverage from: 1984 for most newspapers. Update frequency: Weekly. Abstracts: Yes.

Database service/vendor: Dialog.

Contents: Indexing and abstracting of major news articles in newspapers including *The New York Times, The Wall Street Journal* (indexed by Dow Jones), *Atlanta Constitution, Boston Globe, Chicago Tribune, Christian Science Monitor, The Denver Post, The Detroit News, Guardian & Guardian Weekly* (London), *Houston Post, Los Angeles Times, Times-Picayune, Pravda* (English-language version), *St. Louis Post-Dispatch, San Francisco Chronicle, USA Today,* and the *Washington Times.* The *Black Newspaper Index,* listing citations to articles in nine black newspapers, also is included. All international, national, regional, state, and local news is abstracted, as well as business articles, features, editorials, and commentaries.

225. **New York Times Biographical File**. Producer: The New York Times Company. Printed version: None. Coverage from: June 1980. Update frequency: Biweekly. Abstracts: No.

Database service/vendor: Mead Data Central.

Contents: Full text of selected biographical articles from *The New York Times,* including profiles, interviews, and obituaries.

226. **NEXIS**. Producer: Mead Data Central. Printed version: None. Coverage from: Varies. Update frequency: Daily or weekly. Abstracts: No; full text.

Database service/vendor: Mead Data Central.

Contents: Full text of articles from newspapers, magazines, newsletters, newswires, and special-interest services. Contributing wire services include *Associated Press, Jiji Press Ticker Service, Kyodo English Language News Service, PR Newswire, Reuter's General*

News Report, Reuter's Northern European News Service, United Press International, and *Xinhua (New China) News Agency.* Also included are *BBC Summary of World Broadcasts and Monitoring Report, Christian Science Monitor, Facts on File World News Digest, Manchester Guardian Weekly, The New York Times, The Washington Post,* and *The Information Bank.*

227.   **PAIS International**. Producer: Public Affairs Information Service, Inc. Printed version: *Public Affairs Information Service Bulletin* (entry 180), *Public Affairs Information Service Foreign Language Index.* Coverage from: 1972, *Index*; 1976, *Bulletin.* Update frequency: Quarterly, *Index*; monthly, *Bulletin.* Abstracts: Yes, for some.

Database service/vendor: BRS, BRS After Dark, BRS/Colleague, Data-Star, Dialog, Knowledge Index, TECH DATA.

Contents: Citations to articles, pamphlets, directories, reports, government documents, and yearbooks focusing on political, social, and economic issues. Indexes non-English-language sources as well. Also available on compact disk.

228.   **Readers' Guide Abstracts**. Producer: H. W. Wilson Company. Printed version: *Readers' Guide Abstracts.* Coverage from: 1984. Update frequency: Weekly. Abstracts: Yes.

Database service/vendor: Wilsonline.

Contents: Abstracts to articles indexed in the *Readers' Guide to Periodical Literature* (entries 181, 229). Book reviews, general works, and poems are not abstracted. Also available on compact disk.

229.   **Readers' Guide to Periodical Literature**. Producer: H. W. Wilson Company. Printed version: *Readers' Guide to Periodical Literature* (entry 181). Coverage from: January 1983. Update frequency: Twice weekly. Abstracts: No.

Database service/vendor: Wilsonline.

Contents: Index to articles in almost 200 popular general interest periodicals. Areas covered include journalism, news and current events, advertising and public relations, politics, and education. Available on compact disk. See also *Readers' Guide Abstracts* (entry 228).

230.   **Reuter News Reports**. Producer: Reuters Information Services, Inc. Printed version: None. Coverage from: (see below). Update frequency: Continuously (Mead Data Central usually updates within two days). Abstracts: No.

Database service/vendor: Dialog (1987-), Mead Data Central (April 15, 1979-), NewsNet (current two weeks).

Contents: Full text of news releases from Reuter News Reports wire service, including all English-language news stories filed in 100 bureaus around the world.

231.   **Scarborough Reports**. Producer: Scarborough Research Corporation. Printed version: None. Coverage from: Current. Update frequency: Every two years. Abstracts: No.

Database service/vendor: Interactive Market Systems, Telmar Group, Windsor Systems Development.

Contents: Scarborough Research Corporation maintains separate databases covering five markets: Detroit; Boston; Washington, D.C.; Philadelphia; and New York. Data on newspaper, magazine, radio, television, and magazine audience measurement. Subscription required.

232.   **Science Journalism Database** (SCI-FIND). Producer: Science Journalism Center, University of Missouri. Printed version: In-house files. Coverage from: Current. Update frequency: Varies. Abstracts: Yes.

Database service/vendor: Science Journalism Center, University of Missouri.

Contents: Four thousand abstracts of news articles on science and biomedical topics available free on this menu-driven online file. An index to all listings, from earthquakes to hormones, is available and includes cross-references. For further information, call 314-882-2914.

233. **Scripps-Howard News Service**. Producer: Scripps-Howard News Service. Printed version: None. Coverage from: Current day. Update frequency: Daily. Abstracts: No; full text.

Database service/vendor: The Source.

Contents: Full text of selected stories from Scripps-Howard newspapers such as the *Providence Journal-Bulletin* and the *Pittsburgh Press*.

234. **Simmons 1987 National Study of Local Newspaper Ratings**. Producer: Simmons Market Research Bureau, Inc. Printed version: None. Coverage from: 1987 only. Update frequency: Every two years. Abstracts: No.

Database service/vendor: Interactive Market Systems, Management Science Associates, Market Science Associates, Telmar Group, Windsor Systems Development.

Contents: Survey of newspaper audiences in 56 major markets. Subscription required. Simmons also makes available online a *Study of Media and Markets. Editor & Publisher* reported in a March 1989 issue, however, that Simmons Market Research Bureau "has dissolved its newspaper research division."

235. **Social Sciences Index**. Producer: H. W. Wilson Company. Printed version: *Social Sciences Index* (entry 184). Coverage from: April 1983. Update frequency: Twice weekly. Abstracts: No.

Database service/vendor: Wilsonline.

Contents: Index to articles in 300 international social science periodicals. Subjects covered include demography, economics, international relations, political science, psychology, and area studies. Also available on compact disk. A new database available on DIALOG, *Academic Index*, provides access to the literature of the social sciences and humanities.

236. **Sociological Abstracts**. Producer: Sociological Abstracts, Inc. Printed version: *Sociological Abstracts*. Coverage from: 1963. Update frequency: Varies; 3-5 times/year. Abstracts: Yes, since 1973.

Database service/vendor: BRS, BRS After Dark, BRS/Colleague, Data-Star, Dialog, DIMDI, Knowledge Index.

Contents: Citations and abstracts to journal articles, books, monographs, and conference papers focusing on sociology and allied disciplines. Use of this database in journalism will be a bit limited, but it does turn up articles such as "Barriers of Investigative Sports Journalism; An Empirical Inquiry Into the Conditions of Information Transmission." Also available on compact disk.

237. **Study of Major Market Newspapers**. Producer: Three Sigma Research Center, Inc. Printed version: *Study of Major Market Newspaper Audiences* (82 vols.). Coverage from: 1980 only. Update frequency: Not updated. Abstracts: No.

Database service/vendor: Interactive Market Systems, Market Science Associates, Telmar Media Systems, Windsor Systems Development.

Contents: Audience and demographic data for 240 American newspapers in 30 major markets. Subscription required.

238. **Tass**. Producer: Tass English Language News Service. Printed version: None. Coverage from: (see below). Update frequency: Daily. Abstracts: No; full text.

Database service/vendor: Mead Data Central (1987-), DataTimes and PROFILE Information (November 18, 1985-).

Contents: Full text of English-language news from Tass, official news agency of the Soviet Union.

239. **UPI Database**. Producer: Comtex Scientific Corporation. Printed version: None. Coverage from: (see below). Update frequency: Continuously or daily. Abstracts: No.

Database service/vendor: ALA, Dialcom, Dialog (April 1983-), Mead Data Central (September 26, 1980-), NewsNet (current two weeks), The SOURCE (current week), Western Union Telegraph Company.

Contents: Full text of news stories, columns, features, and commentaries on the United Press International newswire. Each record lists priority of news item (urgent, flash, etc.).

240. **Vu/Text**. Producer: Vu/Text Information Services, Inc. Printed Version: None. Coverage from: Varies. Update frequency: Varies. Abstracts: No; full text.

Contents: This electronic service offers full text of numerous newspaper libraries as well as other databases. It is a subsidiary of Knight-Ridder, which recently purchased Dialog. Coverage and update frequency vary from one database to another. Newspapers currently available full text on Vu/Text include: *Akron Beacon Journal, Anchorage Daily News, The Arizona Republic and Phoenix Gazette, Atlanta Journal and Constitution, The Boston Globe, The Capital* (Annapolis), *The Charlotte Observer, Chicago Tribune, The Columbus Dispatch, Daily News* (Los Angeles), *Detroit Free Press,* the *Electronic Washington Post Library, Fort Lauderdale News and Sun-Sentinel, Fresno Bee, Houston Post, The Lexington Herald-Leader, Los Angeles Times, Miami Herald, Miami News, The Morning Call* (Allentown), *Newsday, El Nuevo Herald, The Orlando Sentinel, Palm Beach Post, Philadelphia Daily News, Philadelphia Inquirer, The Post-Tribune* (Gary), *Richmond News Leader and Times-Dispatch, The Sacramento Bee, San Jose Mercury News, Seattle Post-Intelligencer, St. Louis Post-Dispatch, The State Record* (South Carolina), *Times-Union and Knickerbocker News* (Albany), and *The Wichita Eagle-Beacon.*

241. **Washington PressText**. Producer: PressText News Service. Printed version: (see below). Coverage from: 1981. Update frequency: Daily. Abstracts: No.

Database service/vendor: Dialog.

Contents: Full text of White House and United States Department of State news releases and policy statements. Information also provided by White House Office of the Press Secretary. Covers domestic and international news, and presidential speeches, news conferences, broadcasts, and statements. Items in this database correspond to documents in the *State Department Bulletin,* the *Weekly Compilation of Presidential Documents, Key Officers of Foreign Service Posts,* and other published materials. This database is particularly useful to political reporters.

242. **World Affairs Report**. Producer: California Institute of International Studies. Printed version: *World Affairs Report.* Coverage from: 1970. Update frequency: Monthly. Abstracts: Yes.

Database service/vendor: Dialog.

Contents: News and analysis from *Pravda, Izvestia,* Tass, and the *Literaturnaya Gazeta,* as well as Reuter's News Service, *Le Monde,* and major American newspapers and wires. Emphasis is, obviously, placed on the Soviet view of world affairs. The print version contains graphic and bibliographic material not found online; however, the online version contains more text. Useful in study of Soviet journalism.

The following databases may also provide useful references and information. For further information on individual databases, consult the *Directory of Online Databases* (Cuadra/Elsevier): Knight-Ridder Graphics Network, GraphicsNet, Southam News, Startext (includes articles from the *Fort Worth Star-Telegram*), Newsfile, ELSA, Noticias de Prense Espanola, Radio Resources Network, Northern Ireland News Service, Arab Information Bank, Current Digest of the Soviet Press, XINHUA English Language News Service, Quebac, NEWZ, Deutsche Presse Agentur, Arbitron Radio and Arbitron TV, BBM Bureau of Measurement, Broadcasters Audience Research Board, Mediawire, Newswire ASAP, Nielsen Station Index, Nielsen Television Index, PR Newswire, Public Broadcasting Report, Study of Media and Markets, Television Digest, USA Today Decisionline, and USA Today Broadcast.

Other newspapers available full text online include: *Le Monde, Whig-Standard, Asahi Shimbun, Globe and Mail, The Guardian, Yomiuri Shimbun, Daily* and *Sunday Telegraph,* and the *Times Newspapers* (London).

5
Biographical Sources

243.   Abrams, Alan E., ed. **Journalist Biographies Master Index**. Detroit, MI: Gale Research Company, 1979. 380p. (Gale Biographical Index Series, no. 4). LC 77-9144. ISBN 0-8103-1086-4.

This ambitious index is an offspring of *Biography and Genealogy Master Index* and showing its age now. Sam Donaldson and Linda Ellerbee are considered "unidentified persons" here, and so next to their names are the letters "NF" for "Not Found." (If this is confusing, it might help to know that the editor first identified the journalists to be included, then located biographical sketches in approximately 200 biographical directories, major journalism texts, and historical sources). The subtitle states that this is a "guide to 90,000 references to historical and contemporary journalists." Entries are arranged alphabetically, and list only year of birth/death and title codes for book references. Among the sources indexed are *Who Was Who in Journalism* (entry 266); *American Journalism: A History, 1690-1960* (entry 476); *The American Radical Press, 1880-1960 Authors in the News* (entry 260); *Biography Index* (entry 200); *Blacks in Communications, Journalism, Public Relations, and Advertising; Contemporary Authors* (entry 248); *Famous War Correspondents; The Foreign Press: A Survey of the World's Journalism; Foremost Women in Communications* (entry 256); *A History of American Magazines; The Investigative Journalist: Folk Heroes of a New Era; Lords and Laborers of the Press: Men Who Fashioned the Modern British Newspaper; The New Muckrakers; Overseas Press Club of America and American Correspondents Overseas 1975 Membership Directory; Reporting the News: Selections from Nieman Reports*; and *Who's Who in Graphic Art* (entry 244). Abrams also edited the *Media Personnel Directory* (entry 267). For further references to television journalists, consult the *Performing Arts Master Index* (Gale, 1981).

244.   Amstutz, Walter, ed. **Who's Who in Graphic Art**, vol. 1. Dubendorf, Switzerland: De Clivo Press, 1962. 582p. **Who's Who in Graphic Art**, vol. 2, 1982. 891p. index. ISBN 3-85634-779-8.

Short biographical sketches of contemporary graphic artists, typographic designers, illustrators, and cartoonists accompany examples of their artwork in these two volumes. Cartoon journalism, according to the editor, "hovers on the fringe." Artists are grouped by country and arranged alphabetically. The text is written in English, French, and German; obviously the scope is international. From Walt Disney to Herb Lubalin, names from advertising, printing, and publishing industries are included as well as those "whose rendering of ideas attains a certain artistic level." Examples of cover art, including the curious and understated *New Yorker* covers, magazine illustrations, exhibition posters, book jackets and covers, advertisements, and drawings bring the text to life and provide perhaps the best microscope with which to examine a graphic artist. Each entry contains date of birth and address, and a complete bibliography of works by and about the author. The first volume examines 414 artists. Volume 2 contains sketches of 544 artists from 42 countries, along with a well-illustrated "Short History of the Graphic Arts." Two artist indexes are organized by name and country.

245. Ashley, Perry J., ed. **American Newspaper Journalists, 1690-1872**. Detroit, MI: Gale Research Company, 1985. 527p. illus. index. (Dictionary of Literary Biography, vol 43). LC 85-20575. ISBN 0-8103-1721-4. **American Newspaper Journalists, 1873-1900**. Detroit, MI: Gale Research Company, 1983. 392p. (Dictionary of Literary Biography, vol. 23). LC 83-20582. ISBN 0-8103-1145-3. **American Newspaper Journalists, 1901-1925**. Detroit, MI: Gale Research Company, 1984. 385p. (Dictionary of Literary Biography, vol. 25). LC 83-25395. ISBN 0-8103-1704-4. **American Newspaper Journalists, 1926-1950**. Detroit, MI: Gale Research Company, 1984. 410p. (Dictionary of Literary Biography, vol. 29). LC 84-8182. ISBN 0-8103-1707-9.

"The most important thing about a writer is his writing," according to the Dictionary of Literary Biography Advisory Board, and that is the tone set in these four volumes delineating four distinct periods in journalism history and in journalistic writing and reporting. Experts and scholars contributed these critical and biographical essays ranging in length from 1½ pages to 20 pages. Again, the emphasis is on writing, and each entry contains the essay and usual sketch data along with books written and periodical publications. At the end of each essay is a list of biographies, bibliographies, letters, recordings, references, and locations of papers.

Volume 43 (1690-1872) showcases 66 pioneers of the American press, with some emphasis on the penny press. Among those included are Samuel Adams, Benjamin Henry Day, Frederick Douglas, Joseph Medill, and Sara Payson Willis Parton (aka Fanny Fern). Volume 23 (1873-1900) is the age of New Journalism and, later, yellow journalism, and investigates the lives of 46 journalists such as James Gordon Bennett, Ida B. Wells-Barnett, Henry W. Grady, and Joseph Pulitzer. The years 1901-1925 are chronicled in volume 25, and the 47 essays examine the rise of yellow journalism, jazz journalism, and a new interest in public and community service. "In all," the editor writes, "the first fourth of the twentieth century was a transitional period from the highly personalized journalism of the nineteenth century to the corporate journalism of today." Names such as Elizabeth Cochrane (Nellie Bly), E.W. Howe, W. Randolph Hearst, Adolph S. Ochs, E.W. Scripps, William Allen White, and Melville Stone are entered here. Finally, volume 29 (1926-1950) looks at the growth of mass-circulation magazines, radio, and television, and the rise of interpretive journalism through the lives of 54 journalists such as Walter Lippman, Ralph McGill, H.L. Mencken, Dorothy Day, Red Smith, Ernie Pyle, and Joseph Pulitzer, Jr.

These volumes provide a starting point in the search for basic biographical information on star journalists, fashioned into an attractive, well-illustrated, and highly readable package. *American Magazine Journalists*, edited by Sam Riley, is also part of the Dictionary of Literary Biography series. Titles include *American Magazine Journalists, 1741-1850* (1988), and *American Magazine Journalists, 1850-1900* (1989).

246. Barkley, Jack, comp. **Alphabetized Directory of American Journalists: Associated Press, United Press International, America's Daily Newspapers**. Kokomo, IN: the author, 1978.

It was supposed to be an annual publication, and had it come to pass, would be a source like no other in this incredibly high-turnover field. It held much promise, listing about 20,000 writers, reporters, editors, publishers, and others employed by daily newspapers, United Press International, and Associated Press. It was less of a biographical source than a directory, but touched a much broader base than the *Editor & Publisher International Yearbook*, which lists only newspaper editors, managers, and major columnists. Alas, more than 10 years later, it is not terribly useful for anything.

247.   Butler-Paisley, Matilda, Sheridan Crawford, and M. Violet Lofgren, comps. **Directory of Women and Minority Men in Academic Journalism Communications**. Stanford, CA: Stanford University, 1976.

According to the compilers, this directory "will be useful in identifying women and minority men not only for faculty positions in journalism/communication but also for guest lecturers, professional committee service, etc." A useful source in its time, this subject listing is certainly dated now. Arranged in sections on advertising, broadcasting, business communication, editing, ethics, film, international communication, mass communication, radio, etc., entries contain current position and degree, teaching specialties, and professional experience.

248.   **Contemporary Authors; New Revision Series: A Bio-Bibliographical Guide to Current Writers in Fiction, General Nonfiction, Poetry, Journalism, Drama, Motion Pictures, Television, and Other Fields**. Detroit, MI: Gale Research Company, 1980- . illus. index. ISSN 0275-7176.

The multi-volume *Contemporary Authors* (1962-) still doesn't seem comfortable with its inclusion of journalists. There are "authors" and there are "media people" and though the twain have met, it is still an uneasy alliance. Broadcast journalists, cartoonists, communications theorists, essayists, film critics, gossip columnists, magazine and newspaper editors, music critics, publishers, radio personalities, television writers, and the stars of print journalism are included, though criteria for selection is a bit hazy. Entries offer more than your standard biographical fare. Besides date of birth, address, awards, honors, and education, there are complete lists of writings, works in progress, "sidelights," and a section for avocational interests. The cumulative index (in even-numbered original volumes) provides complete access to all *Contemporary Authors* volumes (Permanent Series, 1st revision, etc.).

249.   **Directory, American Society of Journalists and Authors: A Listing of Professional and Free-Lance Writers**. New York: American Society of Journalists and Authors. 1952- . (Annual). ISBN 0-9612200-5-8. ISSN 0278-8829.

More than 750 brief biographical sketches of members of the American Society of Journalists and Authors, an organization of freelance writers, are included here. Entries are arranged alphabetically and include address, telephone, areas of expertise, publications, etc. Geographical and subject specialty indexes are provided.

250.   Dziki, Sylwester, Janina Maczuga, and Walery Pisarek, comps. **World Directory of Mass Communication Researchers**. Krakow, Poland: Prasa-Ksiazka-Ruch, 1984. unpaged.

Members of the International Association for Mass Communication Research compiled this international directory of communication researchers and say that "the most serious weak point of our Directory is the absence of many names, including leading figures, founding fathers, etc., well-known and recognized in national or even international forums, often people whose names can be found in encyclopedias and other general reference books." Keeping that in mind, users can consult this alphabetically arranged directory for general biographical information as well as individuals' research interests and publications. These interests range from history of the popular press to the documentation of mass communication in Silesia (Poland). The compilers say they know "at least one index in such a directory is a necessity. However, the Directory exists and thus the first step has been made." There is no index, but signs of the zodiac accompany each biographical entry (according to this book, Elie Abel is a Libra).

251.   Gale, Steven H., ed. **Encyclopedia of American Humorists**. New York: Garland, 1988. 557p. index. LC 87-8642. ISBN 0-8240-8644-9.

More than 70 contributors profile 135 humorists from America's colonial period to the present in this alphabetically arranged encyclopedia. There are essays on Roy Blount, Art Buchwald, Jules Feiffer, A.J. Liebling, E.B. White, Ogden Nash, S.J. Perelman, and even

Davy Crockett. Each signed essay contains general biographical information, a biographical essay, a lengthy literary analysis, summary, and selected bibliography. This work "is intended to be the most comprehensive and up-to-date reference text on American and Canadian humorists ever published." It is indeed that, but perhaps a second edition will include Dave Barry. There is a subject and name index.

252.   Green, Charles, and Mort Walker, comps. **The National Cartoonists Society Album**. Brooklyn, NY: National Cartoonists Society, 1980. 174p. ISBN 0-318-15238-4.

This publication of the National Cartoonists Society offers biographical profiles of its members. Short entries were written by the individual editorial, magazine, strip, or advertising cartoonists and illustrators. The book includes photographs of the artists as well as samples of their work.

253.   Havlice, Patricia Pate. **Index to Literary Biography**. Metuchen, NJ: Scarecrow Press, 1975. 2 vols. 1300p. LC 74-8315. ISBN 0-8108-0745-9. **First Supplement**, 1983. 2 vols. 1193p. LC 82-25051. ISBN 0-8108-1613-X.

Numerous journalists are involved in literary pursuits, and their names, from Hemingway to Pulitzer to Rather, are included here. The original index lists references to biographical information of 68,000 authors from the earliest times to the 1970s. The supplement lists 53,000 authors in more than 50 reference sources between 1969-1981. Each alphabetical entry contains the author's real name, pseudonym, date of birth and death, nationality, type of writing, and a letter code to reference sources. This is no replacement for *Journalist Biographies Master Index* (entry 243), but is an excellent, easy-to-use, additional source.

254.   Horn, Maurice, ed. **Contemporary Graphic Artists: A Biographical, Bibliographical, and Critical Guide to Current Illustrators, Animators, Cartoonists, Designers, and Other Graphic Artists**. Detroit, MI: Gale Research Company. index. **Vol. 1**, 1986. ISBN 0-8103-2189-0. **Vol. 2**, 1987. ISBN 0-8103-2190-4. **Vol. 3**, 1988. ISBN 0-8103-4320-7. LC 86-131830. ISSN 0885-8462.

This series offers biographical sketches of graphic artists. More than 100 illustrators, graphic designers, editorial cartoonists, magazine cartoonists, newspaper artists, comic book artists, and animators are profiled in each volume. Most are contemporary names, although some prominent artists from the past are occasionally included. Each entry lists personal and career information, awards, credits, publications, a brief biographical profile, bibliography, and examples of the artist's work. Horn also edited the *World Encyclopedia of Cartoons* (Gale, 1980).

255.   **International Authors and Writers Who's Who**. Cambridge, England: International Biographical Centre, 1986. 879p. index. ISBN 9-003-3288-3.

The introductory material sets the tone: "In this edition, we have bowed to numerous requests (and a few complaints) for the inclusion of magazine and newspaper publishers, editors and leading journalists." The scope is worldwide, though there is a definite British slant, and emphasis is placed on poets, novelists, essayists, and critics. Entries are arranged alphabetically, and include date of birth, address, education, publications, appointments, memberships, and honors. Appendices include lists of pseudonyms, literary agents, literary societies, and Poets Laureate of the United Kingdom. Its use is limited, but at least it is updated frequently (usually every three years).

256.   Love, Barbara J., ed. **Foremost Women in Communications: A Biographical Reference Work on Accomplished Women in Broadcasting, Publishing, Advertising, Public Relations, and Allied Professions**. New York: Foremost Americans Publishing Company, 1970. 788p. index. LC 79-125936. ISBN 08352-0414-6.

Reference sources which address high-turnover professions require almost continual updating. Published in 1970 and exceedingly important in its time, this book now serves as more of a "where was she then" or "who was who" source. For example, the entry for

Jessica Beth Savitch informs us that she has just been hired as an administrative assistant at CBS. Biographical profiles of almost 8,000 women in communications, broadcasting, advertising, public relations, and "allied professions" include date of birth, career information, education, awards and honors, and other who's-who data. Arrangement is alphabetical, with the geographical and subject cross-indexes providing a way to track down names associated with a specific industry (television, radio, newspapers) or profession (management, editing, writing). Some things have changed very little in the 20 years since this was published. The editor writes, "Still, few women are city editors, newscasters of world events, political and editorial writers, officers in publishing firms or radio and television stations."

257. McKerns, Joseph P., ed. **Biographical Dictionary of American Journalism**. Westport, CT: Greenwood Press, 1989. 820p. ISBN 0-313-23819-7.
    The publication of this source on print and broadcast journalists was announced as *Journalism: A Guide to the Reference Literature* was going to press. Biographical sketches of 500 reporters, editors, columnists, editorial cartoonists, photographers, and correspondents are included.

258. Naylor, Colin, ed. **Contemporary Photographers**. 2d ed. Chicago, IL: St. James Press, 1988. (Contemporary Arts Series, vol. 3). ISBN 0-912289-79-1.
    Of limited use, this second edition of *Contemporary Photographers* is nonetheless a beyond-the-coffee-table book and a compelling read. The 750 photographers selected for inclusion are living or recently dead, or those who are "essentially contemporary." Only the biggest names in documentary photography and photojournalism will be found here. More than 175 contributors have written consistently incisive and compelling critical essays on the likes of Ansel Adams, Margaret Bourke-White, Cornell Capa, Robert Capa, Alfred Eisenstaedt, and Paul Strand. Alphabetical entries include basic biographical information, collections, publications, individual exhibitions, and selected group exhibitions. There is no index. See also the *Photographers Encyclopedia International, 1839 to the Present* (Editions Camera Obscura, 1985).

259. **The New York Times Biographical Service**. Monthly. index. LC 70-20206. ISSN 0161-2433.
    This "compilation of current biographical information of general interest" is basically a month-by-month collection of general-interest articles and numerous obituaries in *The New York Times*. It does not concentrate specifically on the journalist or communicator, but those who report the news (especially in television) tend to be the subjects of news and feature stories themselves. An index appears on the inside front cover of each monthly issue, and there is a cumulative index in December. *The New York Times*, with its many guides and indexes, both online and offline, is a most accessible newspaper. This service carries on that tradition, and is worth consulting. *The New York Times Obituaries Index* might also be useful.

260. Nykoruk, Barbara, ed. **Authors in the News**. 2 vols. Detroit, MI: Gale Research Company, 1976. index. LC 75-13541. ISBN 0-8103-0043-5.
    This "special category edition" of *Biography News* is a strange mix of articles and feature stories selected from 50 newspapers and magazines "covering writers and other members of the Communications Media." It was a good idea run amok. These 500 "writers and other members" range from William F. Buckley to Edna Ferber to Jack Kerouac to Phyllis Schlafly. There are articles on Chet Huntley, but none on David Brinkley. There are no updates or later editions. Arrangement is alphabetical by author, and some names are represented by just one article. An annoying graphic device in the shape of an index card contains bibliographic information, and is contorted into uncardlike shapes to fit into open space. Articles are culled from publications such as the *Pittsburgh Press, Atlanta Journal and Constitution, Cincinnati Enquirer, Fresno Bee, Atlantic Monthly, Editor & Publisher, The Quill, Forbes,* and *Esquire*. For those in a hurry and who seek instant gratification, this could be a satisfying source. For others, it will not be.

261. Scheuer, Steven, ed. **Who's Who in Television and Cable**. New York: Facts on File, 1984. 579p. illus. index. LC 82-12045. ISBN 0-87196-747-2.

Prone to using such phrases as "delightfully wacky," and "unabashedly masculine," Scheuer (spelled "Sheuer" on the cover of one copy) is editor and publisher of *TV Key*, a syndicated column about television. He lists approximately 2,000 persons involved in television, video, and cable, including network and public television executives, television journalists, and actors. This source addresses a range of personalities from communications professor Elie Abel to that comedian/announcer/host Gene Rayburn. Entries are arranged alphabetically and occasionally are accompanied by mug shots. (Rayburn has one, Abel does not.) Date of birth is included, though the year often is not, as well as address, education, career highlights, and achievements and awards. There are numerous "NAs" in sections marked for personal information. We do learn, however, that Dan Rather is "known for his impeccable deportment and conservative but casual wardrobe." Corporation and job title indexes are included. Consult this source for initial information, then search elsewhere.

262. Taft, William H. **Encyclopedia of Twentieth Century Journalists**. New York: Garland, 1986. 408p. index. LC 84-48011. ISBN 0-8240-8961-8.

This star-studded sketchbook of nearly 800 well-known, award-winning, and/or highly reputed print and broadcast journalists is invaluable for basic biographical information. Most included are still alive, but those now dead who played major roles in the formation of present-day journalism are included. Excluded are those in advertising, public relations, management, production, etc. Sketches are short, usually four to six paragraphs, but loaded with pertinent information. Length of entry usually is an indication of the importance of the journalist and contributions he or she has made, but that is not always so; the entry for Geraldo Rivera (that "practitioner of advocacy journalism") is about as long as the one for the entire Pulitzer family. Names were culled from various Who's Who publications, *Contemporary Authors* (entry 248), journalism histories, trade journals, and journalism reviews. Arrangement is alphabetical and there is an excellent index of names, subjects, and organizations. Also included is a short essay on journalism awards, useful as a quick overview. See also the *Encyclopedia of American Journalism* (entry 113).

263. Wanniski, Jude, ed. **The MediaGuide**. New York: Harper & Row, 1986- . Annual. index. LC 86-45706. ISBN 0-06-055048-1; 0-06-096124-4 (pbk).

"What we had set out to do was produce a kind of Michelin Guide to the national print media, evaluating the work of the top reporters and columnists and rating them the way Michelin rates the restaurants of Europe," writes Wanniski, a "news gourmet" and former editorial writer (petroleum Writer of the Year in 1976) for the *Wall Street Journal*. Approximately 500 members of the national press were selected for inclusion, and are rated like restaurants and hotels in the AAA travel books. Four stars is exceptional, and a dash means the reporter is "failing in the basic criteria on one or more counts." Journalists are listed alphabetically and rated within the following categories: Financial Reporters and Columnists, Foreign Correspondents, National Security/Diplomatic Correspondents, Political Columnists, Social/Political Reporters, and Social/Political Commentators. Perhaps the most useful element in this guide is the Biographics section, sans stars. It is an alphabetical who's-who listing of about 900 print journalists, many who "didn't make the cut," with emphasis, once again, on the national magazine and newspaper press. In addition, there are overviews of the print media for the previous year, best columns and stories, and major news stories, along with discussions of major newspaper and magazine publications. The 1987 MediaGuide on *Newsweek's* Howard Fineman: "his ego keeps jumping in before the talent we think is there, snotty 'I know it all' little political pieces appear with too much regularity." Wanniski and his crew are occasionally on target, if less than tactful themselves.

264.   **Who's Who in the Press: A Biographical Guide to British Journalists.** 2d ed. Carrick Publishing Company, 1986. 133p.

265.   **Who's Who in U.S. Writers, Editors, and Poets.** Highland Park, IL: December Press, 1986- . Annual. ISBN 0-913204-18-8. ISSN 0885-4521.

Biographies of approximately 7,000 poets, novelists, short-story writers, journal and book editors, journalists, nonfiction writers, critics, playwrights, and scriptwriters are included. Entries are alphabetically arranged and list general biographical information as well as a full publishing history. According to the introduction, "Inclusion is intended to be a mark of literary/publishing distinction and achievement." Names range from John N. Berry III, editor-in-chief of *Library Journal*, to author Stephen King, with emphasis on novelists and the periodical press. This is an unusual, eclectic biographical collection, a mini *Contemporary Authors* (entry 248).

266.   **Who Was Who in Journalism, 1925-1928.** Detroit, MI: Gale Research Co. (c1925, c1928) 1978. 664p. (Gale Composite Biographical Dictionaries, no. 4).

Nearly 4,000 early twentieth-century newspaper and magazine journalists are included in this biographical source comprised of material from the 1925 and 1928 editions of *Who's Who in Journalism*. Every page places the reader squarely back in this period of journalism history, with biographical sketches of the American and Canadian publishers, editors, reporters, writers, and teachers who made journalism yellow or aimed for higher ground. Adolph S. Ochs, Joseph Medill Patterson, Eugene C. Pulliam, William Randolph Hearst, R.W. Bingham, and Henry Justin Smith are all listed here, with entries arranged alphabetically and reproduced as they appeared in the original volumes. Biographical information includes date of birth, home address, present position and other career information, education, and published writings. Also included are lists of syndicates, foreign news agencies, clubs and associations, schools of journalism, and a bibliography. An eight-page "Codes of Ethics" section contains the Journalist's Creed ("I believe that no one should write as a journalist what he would not say as a gentleman") and "Commandments" for desk men, such as "Boil it down. Reporters' jargon is always susceptible of condensation." This is an important historical source, and is included in *Journalist Biographies Master Index* (entry 243).

6
Directories, Yearbooks, and Collections

Directories and Yearbooks

Directories of individual organizations are listed in the Chapter 12 (Societies and Associations) entries.

267.   Abrams, Alan E., ed. **Media Personnel Directory**. Detroit, MI: Gale Research Company, 1979. 262p. LC 79-12885. ISBN 0-8103-0421-X.
Useful to journalists and media specialists in its time, this alphabetical guide to major business and editorial personnel at more than 700 periodicals in the world is dated. Included are publishers, editors, columnists, art directors, book reviewers, correspondents, bureau chiefs, sales and production managers, and other management personnel. Job title, last reported place of service, address, and telephone number are provided. An index of periodicals included lists titles ranging from the *Aerospace Historian* to the *Prairie Schooner*. Abrams also edited the *Journalist Biographies Master Index* (entry 243).

268.   Allen, Martha Leslie, ed. **Index/Directory of Women's Media**. Washington, D.C.: Women's Institute for Freedom of the Press, 1975- . Annual.
The mission of the Women's Institute for Freedom of the Press is to aid "networking among women, women's organizations, and women's media, nationally and internationally." Their vehicle is this index and directory to "media primarily owned and operated by, for, and about women." The Women's Media Groups section is divided in sections on periodicals, presses/publishers, news services, columns, radio-television groups, regular programs-radio/television, video and cable, film, multi-media, music, art/graphics/theater, writers' groups, editorial and public relations, speakers' bureaus, courses, distributors, media organizations, bookstores, library collections, and directories. Within these sections, entries are arranged by zip code. International entries are arranged alphabetically by country at the end of each section. Fortunately, there is a list of zip codes by state, and several alphabetical cross-indexes. Listings contain address, telephone number, brief description of services, etc., and contact.
Inclusion in the second section, the Directory of Media Women and Media-Concerned Women, is voluntary, and many names listed here are associates of the Women's Institute for Freedom of the Press. These listings are alphabetical (but there is a zip code and country cross-index) and include address, some telephone numbers, and a sentence or two on media interests and professional accomplishments. Interspersed throughout the volume are previously published essays and reports such as "A Radical Feminist Analysis of Mass Media."

Every five years since 1972, The Women's Institute has also cumulatively indexed and annotated *Media Report to Women* and published it in this volume. Indexed by subjects such as broadcasting, censorship, discrimination, feminist journalism, First Amendment free press right, journalism and communications schools, news coverage, news definition, and ownership of media, it is an important tool in researching the role of women in the media. Also useful is the Women's Institute for Freedom of the Press's *Women in Media: A Documentary Source Book.*

269. Anderson, Elizabeth L., ed. **Newspaper Libraries in the U.S. and Canada**. 2d ed. New York: Special Libraries Association, 1980. 321p. index. LC 80-25188. ISBN 0-87111-265-5.

Five practical indexes make this a most accessible directory. In addition to a personnel index, there are separate indexes for U.S. cities and newspaper groups as well as Canadian cities and newspaper groups. More than 300 newspaper libraries are listed here, representing newspapers with circulation over 25,000. (Most newspapers with 100,000 daily circulation are included.) Washington, D.C. bureau libraries also are listed. Entries are arranged by state, then alphabetically by city within state. Canadian listings follow United States entries. Newspaper name, address, telephone number, circulation figures, library personnel, public access and limitations, services, hours, resources, microform, newspaper indexes, special collections, automation and electronic systems, and products for sale are included. Entries also indicate the year in which each library was established. Nameplates for some newspapers are even included, useful when seeking a newspaper's exact title. Members of the News Division (then the Newspaper Division) of the Special Libraries Association revised, organized, and synthesized this information which is unlikely to be found anywhere else. A new edition would be welcomed.

270. **Bacon's Radio/TV Directory**. Chicago, IL: Bacon's Publishing Company. Annual. index. ISSN 0891-0103.

Nearly 10,000 television and radio stations in the United States, as well as major networks, are listed here. In separate sections on radio and television, entries are arranged by state, city, and call letter, and include frequency or channel, address, telephone, network affiliation, staff, station profile, and programs. Cable systems are listed by state, city, and system name, and include address, telephone, profile, and programs. Call letter, program, and geographical indexes are provided. Bacon's also publishes the annual *Bacon's Media Alerts*, a directory of editorial calendars from major newspapers and business, trade, professional and consumer magazines.

271. **Benn's Media Directory**. Kent, England: Benn Business Information Service. 2 vols. Annual. ISSN 0269-8358.

Formerly *Benn's Press Directory*, this became a directory of media with the 134th edition in 1986 when it began to cover broadcasting and electronic publishing as well. One volume is devoted entirely to the United Kingdom. A national newspaper section is followed by listings of newspapers in Greater London, English provinces, Wales, Scotland, Northern Ireland, Isle of Man, and the Channel Islands, further subdivided by city/town. Also included are local free-distribution newspapers, periodicals, and free-distribution magazines. Entries contain date established, address, brief description, personnel, etc. The broadcasting section serves as a comprehensive guide to the BBC, IBA, commercial television (including cable and satellite), radio, and electronic publishing. Alphabetical lists of agencies and sources in the communications industry and national and international media organizations are included. There are numerous indexes scattered throughout this volume as well as a master index. The international volume offers a media directory organized alphabetically by country, from Botswana to Zimbabwe. More generous indexing would greatly enhance this international volume. As it stands, there are only country/area and advertiser indexes.

272.   **Black List: The Concise and Comprehensive Reference Guide to Black Journalism, Radio and Television, Educational and Cultural Organizations in the U.S.A., Africa, and the Caribbean.** 2 vols. 2d ed. New York: Panther House, 1974. LC 73-89092. ISBN 0-87676-541-X.

Black List is a reference guide to black journalism, radio, and television in the United States, Africa, and the Caribbean. According to the introduction, "Media of countries and territories which are not controlled by blacks but having substantial black populations—sometimes exceeding the ruling minority such as South Africa—are included." Volume 1 lists television broadcasting stations arranged by state and call letter, radio stations (with a large portion of programming aimed at black audiences), newspapers, publishers, educational institutions, etc., in the United States. Volume 2 is a country-by-country description of black media, including lists of media organizations, news agencies, and United States embassies. Unfortunately, much of the information is dated. For example, the listing of estimated black populations in 50 United States cities is based on 1971 estimates. There is no index. Researchers of the black press might also be interested in Hans Zell's fourth edition of *The African Book World and the Press: A Directory* (K. G. Saur, 1988).

273.   **Black Media Directory.** Livingston, NY: Burrelle's Media Directories, 1983-84. 154p.

Another *Black Media Directory* (to be published in 1989 by Alliance) will update this directory. The first section of *Black Media Directory* focuses on print media, with sections on national newspapers, national periodicals, national syndicated columns, college publications, state and local newspapers, and print ownership groups which are black-owned or have a black focus. Entries are arranged alphabetically within these sections and include address and telephone, advertising rates, publisher, and editors. Part 2 lists television and radio stations which are black-owned or offer black programming. There are more than 1,100 entries. There also is a name, banner, and call-letter index which has some peculiarities. Columnists Carl Rowan and William Raspberry, for example, are indexed under their first names. Burrelle's also publishes a *Women's Media Directory*, 1983-84, and a *Hispanic Media Directory*, 1983-84, which are similar in format to the *Black Media Directory*.

274.   **Broadcasting/Cablecasting Yearbook.** Washington, D.C.: Broadcasting Publications, 1935- . Annual. LC 82-643037. ISSN 0734-7196.

This important directory is crammed with up-to-date information on all aspects of the Fifth Estate in the United States and Canada. The first section offers a historical overview of the industry as well as current growth and developments. Radio listings, arranged geographically, offer call letters, address, telephone number, programming information, and personnel. Also in this section are cross-referenced lists of AM and FM stations by call letters and frequencies. Most television listings, also arranged geographically, include call letters, address, telephone number, personnel, and Arbitron circulation figures. There also are separate sections on cable, satellites, programming, advertising and marketing, technology, professional services and associations, and broadcast education. A separate index accompanies each section and there is also a general index. See also the annual *Television and Cable Factbook* (entry 313) and *World Radio TV Handbook: The Authoritative Directory of International Radio and Television* (Billboard). The annual *Kemp's International Film and Television Yearbook* (Kemp's Group) emphasizes British film and television, and might also provide useful information. The annual *CPB Public Broadcasting Directory* (Corporation for Public Broadcasting) offers data on, obviously, public broadcasting stations.

275.   **The CFJ Directory: A Register of Education, Training, Fellowship and Intern Programs for Journalists Worldwide.** Reston, VA: Center for Foreign Journalists, 1986- . Annual.

More than 200 organizations in 80 countries are listed and, according to the introduction, the "main criteria for an entry continues to be that an organization offers programs for foreign participants from beyond the institution's national boundaries." Entries are arranged in sections on Africa, Asia and Pacific, Europe, Middle East, Latin America and the Caribbean, and North America, subdivided by country, and list address, telephone, contact person, and a brief description of the program. Country and program indexes are provided.

276. **Circulation**. Malibu, CA: American Newspaper Markets, 1961- . Annual.

The preface indicates this "annual analysis of penetration and circulation of major print media" is arranged in a "user friendly" format, and it offers carefully worded definitions and guidelines for using the facts and figures. This annual "helps answer two basic questions in the selection of media, particularly newspapers: 1. Is this newspaper, supplement, or magazine needed for the optimum media buy? 2. If so, what does it deliver?" Each section begins with scope notes and an explanation of what will follow. Sections include a metropolitan-area print analysis, state analyses, television viewing areas (ADI and DMA), newspaper ratings study (including excerpts from Simmons and Scarborough Studies), and analytical tables and rankings. See also Standard Rate and Data Service's *Newspaper Circulation Analysis* (entry 310). The new biannual *Newspaper Datatrak* (Media Market Guide) might also be useful. The Audit Bureau of Circulations also offers several Blue Books to its members only: *Canadian Weekly Newspapers, U.S. Daily Newspapers, U.S. Weekly Newspapers*, and *Publisher's Statements*.

277. Clark, Bernadine, ed. **Writer's Resource Guide**. 2d ed. Cincinnati, OH: Writer's Digest, 1983. 473p. index. LC 82-25919. ISBN 0-89879-102-2.

Written with the same bubbling enthusiasm found in other Writer's Digest publications, this guide aims at the writer seeking information sources and background information on practically any subject. The book stresses that there are experts and agencies out there with just the information you seek, no matter what it is. (Sure enough, there is a group interested in the study of transportation fare tokens. Call the American Vecturist Association.) More than 1,600 entries are numbered and organized by subject, then arranged alphabetically within subjects. According to the introduction, each resource, be it an association, organization, museum, library, or company, "identifies itself as willing to share information." That in itself may be the book's biggest asset. Included are six essays on how to do research, as well as some short "Behind the Byline" essays by such notables as Ellen Goodman, Matthew Lesko, Edwin Newman, and Nikki Giovanni within the subject sections. Subjects include business, education, communications/entertainment, environment, government and military, law, human services, health and medicine, farming, and information services. Each section also contains a short bibliography of related reference materials. Entries are similar to those in *Writer's Market* (entry 320), and offer a description of the organizations, contact person, services available, restrictions of use, costs, response time, and helpful hints or tips. There are subject and title indexes. Of course, much of the information here may be found in the *Encyclopedia of Associations* (Gale, annual), *Foundation Directory* (Foundation Center, irregular), *World of Learning* (Europa, annual), or Matthew Lesko's publications. (*Information U.S.A.*, Viking Press, 1983, etc.), but this is a convenient one-volume directory.

278. Claxton, Ronald H. **The Student Guide to Mass Media Internships**. San Marcos, TX: Intern Research Group, Department of Journalism, Southwest Texas State University. 2 vols. 1979- . Annual. ISSN 0730-5117.

Volume 1 focuses on internships and training programs available in print media, and is divided into sections on daily newspapers, weekly newspapers, newspaper groups, news services and syndicates, miscellaneous internships, magazines, book publishers, etc. Within these sections, entries are arranged by state and publication, and include a description of the internship, number of internships available, address, circulation, application information, etc. Volume 2 lists programs available in broadcasting, with separate sections for television stations, cable, and radio. It is similar in format to volume 1. This directory aims at mass communications students, but does list some programs for recent graduates. Also useful might be *Internships; Volume 2: Newspaper, Magazine and Book Publishing* (Career Press).

279. **Directory of the College Student Press in America**. Dario Politella, ed. 6th ed. New York: Oxbridge Communications, 1986. 291p. LC 78-120744. ISBN 0-917460-07-3. ISSN 0085-0020. (A 1989 edition, now entitled **The College Media Directory**, was published as this book was going to press.)

No longer just a press directory, the sixth edition has outdone itself and included radio and television stations run primarily by college students. More than 6,000 newspapers, magazines, handbooks, law reviews, yearbooks, and stations from 3,610 two- and four-year colleges and universities, satellite campuses, and specialized schools are listed. The editor states that the purpose of the directory is threefold: to provide "the most complete guide to the college student media anywhere ... the most extensive listing of institutions of higher learning in the United States ... the most complete and authoritative data for those who seek effective means of reaching the 12,000,000 + students of all ages who make up the American campus community." Whether it succeeds in all these endeavors is questionable, but it is a handy and well-organized record of college student media. Listings are arranged by state, then alphabetically by college. Entries contain address, telephone number, name of president, chancellor, or director, director of student activities, reference librarian, type of college, enrollment and ratio of men/women students, title of publication and type, adviser, year established, frequency, annual subscription rate, single copy price, circulation, advertising cost, trim size, use of color, method of printing, annual budget, and financing. Information for radio and television stations includes call letters, programming, telephone number, station manager, program manager, and engineer. Unfortunately, there are no indexes at all. Even an index of publication titles would make this directory far more accessible.

280. **Directory of Editorial Resources**. Alexandria, VA: Editorial Experts, 1981- . Biennial. index. ISBN 0-935012-09-5.

Defined as a "quick reference listing of opportunities for writers, editors, and publications managers," this directory and handbook aims at book and magazine editorial staffs. It is divided into chapters on useful books, directories, periodicals, professional organizations, training opportunities, and grammar hotlines. The books section lists dictionaries and stylebooks, publications on grammar, writing, language usage, production, newsletters, general reference, and clip art, and sources for cartoons and editorial fillers. Each listing has a two- or three-line annotation.

281. **A Directory of Major Newspapers and Their Op-Ed Policies**. Washington, D.C.: Campaign for Political Rights, 1982. 28p. ISBN 0-910175-01-4.

The Committee for Political Justice interviewed various editors of the top 160 United States newspapers, based on circulation. The committee was primarily interested in finding out which newspapers considered and published opinion articles by nonstaff writers. According to the directory, "Publishing op-ed articles in this manner has enabled many organizations and individuals to communicate their views to a large number of people and it has helped enhance their credibility in the eyes of the newspaper and its readers." Compiled by the Campaign for Political Rights, the directory is arranged alphabetically by state and newspaper. Circulation figures, culled from the *1980 World Almanac*, are included along with address, telephone number, editor and/or editorial editor, percentage of unsolicited pieces published, when published, word length and other requirements, and whether a newspaper is willing to print previously published articles. This, of course, would be of particular interest to lobbyists and organizations seeking to spread a viewpoint. Also included is a listing of the more than 30 newspapers that do not publish opinion pieces by nonstaffers.

282. Drake, Judith. **News Bureaus in the U.S.** New York: Billboard Publications, Inc. (formerly Larimi Communications). Annual.

This annual directory of print media news bureaus updates Weiner's *News Bureaus in the U.S.* (entry 316).

283. Drake, Judith. **Syndicated Columnists Directory**. New York: Billboard Publications, Inc. (formerly Larimi Communications). Annual.

More than 1,600 syndicated columnists and syndicates are listed in this new annual looseleaf publication which updates Weiner's *Syndicated Columnists Directory* (entry 317). Entries are arranged alphabetically by subject (advice, books, entertainment, sports, etc.), and include address, telephone number, syndicator, format, length, and frequency of publication.

284. Dziki, Sylwester. **World Directory of Mass Communication Periodicals**. Krakow, Poland: Press Research Centre, 1980. 218p.

According to Walery Pisarek, director of the Press Research Centre, "In its present version this Directory is beyond a doubt the most comprehensive and most complete annotated bibliography of mass communication periodicals." More than 500 scientific and professional journals, periodicals, magazines, newsletters, and other publications from 55 countries are listed. A large number of titles are published in the United States, Great Britain, France, Germany, Australia, and Czechoslovakia. Entries are numbered, arranged alphabetically by title, and include address, publisher, editor, brief description, target audience, circulation, frequency of publication, etc. Some entries are incomplete, such as the entry for *MORE: The Media Magazine*; though an address and editor are still listed, the entry does not indicate that *MORE* ceased publication in 1978. Titles range from the familiar *Journal of Communication* to *Korrespondent*, a monthly journal published in the Soviet Union which focuses on sociopolitical issues of journalism. Excluded are film, theater, book publishing, photography, and advertising periodicals. Country, town, language, and other indexes are provided.

285. **Editor & Publisher International Yearbook**. New York: Editor & Publisher, 1920-21- . Annual. index. ISSN 0424-4923.

This yearbook, claiming to hold more than 250,000 facts about newspapers, touts itself as the encyclopedia of the newspaper industry. That is no misnomer, as it is possibly the single most important one-volume source on the newspaper industry. The bulk of the annual is its state-by-state listing of daily newspapers, arranged alphabetically by city and newspaper. Entries include address, telephone number, circulation, price, advertising and representatives, news services, politics, date established, special editions and sections, supplements, market information, mechanical specifications, commodity consumption, and equipment. A detailed personnel list contains names in general management, advertising, circulation, finance, human resources, information services, marketing, news, and production, as well as news executives, editors, and managers.

Weekly newspapers are arranged alphabetically by state, then by principal community or neighborhood served. Foreign language, religious, college, and black newspapers are also listed. Daily Canadian newspapers are listed by province, and there is a separate list for weeklies.

The section entitled "Papers Published in Foreign Countries" offers an overview of the British press and a list of newspapers in the British Isles. Newspapers of Europe are arranged by country, then alphabetically by newspaper. Brief entries contain address, circulation, editor-in-chief, business manager, etc. Other sections list news and syndicate services, suppliers and services, organizations, associations and press clubs, schools and departments of journalism (from the AEJMC's *Journalism and Mass Communication Directory*, entry 302), a rather dated section on films about newspapers, and a directory of the Foreign Press Association.

The list of top minimum pay scales for reporters and the 100 top daily newspapers are two frequently consulted features. When searching for specific information, remember that the table of contents serves as a better index than the index does. Whether studying the newspaper business or figuring out where (and to whom) to send clips, one will, of necessity, consult this source.

286. **Editor & Publisher Market Guide.** New York: Editor & Publisher, 1924- . Annual.
Market data on United States and Canadian daily newspapers appears in this annual. The first section, covering market rankings, lists metropolitan statistical areas (MSAs) and MSA rankings by population, disposable income, household income, retail sales, etc. County and city rankings are included as well. Section 2, arranged alphabetically by state, surveys daily newspaper cities, and includes state maps and data on passenger autos, industries, shopping centers, banks, population, and even tap water. Section 3, arranged alphabetically by province, details Canadian newspaper market surveys, and the last section contains numerous population, income, retail sales, and food sales tables. The general index, located in the front of the volume, is skimpy, but it should lead you well enough through the vast amount of material here.

287. Elmore, Garland C. **Communication Media in Higher Education.** Annandale, VA: Association for Communication Administration, 1987. 529p. index.
Almost 600 undergraduate and graduate departments and programs in media studies are detailed here. *Communication media* is defined as radio, television, film, communication technologies, and related media. It aims primarily at scholars and educators, according to the foreword written by Samuel L. Becker, J. Robert Wills, and Robert E. Davis, as "it should facilitate the development of a more cohesive national community of teachers/scholars in media studies." The second "key audience," though perhaps the group that will use this best, are counselors and students seeking in-depth information on communication and media programs. The book also aims at industry personnel with hiring responsibilities. "It was not long ago that a college degree in broadcasting, journalism, or film was considered by those in the industry to be more of a hindrance than a help. This is no longer the case; in fact, quite the opposite." Some might argue with that statement; indeed, it all depends on which managing editor or newsroom editor you ask.
Part 1 is a directory of institutions, containing state-by-state listings of universities and colleges. Each entry lists program, department or school, address, telephone number, chief administrators, curriculum, facilities, and full-time faculty. Part 2 is a directory of degree offerings listing institutions with associate's, bachelor's, master's, and doctoral degree programs in radio, television, or film. Names, addresses, and phone numbers of more than 1,700 full-time media faculty members make up part 3. Entries are alphabetical and include rank, highest degree earned, and research emphasis. Objectives and criteria for inclusion are clearly spelled out in the preface, and an impressive number of both renowned and lesser-known programs are included. However, one might ask why the University of Kansas, Northeastern University, and Emerson College, for example, are not listed: did they not meet the criteria, or did they simply not respond?

288. Elving, Bruce F. **FM Atlas and Station Directory.** 11th ed. Adolph, MN: FM Atlas Publishing, 1988. 176p. maps. LC 88-80373. ISBN 0-917170-07-5. The twelfth edition of the directory (1989, LC 89-083679, ISBN 0-917170-08-3) was published as this book was going to press.
"Just as FM is infinitely superior to AM, metric is superior to the other system, and we hereby kiss that system goodbye (except for the printing dimensions of these book pages, and that could change, if we could go with a printer that orders its book stock in meters and centimeters)." Thus, Elving sets the tone in this directory of FM radio in the United States, Canada, and Mexico. Included are maps illustrating distribution of FM stations arranged in geographical order from east to west, and in Canada, west to east. Fortunately, there is a maps index for those who do not have a sense of direction. Part 1 of the station directory is organized alphabetically by state or province, then subdivided by city. Mexico, Puerto Rico, and the Virgin Islands are included. Part 2 contains FM stations listed by frequency, subdivided by cities. No U.S. territories are listed here. This is an essential title for those researching FM radio, but be forewarned that it does not contain detailed descriptions of individual stations, personnel, addresses, or telephone numbers. For information on radio markets, see the annual *Duncan's Radio Market Guide* (Duncan's American Radio).

289.   **Faculty Directory of Higher Education: A Twelve Volume Subject-Classified Direc-tory Providing Names, Addresses, and Titles of Courses Taught for More than 600,000 Teaching Faculty.** Vol. 2: **Communications Faculty**. Detroit, MI: Gale Research Company, 1988. ISBN 0-8103-2750-3. ISSN 0894-9476.

More than 20,000 United States college and university faculty members in communi-cations, as well as faculty of selected Canadian institutions, are listed in this volume of the 12-volume set. Faculty members in journalism, mass communication, radio, television, speech, and audiology programs are included. These names, which were culled from CMG Publishing Company's mailing lists to college and university faculty, are arranged alpha-betically. Individual entries list institution, department, address, and course titles. A two-volume index provides access to the entire set.

290.   Fry, Ronald W., ed. **Magazines Career Directory**. 2d ed. Hawthorne, NJ: Career Press, 1987. (Career Directory Series). index. ISBN 0-934829-17-9; ISBN 0-934829-11-X (pbk). ISSN 0889-8502.

In the second edition, the tone is set in the first chapter, "Are You a Magazine Per-son?" Barrie J. Atkin, Director of Corporate Planning at Rodale Press, asks, "Do you carry magazines everywhere—to the gym, to bed, to the bathroom ...? Do you get a thrill from seeing your name in print ...? Do you like working with interesting, creative, dynamic people, many of whom have big egos and strong opinions?" Similar in scope and format to the *Newspapers Career Directory* (entry 291), essays by various magazine profes-sionals explore opportunities in editorial, advertising sales, circulation, art and design, production, public relations, and starting your own magazine. The section on job hunting covers networking, resumes, and interviewing. Aimed at recent college graduates and those looking for first jobs, the job opportunities databank lists entry-level positions as well as internship programs with various magazine publishers from *American Baby* to The New York Times Magazine Group. Listings include contact, type of magazines published, mag-azine titles, entry-level hiring the previous year, estimated current entry-level hiring, and general hiring outlook. According to the foreword, "If you're sure you want to be in 'editorial,' but don't know the differences between the editorial functions at a magazine, newspaper, and publishing house, these three volumes [in Career Directory Series] will help you explore all three industries before you make the mistake of breaking into the wrong one!" The fledgling journalist might use this directory as a marketplace of ideas.

291.   Fry, Ronald W., ed. **Newspapers Career Directory**. Hawthorne, NJ: Career Press, 1987. 238p. (Career Directory Series). index. ISBN 0-934829-21-7; ISBN 0-934829-15-2 (pbk). ISSN 0889-8499.

Written with sometimes annoying gung-ho spirit, and with lots of italics and exclama-tion marks, this is more of a career guide than it is a directory. Nevertheless, the foreword material states that "this volume is *not* a typical career guide—you know, those books that promise to tell you how to get a job in some field or profession (invariably written by a freelancer who's never *worked* one day in that field!) ... It's a process of discovering *what* you want to do, *where* you want to do it, and then, and *only* then, *how* to break down the paper's front door." Alvah Chapman, Jr. writes about the mission of newspapers in the introductory essay. Working journalists describe, in essay format, opportunities in the newspaper business in general, editorial ("Don't Stop the Presses! Getting Into Editorial at Large Papers"), advertising, art and design, circulation ("The Newspaper's Most Misunder-stood Soft Drink"), promotion, production, and finance. Section 8 details the job search process, with emphasis on career objectives, networking, resumes, and interviewing.

The job opportunities databank lists entry-level jobs available at more than 100 news-papers and groups. Entries are arranged alphabetically by newspaper, include address, tele-phone number, contact, and (when available) entry-level hiring for previous year, antici-pated hiring, and general outlook, although most entries indicate that the hiring scene is "not as good as last year" or "same as last year." The databank also contains internship and training program listings, arranged alphabetically by newspaper or group. Information included is contact, type of internship offered (salaried, nonsalaried), internships available the previous year, and training available.

Other books in this Career Directory Series center on magazines (entry 290), book publishing, public relations, advertising, and marketing and sales. This title will be most useful to students who have not quite made up their minds about the journalism business, and for those who are seeking internships. The editor frequently refers the user to the *Editor & Publisher International Yearbook* (entry 285) for further information and ideas. This is not a bad suggestion.

292. Gadney, Alan. **How to Enter & Win Non-Fiction & Journalism Contests**. New York: Facts on File, 1981. index. LC 81-2179. ISBN 0-87196-518-6; ISBN 0-87196-553-4 (pbk).

A previous edition of Gadney's guide (*Gadney's Guide to 1800 International Contests, Festivals, & Grants* [Festival Publications, 1980]), which is still in print, lumped journalism, film, video, photography, broadcasting, writing, poetry, and playwriting into one volume. Now nonfiction and journalism have their own volumes in this series of international contest/grant guides. Almost 400 contests, events, and grants are grouped according to subject, and contain addresses, code numbers, dates, deadlines, requirements, eligibility and fee information, awards, judging, theme, sponsors. More than 90 awards, competitions, and contests are listed in journalism categories, subdivided into general; business, financial, industrial; children, student, youth; health, medical, mental health; humanitarian, religious, social concern; legal, political, freedom, international; lifestyle, consumer, women; regional, state; scientific, technical, environmental; sport, hobby, travel; other; intern, training programs; residence fellowships; and scholarships, fellowships, grants. When used with the *Journalism Career and Scholarship Guide* (entry 303), one has an impressive selection of competitions and prizes to consider. Indexes provide subject and event/sponsor/award access, and they should be used, since some journalism awards and contests are listed in other sections.

Gadney promised updates every two or three years, but there is no update as of this writing, and this is out of print. Gadney is also the author of the Facts on File publications *How to Enter and Win Design and Commercial Art Contests* (1982), *How to Enter and Win Color Photography Contests* (1982), *How to Enter and Win Black and White Photography Contests* (1982), as well as titles such as *How to Enter and Win Wood and Leather Crafts Contests* (1983), all currently out of print.

293. **Gale Directory of Publications**. Kay Gill and Donald P. Boyden, eds. 2 vols. Detroit, MI: Gale Research Company, 1869- . Annual. index. ISSN 0892-1636.

This granddaddy of periodical directories, known in its lifetime as the *American Newspaper Annual, N. W. Ayer and Son's Directory of Newspapers and Periodicals*, and the *Ayer Directory of Publications*, to name a few, is a geographic guide to newspapers, magazines, and journals in the United States and Canada. Volume 1 is the catalog of publications arranged by state or province. State descriptions, as well as a list of counties and population, newspaper, and periodical statistics, are included. Entries are numbered and contain address, telephone number, description, date publication was established, frequency, format, contacts, ISSN, subscription cost, circulation, and advertising rate. The second volume, consisting of indexes and maps, also lists newspaper feature editors (50,000 or more circulation) arranged by state and city, then alphabetically by newspaper. In addition, there are separate geographical indexes for agricultural, college, Jewish, black women's, Hispanic, daily newspapers; daily periodicals; weekly, semiweekly, and triweekly newspapers; and free newspapers and shoppers. Other indexes, arranged by subject, then geographically, are general circulation magazines; trade, technical, and professional publications; newsletters; agricultural publications; foreign language publications; and fraternal publications. To be included, four or more issues or editions must be published annually. There is an alphabetical title and key-word index. See also the *Gale Directory of International Publications*.

294. Garner, Ana C., and Carolyn Stewart Dyer, comps. **The Iowa Guide: Scholarly Journals in Mass Communication and Related Fields**. 3d ed. Iowa City, IA: University of Iowa, Iowa Center for Communication Study, School of Journalism and Mass Communication, 1989. 70p.

According to the introduction, the purpose of this guide is to "help journalism and mass communication researchers find appropriate journals in which to publish their work and to help them prepare manuscripts for publication in those journals." The introduction also lists criteria for journal selection and describes the directory format. In the directory portion, entries are arranged alphabetically by title and include the following information: focus, affiliation, readership, editor, address, telephone number, frequency of publication, circulation, query, blind referee, review period, acceptance rate, abstract, style guide, preferred length, illustrations, foreign languages, and additional notes. Titles included range from *Communication Research* to the *International Journal of Mass Emergencies and Disasters*. This is the *Writer's Market* for scholarly mass communication publications.

295. Godfrey, Donald G., comp. **A Directory of Broadcast Archives**. Washington, D.C.: Broadcast Education Association, 1983. 90p.

Recordings available at the Pacifica Tape Library, Broadcast Pioneers Library, Public Television Archives, Vanderbilt Television News Archive, and even the Celia Nachatovitz Diamant Memorial Library of Classic Television Commercials are listed in this directory of approximately 70 radio and television program archives. Organized alphabetically by state, entries offer addresses, telephone numbers, contact, types of recordings available, program types, subject content of collection, and accessibility of the collection (card catalog, catalogs, indexes, on-site facilities, tape availabilities, finding aids, and restrictions). There is also a brief section on Canadian and British collections. Information was garnered from a questionnaire, and some entries are quite spare. A curious listing of "other known collections" appears at the end of the volume, and sometimes lists only an individual's name and address with a miniscule description of the individual's collection ("still active in issuing albums") or no description at all.

296. **Grants and Awards Available to American Writers**. New York: PEN American Center, 1969- . Biennial. index. ISSN 0092-5268.

For this publication's purposes, a *writer* is someone who pens fiction, poetry, drama, journalism, general nonfiction, and children's literature. Only those grants or awards which involve $500 or more, publication of a manuscript, or carry special distinction are included. More than 30 journalism awards are listed, such as the Penney-Missouri Newspaper Awards, Alicia Patterson Foundation Fellowship Program, the Pulitzer Prizes, Ernie Pyle Memorial Awards, and even the Eclipse Awards for "outstanding magazine and newspaper writing on thoroughbred racing." There is also a section of awards and grants available to Canadian writers. Each entry is coded to designate the subject area (journalism, drama, etc.), describes the award, and lists address, deadline, and restrictions. There are award, organization, and subject indexes. For a wider selection of awards, see the *Journalism Career and Scholarship Guide* (entry 303) and *How to Enter and Win Non-Fiction and Journalism Contests* (entry 292).

297. Hall, John, comp. and ed. **International Directory of Writer's Groups & Associations**. Alexandria, MN: Inkling Publications, 1984- . Biennial. index.

More than 2,000 local, regional, national, and international writers' groups, from the Society of Professional Journalists, Sigma Delta Chi to the United States Harness Writers Association, are listed alphabetically in this highly accessible source. There are also an individual name index and a geographical index, as well as a geographical listing of conferences and workshops. A section on how to organize a writers' group is included as well. Each entry contains address, telephone number, officers, dues, publications (the Alaska Press Women publish a monthly entitled "Artic-Ulation"), affiliated societies, and national organizations. This should be especially useful when seeking a speaker, specialist, or writing consultant.

298. **The International Directory of News Libraries**. 2d ed. Bayside, NY: LDA Publishers, 1988. ISBN 0-935912-38-X.

More than 600 news and media libraries in the United States and Canada are chronicled in this directory. Entries are numbered, arranged by state or province, subdivided by city, and include address, telephone number, hours, brief history, duplication equipment, services offered to other libraries, resources, online information systems, access privileges, computers, and personnel. An alphabetical list of libraries is provided in which, as one might expect, most are newspaper libraries. There are listings, however, for the libraries of the American Newspaper Publishers Association, CBS News, National Association of Broadcasters, etc. This is invaluable to the news librarian and important to researchers seeking a new angle on media research, but it is important to note that most news libraries are not open to the public and offer services only to other news libraries. Numerous indexes are provided.

299. **International Media Guide: Newspapers Worldwide**. South Norwalk, CT: International Media Enterprises. Annual. LC 75-646471. ISSN 0093-9447.

Aimed at media planners, the publisher assumes the user is familiar with the contents. Introductory material is located in the "Media planners please note" section. This guide to newspapers and Sunday magazines is divided geographically into sections on multicontinental publications, and those published in Asia/Pacific, Europe, Latin America, Middle East/Africa, and North America. Fortunately, an alphabetical list of titles with a country code is included. Entries consist of address, telephone number, general description, U.S. representative, advertising rates and data, local currency and U.S. equivalent, circulation, mechanical data, and current tax situation. This certainly does not displace the *Editor & Publisher International Yearbook* (entry 285), but it does offer useful additional data.

300. **International Television & Video Almanac**. New York: Quigley Publishing, 1955- . Annual. LC 56-2008. ISSN 0539-0761.

With the publication of the 1987 annual, video was added to the title to reflect the "burgeoning home video market." Still, this is largely a who's who in motion pictures and television source, with alphabetical listings for persons such as Hugh Downs and John Travolta. Sections on home video, companies, cable television, television stations (including channel allocations and personnel), advertising agencies, television programs, organizations, and the press (trade and newspaper) include basic address information and round out the contents. Emmy Award winners are listed, including awards for television journalism. An ample services section features everything from animals and trainers to government film bureaus and trailers. To make it truly an international almanac, the industry in Great Britain and Ireland as well as the "world market" is profiled. The annual *International TV and Video Guide* (Tantivy Press, Zoetrope) might also provide useful information.

301. Johnson, Ben, and Mary Bullard-Johnson. **Who's What and Where: A Directory and Reference Book on America's Minority Journalists**. 2d ed. Columbia, MO: Who's What and Where, 1988. 735p. index. LC 88-50602. ISBN 0-9614418-2-8.

More than 4,000 black, Hispanic, Asian-American and Native American journalists are listed in this alphabetical guide of "thumbnail biographies." Each entry contains minority status, current position, address, and telephone number; some entries list educational background and career history. There also are chapters on affirmative action, hiring minority journalists, language, multiculturalism, internships, etc., and a section on the history of minority journalism. An appendix names local minority organizations (no addresses), and minority Nieman Fellows, Knight Fellowships, MMP Fellows, and columnists. This is an important source.

302. **Journalism and Mass Communication Directory**. Columbia, SC: Association for Education in Journalism and Mass Communication (AEJMC), University of South Carolina, 1983- . Annual. ISSN 0735-3103.

A wealth of information on journalism education and educators is neatly arranged in this paperbound volume. Listed first are schools and departments of journalism and mass communication, arranged alphabetically by state. There are some listings for Puerto Rico, Canada, Australia, and England as well. Entries for schools and departments affiliated with the Association of Schools of Journalism and Mass Communication include address, telephone number, major sequences or program specialties, faculty, and educational facilities. Two-year colleges are not represented here.

There are listings for information centers and special interest groups, journalism education organizations, media and professional associations, fellowships and foundations, and professional and student societies. The bulk of the directory is the annual AEJMC membership roster, arranged alphabetically and including addresses, telephone numbers, and biographical information. Also useful might be the *AWP Catalog of Writing Programs* (Associated Writing Programs, 1984). Though creative writing is emphasized, professional writing courses are included.

303. **Journalism Career and Scholarship Guide**. Princeton, NJ: Dow Jones Newspaper Fund, 1962- . Annual.

The Newspaper Fund is to be commended for consistently publishing an inexpensive, high-quality, and timely account of the state of journalism careers, education, and financial aid. Endorsed by the Association for Education in Journalism and Mass Communications, this is an essential source for anyone seeking a journalism scholarship. Section 1 offers an overview of the field, with essays aiming at students who have not yet made career choices ("What Do Reporters and Editors Do?", "The Graduates Advise Future Grads"). Also included is a newspaper salary report, a report which might lead some budding journalists to other, more lucrative job markets. Section 2 details universities offering journalism majors, and lists the "Journalism Ivys," colleges accredited by the Accreditation Council on Education in Journalism and Mass Communications. The Directory of Journalism Scholarships, section 3, lists universities offering news/editorial scholarships. Organized alphabetically by state, each entry contains address, telephone number, and contact person.

Other grants and scholarships listed in separate sections in the directory include general scholarships, continuing education grants, and minority scholarships. (Available under separate cover, but containing the same information found here under minority scholarships, is a booklet entitled *Journalism Career Guide for Minorities*, also published annually by Dow Jones.) *Financial Aid for Minorities in Mass Communications* (Garrett Park Press, 1981) and Alfred Balk's 32-page *Directory of Media Studies Centers, Midcareer Fellowship and Training Programs for Journalists* (Gannett Center for Media Studies, 1989), might also provide some useful information. In addition, *Editor & Publisher* publishes an annual "Directory of Journalism Awards and Fellowships" in a late December issue.

304. La Brie, Henry G., III. **A Survey of Black Newspapers in America**. Kennebunkport, ME: Mercer House Press, 1979. 72p.

Though less useful as a directory than as a record of black publishing, this is a guide to nearly 200 black newspapers in the United States. The third edition was published in 1973 as *The Black Newspaper in America: A Guide*. Entries are arranged by state, then newspaper, and list address, telephone number, circulation, advertising rate, publisher, editor, method of printing, size of paper, when published, total number of employees on staff, and number of white employees. Included are biweekly or monthly black newspapers, and a state-by-state list of black newspapers no longer published.

305. **Literary Market Place**. New York: Bowker, 1940- . Annual. index. LC 41-51571. ISSN 0161-2905.

Though this is a directory of American book publishing, its usefulness does not end with the book trade. *Literary Market Place* offers a wealth of information on the mass media. United States book publishers receive the most attention, and publishers are classified geographically and by subject and activity. Other main sections center on associations and organizations, including advertising, magazine, press, film, music, radio, and television associations. Other useful features are a subsection on columnists and commentators, listings of radio, television, and cable networks, and radio and television programs featuring books. A section on newspaper and magazine publishing, arranged by state and city, lists newspapers, newspaper magazine sections, and general-interest and specialty magazines which have book reviews and/or features on books and authors. Entries include address, telephone number, brief description of the book review section, review editor, and circulation. There also is a section on news features and syndicates. However, the *International Literary Market Place*, another annual from Bowker, offers no such information on the mass media in territories or countries beyond North America. It is limited primarily to book trade information.

306. **Magazine Industry Market Place: The Directory of American Periodical Publishing**. New York: Bowker, 1980- . Annual. index. LC 79-6964. ISSN 0000-0434.

Divided into 40 sections on various aspects of magazine publishing, the first three chapters on publications and publishers make up the bulk of this directory. Section 1 is an alphabetical listing of periodical titles, which includes publisher, address, telephone number, personnel, branch offices, circulation, printing process, printer, frequency of publication, advertising, and other notes. It is followed by two indexes which classify periodicals by type and subject. Section 2 lists publishers of multiple periodicals, and section 3 contains micropublishers. Other sections focus on trade newsletters and magazines, reference books, national associations, exhibits and awards, advertising agencies, networks, public relations agencies, individuals and firms providing services and supplies, direct mail, and promotional services. A "yellow-pages" section includes telephone numbers of individuals and companies in the main directory.

307. McDarrah, Fred W. **Stock Photo and Assignment Source Book**. 2d ed. New York: Photographic Arts Center, 1984. 324p. index. ISBN 0-913069-01-9.

McDarrah, picture editor of *The Village Voice*, anticipating the needs of picture editors, art directors, and graphic designers everywhere, has subtitled this well-researched book "Where to Find Photographs Instantly." Aimed at anyone in mass communications who has to locate or assign photographs, this volume contains more than 4,000 entries highlighting sources, agencies, and photographers in the United States and Europe. According to McDarrah, "this is the only source book that provides a comprehensive guide to working press and editorial photographers who are ready to shoot and deliver assignments instantly."

Arranged in 10 categories, each entry contains address, telephone number, cable address, personnel, photographer's assignment specialty, and description of photographs in stock. Listings are arranged alphabetically by state. A general-sources section spotlights the major world photojournalism sources, news agencies, syndicates, and individual photographers. Foreign sources follow these, and are listed alphabetically by country. Other sections include business, historical, official, public information, newspaper, media (film libraries and television stations), and reference sources. Photography associations are listed as well. There are separate name and stock photo indexes.

McDarrah has created and revised an excellent source to consult when speed is of the essence (and when isn't it?). Also useful are *World Photography Sources* (Directories, 1982); *Directory of Art Libraries and Visual Resource Collections in North America* (Neal-Schuman, 1978); and *Picture Researcher's Handbook* (Van Nostrand Reinhold UK Co., 1986).

308. **National Directory of Community Newspapers**. Minneapolis, MN: American Newspaper Representatives, 1920- . Annual.

Community newspapers are organized by state and city, then arranged alphabetically by title. Entries include address, telephone number, day published, circulation, publisher, county, etc.

309. Newmyer, Marina, ed. **Washington Blackbook: The Directory to the Washington Press Corps.** Lanham, MD: Madison Books, 1988. 565p. index. LC 88-5181. ISBN 0-8191-6878-5.

This book (which is literally black) offers the following observation in the introduction: "There is no single city in America with the concentration of journalists found in the Capital. And there is certainly no city in the country where journalists are more talented, more sophisticated or more powerful than those who work in the shadows of the Capital and the White House." Those who work in the shadows are listed in the personnel index. There is a media index as well. Divided into sections on newspapers, magazines and newsletters, electronic media, wire services (print and broadcast), television and radio programs, multititle publishers, and freelancers, entries are spare or, according to the introduction, arranged in a "highly streamlined format." Names, titles, addresses, and contacts are included. Whether you are a publicist searching for a media contact or a journalism student considering the job market in D.C., this directory should set you on the right track. The new *Power Media Selects: The Nation's Most Influential Media Elite* (Broadcast Interview Source, 1989) and the *News Media Yellow Book* (Monitor Publishing Company), a new semi-annual directory of the media in Washington, D.C., and New York City, might also be useful.

310. **Newspaper Circulation Analysis.** Wilmette, IL: Standard Rate and Data Service, 1957- . Annual. index.

Concerned with newspaper circulation and market penetration, this source guides the user through a maze of metropolitan areas, television market areas, penetration levels, newspaper designated markets, and city zones. There are sections on metropolitan area circulation and market data analysis; newspaper circulation and market data applied to television markets; county circulation, with geographic analysis of circulation and penetration for all daily newspapers and newspaper groups in the United States; newspapers and newspaper groups arranged alphabetically by state; and 36 ranking tables. Advertising and marketing specialists will use this source most efficiently, but anyone with a need for detailed circulation analysis will be able to find it here. See also *Circulation* (entry 276).

311. Nordland, Rod. **Names and Numbers: A Journalist's Guide to the Most Needed Information Sources and Contacts.** New York: John Wiley & Sons, 1978. 560p. index. LC 78-18903. ISBN 0-471-03994-2.

Nordland says this "was developed as a professional tool for the working press, and it is intended to fulfill the serious need for a national directory of information sources and contacts," and that it would "take dozens of specialized directories to duplicate even a portion of this directory." It is now dated; while this book is still an excellent book of ideas and sources for the information-gatherer, one would be wise to seek out all those specialized directories. More than 20,000 listings are organized into three main sections. Useful logistics provides information on "getting around," toll-free numbers, unpublished numbers, and information on automobile, airline, and hotel reservations. The information sources and contacts section is a directory of the federal government and regional, state, city, and county governments. It also details police and emergency agencies; major American businesses; federal, state, and local consumer offices; labor unions; education organizations; arts and entertainment organizations; the National Weather Service; major international organizations; and the "Most Newsworthy Americans." A section on the media lists media organizations, daily newspapers, leading magazines, book publishers, wire services, broadcasting networks, all-news radio stations, television stations, public relations firms, national journalism awards, and press clubs.

312. **Photographer's Market.** Cincinnati, OH: Writer's Digest, 1978- . Annual. index. LC 78-643526. ISSN 0147-247X.

Photographers seeking a marketplace will do well to consult this Writer's Digest source. The markets are identified as and arranged according to the following categories:

advertising and public relations firms; audiovisual, film, and video firms; book publishers; businesses and organizations; galleries; newspapers and newsletters; paper products; publications; record companies, and stock photo agencies. Publications aimed at editorial photographers are further subdivided into association, company, consumer, and trade press. All entries are arranged alphabetically within categories. The newspapers and newsletters category is said to include publications ranging from general to special interest. Since there is no subject organization within categories, one finds, in a recent volume, the *Los Angeles Times Magazine* sandwiched in between *The Liquor Reporter* and *Maryland Farmer, Virginia Farmer, Georgia Farmer,* and *Alabama Farmer* which are all in the same section as *Mom Guess What Newspaper, Weekly World News, Parade* and the *Times-Picayune.* Entries are detailed, and include address and telephone number, contact information, brief description, photos purchased and assignments given, photo needs, photo specs, reporting time, pay scale, rights purchased, and, as usual, advice and tips. A services and opportunities section lists contests and workshops. A publication and organization index is included.

Freelancers and beginning photographers will obviously find this a most useful guide, as the editors indicate that "those companies not interested in hearing from new photographers are not included." However, established photographers seeking a new market might get some ideas here as well. A recent *Photographer's Market* included more than 2,500 listings. The *Writer's and Photographer's Guide to Newspaper Markets* (Helm, 1981) might also provide useful information.

313. Television and Cable Factbook. Washington, D.C.: Television Digest, 1945- . 2 vols. Annual. LC 83-647864. ISSN 0732-8648.

A television station volume and a services volume make up this factbook. It is loaded with current information on the United States and Canadian markets, including lists of station by call letters, television markets, a station directory with demographic data, foreign language programming, translators, public television, buyer's guides, and sections on group and newspaper ownership of television stations. The services volume includes a directory of cable systems and information ranging from sales and transfers of television stations to television set makers. "Television Digest," the Factbook's weekly newsletter, serves to keep this valuable annual publication up to the minute. See also the *Broadcasting/Cablecasting Yearbook* (entry 274).

314. TV News. New York: Larimi Communications Associates. Annual. ISBN 0-935224-43-2.

Local and network news programs in the United States and Canada are detailed in this accessible and important annual. Stations are arranged alphabetically by state, city, and call letter. Canadian stations follow, arranged alphabetically by province, city, and call letter. Entries contain address. telephone number, news directors and assignment editors, news and public affairs programs produced (including titles, times, anchors, and brief description), and satellite video usage. Special features are listings of subjects covered by news departments and a "wants" wishlist (tapes and guests on agribusiness, consumerism, minority issues, etc). The national networks also are covered, and entries list officers, managers, news executives, and bureau chiefs, and descriptions of news programs produced. Regional networks, news services, and Canadian networks are highlighted as well. For quick reference, there are state (or province) and city listings, complete with call letters, address, and telephone number. There are even separate indexes for United States and Canadian call letters. Though Larimi specializes in serving the public relations industry, this is one of its many sources which ably serves journalists as well, whether they are searching for a contact or an address.

315. Veciana-Suarez, Ana. **Hispanic Media, USA.** Washington, D.C.: The Media Institute, 1987. 225p. index. LC 87-60208. ISBN 0-937790-35-4.

Divided into two major parts, the first is a narrative description of Hispanic newspapers, television, and radio in the United States. Spanish-language dailies in Los Angeles,

New York, and Miami, as well as the weekly Spanish-language newspapers of Texas, are highlighted, with emphasis on advertising, news coverage, and editorial policy. The Spanish Language Communication Corporation, Univision, and Telemundo are described in the television section. The radio markets in Los Angeles, New York, South Florida, and Texas also are explored. There are sections on wire services and English-language media aimed at Hispanics. The directory is subdivided into print media, electronic media, and Hispanic media organizations, then further subdivided geographically (east, south, midwest, west, Texas, California) and arranged alphabetically. Entries for newspapers contain address, telephone number, publisher, editor, circulation, language, frequency of publication, distribution, regularly published sections, and type of news. Station entries usually contain just the address, phone, news director, and assignment editor. The author indicates that this is not a comprehensive directory, and "only electronic outlets which devote at least one-half of their air time to Spanish-language broadcasting were surveyed ... outlets which did not respond to the questionnaire were not included in this directory." There is a dearth of information available on the Hispanic media. Even though it is not comprehensive, this book is a useful and welcome source.

316.   Weiner, Richard, ed. **News Bureaus in the U.S.** 7th ed. New York: Public Relations Publishing Company, 1984. 182p. LC 80-83995. ISBN 0-913046-019.

"It is in a spirit of mutual service to publicists and journalists that this book is directed," according to Weiner. Excluded are bureaus for medium to small newspapers, broadcast media, stringers and correspondents. What exactly is included? A brief but chatty overview of news bureaus is included in the introduction, although an alarming number of typos are to be found and cast some doubt as to the care with which this edition was pulled together. Only major newspapers and selected magazines (including *Progressive Grocer* and *Rolling Stone*) are listed. Entries, listed, by state and subdivided by city, contain address, telephone number, short description, circulation, bureaus and addresses, contacts and telephone numbers. More than 20 cities are labeled news bureau centers and all bureaus in these cities are also listed in state sections. Included is information on some syndicated columnists in major cities (also to be found in Weiner's *Syndicated Columnists Directory*, entry 317). Publicists may find ample enough information here, but the most up-to-date information will be found in Drake's update, *News Bureaus in the U.S.* (entry 282).

317.   Weiner, Richard, ed. **Syndicated Columnists Directory**. New York: Public Relations Publishing Company, 1984. 104p. index. LC 82-80079. ISBN 0-913046-14-0.

Aiming primarily at public relations personnel, Weiner directs his comments toward them, and cites his three rules in handling columns and columnists: know the column, know where to find the columnist, and know how to communicate with the columnist. He also cautions the publicist not to bother the columnist ("Do not mass mail to most columnists ... Don't flood columnists with news releases ... A flood of mail from overly aggressive or unprofessional publicists can cause considerable annoyance among columnists"). This is not a who's who of columnists, nor is it a biographical source. It is simply a list of names, addresses (some home), and some telephone numbers of about 1,000 major syndicated columnists (local columnists are not included), subdivided into subject sections ranging from advice and automotive to books and sports. Names are arranged alphabetically within subject sections, and there is a name index.

The introduction of this 1984 edition states that Burt Garnett is the oldest columnist, and that in 1983 he started a weekly column entitled "Century Bound." When he turned 100, his "Century Bound" column became "Century Found." "May all columnists live as long as Burt Garnett," Weiner says. Garnett died in 1988, at the age of 101.

For timely information, consult Drake's update, *Syndicated Columnists Directory* (entry 283) and *Editor & Publisher*'s "Syndicate Directory," published in the last issue in July, complete with columnist, frequency of column, size, format, and address of syndicate only. Both of these have their strengths and weaknesses, but are useful and certainly more timely than Weiner's directory.

318. **Willing's Press Guide**. West Sussex, England: British Media Publications, 1874- . Annual. ISSN 0000-0213.

This guide describes the newspaper and periodical press in the United Kingdom, and includes sections on major publications of Europe, Australasia, Far East, Middle East, Africa, and the Americas. Entries are arranged by country within these sections, and include title, address, telephone numbers, subscription information, circulation, publication date, publisher, editor, advertising manager, and circulation manager. There is a classified index as well as a newspaper index of London, and separate regional and provincial indexes of newspapers in England, Wales, and Scotland.

319. **The Working Press of the Nation. Vol. 1: Newspaper Directory. Vol. 2: Magazine Directory. Vol. 3: TV and Radio Directory. Vol. 4: Feature Writer and Photographers Directory. Vol. 5: Internal Publications Directory**. Burlington, IA: National Research Bureau, 1949- . Annual. indexes. LC 46-7041. ISSN 0084-1323.

This five-volume opus is essential for basic information on the media. Volume 1, similar to the *Editor & Publisher International Yearbook* (entry 285), is first and foremost a directory of daily newspapers organized alphabetically by state and subdivided by city and newspaper. Entries include address, telephone number, publishing company, circulation, wire services, deadlines, and management and editorial personnel. Weekly newspapers are given much the same treatment, with far more detailed information appearing here than in the *Editor & Publisher International Yearbook*. Other sections include special-interest, religious, black, national, and foreign-language newspapers. There are listings of news and photo services, feature syndicates, and newspaper-distributed magazines. One index lists newspapers by largest metropolitan areas, another indexes editorial personnel by subject. Other indexes list newspapers with Sunday supplements and TV supplements.

Volume 2 is a magazine directory arranged by subject. Section 1 is the comprehensive index of magazine subjects with assigned group numbers, section 2 is an alphabetical index of magazine titles, and section 3 is an alphabetical cross-index of magazine subjects and related subject groups. Publication descriptions are listed alphabetically by title within subject groups in sections 4-6; service, trade, professional, and industrial publications comprise section 4. Other sections include farm and agricultural (from beekeeping to rural electricity), and consumer publications.

The TV and Radio Directory is volume 3. Commercial radio and television are listed alphabetically by state, city, and call letters in separate sections, as are public/educational radio and television stations. There also are separate sections on local radio and television programming, organized by subject, and by state and city within subject. Listings include station name, call letters, program name, broadcast days and times, and names of host or announcer. Personnel and headquarters and division location are listed for the radio and television networks section. There are indexes of radio and television stations by metropolitan and nonmetropolitan area, listed alphabetically by state, as well as indexes of radio and television personnel, arranged by subject, then state.

Volume 4 centers on feature writers and photographers, with separate sections on each. Each entry is arranged alphabetically and contains address, telephone number, professional affiliations, subject areas, and publications in which photographs or articles have appeared. There are separate indexes for each, listing writers and photographers by subject specialty.

The Internal Publications Directory is volume 5. The first section lists publication sponsors alphabetically and includes title, editor, brief description, frequency of publication, circulation, and editorial policy. The three indexes allow the user to search internal publications by editorial interest ("editorial material in which the editor expressed interest"), title, or industry.

320. **Writer's Market**. Cincinnati, OH: Writer's Digest, F & W Publications, 1930- . Annual. LC 31-20772. ISBN 0-89879-274-6. ISSN 0084-2729.

The freelance or part-time writer in search of a market or in search of an idea to market will get some good leads from this annual publication. It does tell, as its subtitle promises, where to sell what one writes, be it gags, scripts, greeting cards, business articles, or romance novels. This Writer's Digest book also offers realistic advice on the writing profession and on working with publishers and editors. The bulk of material here is on the markets, which are subdivided into sections on book publishers; book packagers and producers; consumer publications (further subdivided into almost 50 subject headings such as art and in-flight magazines); trade, technical, and professional journals (also subdivided by subject); scriptwriting, gag writing, and greeting card publishers. Entries list address, telephone number, publisher and/or editor, short description of the publication, circulation, response time, what kind of nonfiction and/or fiction needed, payment, photo needs, information on columns and departments, fillers, and advice. Under Journalism and Writing, for example, the following tip in the 1988 *Writer's Market* is offered for those seeking to publish in *JQ*: "Query letters don't really help the author or me very much. We can't make commitments on the basis of query letters, and we are not likely to reject or discourage the manuscript either, unless it is clearly outside our scope. Do a good piece of research. Write a clear, well organized manuscript."

The services and opportunities section lists author's agents and contests and awards. The book publishers subject index, subdivided by fiction and nonfiction, and general index allow easy access to subject areas and journal titles. *Writer's and Photographer's Guide to Newspaper Markets* (Helm, 1981) might also provide useful information.

321.   Wynar, Lubomyr R. **Guide to the American Ethnic Press: Slavic and East European Newspapers and Periodicals**. Kent, OH: Center for the Study of Ethnic Publications, Kent State University, 1986. 280p. index. LC 86-18825.

Wynar narrows his subject matter in this detailed guide to include only Slavic and East European newspapers and periodicals published in the United States. Similar to *Encyclopedic Directory of Ethnic Newspapers and Periodicals in the United States* (entry 322) in scope and format, researchers and scholars will be able to locate information on 17 ethnic groups. Almost 700 of the 770 questionnaires sent to Slavic and East European presses were answered and returned; the 580 titles included here are numbered and arranged alphabetically within ethnic sections, and each section is usually subdivided into native-language and English titles. Entries contain address, sponsoring organization, date established, editor, language, frequency, circulation, subscription, and brief description. When available, library holdings are included. Wynar notes in his essay on the "Nature of the Slavic and East European Press" that "many ethnic serials are not deposited in the Library of Congress or other major American libraries" and "at the present time, there is no systematic approach to the preservation of all East European and Slavic serials published in this country." In view of that, his directory is all the more important.

322.   Wynar, Lubomyr R., and Anna T. Wynar. **Encyclopedic Directory of Ethnic Newspapers and Periodicals in the United States**. 2d ed. Littleton, CO: Libraries Unlimited, 1976. 248p. index. LC 76-23317. ISBN 0-87287-154-1.

The ethnic press in the United States is defined, identified, and described in this scholarly guide emphasizing non-English-language newspapers and periodicals. Lubomyr Wynar, also the author of *American Ethnic Groups: A Guide to the Reference Sources* (Libraries Unlimited, 1987) and *Slavic Ethnic Libraries, Museums and Archives in the United States* (American Library Association, 1980), has revised his 1972 edition to include 63 ethnic groups, eight of which were not covered in the first edition: Argentinian (see Spanish press), East Indian (see Indian press), Egyptian and Pakistani (see Arabic press), Basque, Iranian, Irish, and Scottish. The black and American Indian presses are excluded, as each has been covered in numerous separate volumes.

The introduction explains methodology and scope, and introduces useful statistical data. An essay on the nature of the ethnic press addresses the history of the ethnic press as well as its current role. Arrangement is primarily by individual ethnic group (except in the case of Arab, Spanish, and Jewish presses), then alphabetically by publication. Entries contain title and title translation, address, telephone number, year of origin, editor, languages used, sponsoring organization, circulation, frequency, subscription rate, and description. The authors offer a title index and indicate that the table of contents should be used as a subject index. Slavic and East European newspapers and periodicals are awarded their own volume in Wynar's *Guide to the American Ethnic Press* (entry 321), but a third edition would be welcome.

Selected Annual Collections, Reviews, and Competitions

323. **Alternative Press Annual**. Philadelphia, PA: Temple University Press, 1983-1986. LC 85-643432. ISSN 0748-9463.
Reprints of articles, poetry, cartoons, and photographs from alternative magazines and newspapers.

324. **APME Red Book**. New York: Associated Press, 1950- . LC 49-18124.
Record of annual convention of the Associated Press Managing Editors.

325. **ASNE: Proceedings of the American Society of Newspaper Editors**. Washington, D.C.: ASNE, 1923- .
Formerly *Problems of Journalism*, this is an account of the annual ASNE convention and major committee reports.

326. **Best Editorial Cartoons of the Year**. Gretna, LA: Pelican Publishing Company, 1973- . LC 73-643645. ISSN 0091-2220.
Cartoons by members of the Association of American Editorial Cartoonists.

327. **Best Newspaper Writing**. Don Fry, ed. St. Petersburg, FL: The Poynter Institute for Media Studies, 1979- . LC 80-646604. ISSN 0195-895X.
Winners of the American Society of Newspaper Editors Writing Awards sponsored by ASNE and The Poynter Institute.

328. **Best of Newspaper Design**. Glen Cove, NY: PBC International, 1979/80- . LC 83-641901. ISSN 0737-2612.
Annual winners of Society of Newspaper Design competition. Also of interest might be *Typography: The Annual of the Type Directors Club* (Watson-Guptill).

329. **Best of Photojournalism**. Columbia, MO: National Press Photographers Association and University of Missouri School of Journalism, 1977- . LC 77-81586. ISSN 0161-4762.
Winners of "Picture of the Year" competition sponsored by the NPPA and the University of Missouri School of Journalism.

330. **Broadcast Designers' Association Annual International Design Competition**. San Francisco, CA: Broadcast Designers' Association, 1980- .
BDA award-winning television and advertising graphics.

331. **Communication Yearbook**. Newbury Park, CA: Sage Publications, 1977- . LC 76-45943. ISSN 0147-4642.
Annual publication of the International Communication Association, containing current reports on and commissioned articles of issues in communication. Sage also publishes the *Sage Annual Reviews of Communication Research. Communications Law* (entry 332) contains technical articles on press freedom and law.

332. **Communications Law**. New York: Practicing Law Institute, 1982- . LC 79-643817. ISSN 0898-2457.
A collection of technical articles on press freedom, press law, libel, etc.

333. **Graphis Design Annual: The International Annual of Advertising and Editorial Graphics**. New York: Watson-Guptill, 1952/53- .
   Includes sections on magazine covers and newspaper and magazine illustrations. Also of interest might be the Society of Illustrators' *Illustrators* and *Publication Design Annual* (Madison Square Press), *Art Directors Annual* (ADC Publications), and *American Illustration Showcase* (American Showcase, Inc.).

334. **Mass Communication Review Yearbook**. Newbury Park, CA: Sage Publications, 1980-1988. ISSN 0196-8017.
   Published in conjunction with the Center for Research in Public Communication, this anthology of published studies and original contributions in mass communication was discontinued in 1989.

335. **Photographis: The International Annual of Advertising and Editorial Photography**. New York: Watson-Guptill, 1966- . LC 66-4571.
   International collection of photographs used in advertising, newspapers, and magazines.

336. **The Pulitzer Prizes**. Kendall J. Wills, ed. New York: Simon and Schuster, 1987- . LC 88-641507. ISSN 0896-2197.
   Collection of Pulitzer Prizes in journalism (articles, photographs, and editorial cartoons).

337. **The Silver Book Photography**. New York: Annuals Publishing Co., 1982- . ISSN 0737-2841.
   Advertising, editorial, etc., photographs by members of the American Society of Magazine Photographers.

7
Handbooks and Manuals

This chapter emphasizes reference handbooks and manuals. Most journalism textbooks are excluded. Books of newspaper, publishing, and broadcast style, as well as English language usage, are in Chapter 8.

338. Bann, David. **The Print Production Handbook**. Cincinnati, OH: North Light Publishers, 1985. 160p. index. ISBN 0-89134-160-9.

Editors, publishers, and journalists with little knowledge of newspaper, magazine, and book production will be able to understand and use this book. Bann says, "Also, the barrier between print and the outside world is starting to crumble, as journalists, authors, advertisers and so on become involved in various parts of the process." This is an attractive book, full of illustrations and graphics, with pages color-coded by chapter. The editor and editorial director are credited, and so are the art editor, art director, and designer. There are chapters on printing processes, preparation for printing (proofing, electronic page planning, platemaking), typesetting, paper and ink, finishing and binding, and working with the printer (buying print and paper, estimates, etc.). The extensive glossary stands alone as a valuable reference. The *Handbook of Advertising Art Production* (Prentice-Hall, 1984) and *Graphic Designer's Production Handbook* (Hastings House, 1982), to name two related titles, may also provide useful information.

339. **Black Press Handbook: Sesquicentennial, 1827-1977**. Washington, D.C.: National Newspaper Publishers Association, 1977. 116p.

Though haphazardly organized, this handbook does mark the 150th anniversary of the black press and the birth of *Freedom's Journal*. There are several pages of advertisements before the table of contents appears on page 6. Included are articles on "The Black Press Assessed," "Challenges Still Confront Black Press," the Black Press Archives, and a brief history of the black press. The directory, now out of date, lists National Newspaper Publishers Association member newspapers by state, and includes address, telephone number, and circulation. Managers and editors are listed with biographical information. There is no index.

340. Cooper, Louis F., and Robert E. Emirtz. **Pike and Fischer's Desk Guide to the Fairness Doctrine**. Bethesda, MD: Pike & Fischer, 1985. 183p. index. LC 85-063130.

Broadcast managers, radio and television journalists, and journalism students will find in this book a detailed explanation of the fairness doctrine, a regulation which required that broadcasters provide balanced coverage of controversial topics.

341.   Dill, Barbara. **The Journalist's Handbook on Libel and Privacy**. New York: Free Press, 1986. 262p. index. LC 86-551. ISBN 0-02-908070-3.

Dill designed this to be a "comprehensive newsroom handbook on libel and privacy," and offers discussion and examples of court cases on libel law, actual malice, due care, opinion privilege, privacy law and embarrassment, and false light. (Remember the Cherry sisters' libel case? "The reviewer had depicted the youngest of the sisters, Addie, as 'the flower of the family, a capering monstrosity of 35,' and he wrote that when Addie and her sisters Effie and Jessie sang a eulogy to themselves, 'The mouths of their rancid features opened like caverns, and sounds like the wailing of damned souls issued therefrom.' " The judge agreed with the reviewer).

A 60-page question-and-answer chapter lists more than 150 questions grouped in sections such as "A Suit is Filed," "Before the Trial," "At the Trial," "Reporting and Editing Process," "Official Proceedings," "Privacy," and "Photography." Journalists seeking quick answers to one or two questions are more likely to consult this chapter, as questions such as the following are answered: "Does personal information about a reporter come out in a libel trial?" "What about name-calling? Is that opinion?" "Is there any forgiveness for mistakes in 'hot news,' when a story is produced on deadline?" and "How protective is 'allegedly'?" A table of cases and a subject index guide the user through the libel and privacy maze.

Rodney A. Smolla's *Law of Defamation* (Clark Boardman, 1986) and Bruce W. Sanford's *Libel and Privacy* (Prentice-Hall Law and Business, 1985, with supplements) also provide useful information. Michael G. Crawford's *The Journalist's Legal Guide* (Carswell, 1986), and Robert Martin and G. Stuart Adam's *A Sourcebook of Canadian Media Law* (Carleton University Press, 1989) focus on press law in Canada. See also *Media Law: A Legal Handbook for the Working Journalist* (entry 347) and *News Media and the Law* (entry 534).

342.   Dougherty, John L., comp. **Learning in the Newsroom: A Manual for Supervisors**. Reston, VA: American Newspaper Publishers Association Foundation, 1973. 201p. **Supplement I**, 1975, various pagings.

A great deal of sage advice is hidden in this disorganized, looseleaf collection of tips in training and orienting new staffers and interns. Aiming at city editors and managing editors, Dougherty calls this color-coded guide a "giant check list." Yellow pages are tips for editors; pink pages are checklists and memos. The white pages are handouts for new employees, "if you like them," Dougherty says (it is difficult to tell if he is referring to the new people or the handouts). There are sections on orientation, new reporters, writing examples, interviewing, obituaries, beat reporting, etc. Unfortunately, there is no index.

343.   Edelson, Edward. **The Journalist's Guide to Nuclear Energy**. Bethesda, MD: Atomic Industrial Forum, 1985. 61p.

Edelson, *New York Daily News* science editor, has fashioned a unique handbook for the science writer, a "road map that will guide him accurately and dispassionately through those aspects of nuclear energy that make the news: safety, waste, radiation, and economics." Brief chapters cover history, reactors and safety, Three Mile Island, accidents, radiation, waste management, economics, etc. He includes a three-page glossary and a list of basic information sources. *The Environmental Reporter's Handbook*, published by the Hazardous Substance Management Research Center, might also be useful.

344.   Field, Janet N. **Graphic Arts Manual**. New York: Arno Press, 1980. 650p. index. LC 79-6549. ISBN 0-405-12941-6.

This thoughtfully designed manual of graphic arts technology and processes, aimed at art directors, production managers, editors, designers, graphic artists, and students, offers both introductory and technical material. Essays by more than 90 contributors are organized in sections on color, design, manuscript preparation, typography, composition, art preparation, photography, graphic arts photography, platemaking, printing, substrates, inks, binding, fulfillment, and trade practices. The first article in each section usually presents a general overview of the subject. For example, the design section opens with a discussion of "Principles of Design" and is followed by "The Grid System," "Magazine Design," "Newspaper Design," "Annual Reports," etc. Headings and subheadings are printed in color, and there are more than 400 color and black-and-white illustrations listed in a separate table of contents. In the foreword, Louis Silverstein, then assistant managing editor of *The New York Times*, says, "The *Graphic Arts Manual* presents a view of the graphic arts as an industry—a very large one that touches and services virtually every other business enterprise of any size." This takes up where *Pocket Pal* (entry 360) leaves off, and though it will not fit in a pocket, graphic artists and designers should have it close at hand.

345.   Finnegan, John R., Sr., and Patricia A. Hirl. **Law & the Media in the Midwest**. St. Paul, MN: Butterworth Legal Publishers, 1984. 352p. ISBN 0-86678-119-6.
        Dedicated "to all the hardy and irrepressible souls who gather the news for the doorsteps and airwaves of the Midwest," this handbook answers questions about media law in Illinois, Iowa, Minnesota, Nebraska, North Dakota, South Dakota, and Wisconsin. It aims at working journalists, editors, publishers, and broadcasters. Separate chapters on access to places, meetings, records, and courts, and protecting sources offer an overview of the issue, introduce some hypothetical questions, and then give a state-by-state account of answers to those questions on media law. The chapter on libel addresses confidential sources and defenses for libel. There also is a valuable explanation of how to use law books and references cited throughout the book. Although there is an index of statutory materials, use is hindered by the lack of a subject index. At times, one resorts to flipping through chapters to find information on reporters' privilege or the Freedom of Information Act, for example. Nevertheless, Finnegan, then vice-president and editor (now senior vice-president and assistant publisher) of the *St. Paul Pioneer Press and Dispatch*, and Hirl, a media lawyer, have produced a timely and useful sourcebook on media law for the nonspecialist.

346.   Freedman, Helen Rosengren, and Karen Krieger. **The Writer's Guide to Magazine Markets: Nonfiction**. New York: New American Library, 1983. 363p. index. LC 83-13153. ISBN 0-452-25652-3.
        Aimed at freelance writers, "this book does not guarantee success. But it does contain a wealth of 'bottom line,' honest information about varying policies at magazines, different editors' personal preferences regarding the submissions process, and their tips for writers trying to break in." Most of the magazine titles listed are national consumer and newsstand publications. They are listed alphabetically by magazine title, and entries include a brief description of the publication, freelance possibilities, sample copies, submissions, and rejections. Essays on "How to Get an Article Published" and "How to Submit an Article or Idea" are included. See also *Writer's Market* (entry 320).

347.   Galvin, Katherine M. **Media Law: A Legal Handbook for the Working Journalist**. Berkeley, CA: Nolo, 1984. 228p. LC 84-060496. ISBN 0-917316-75-4.
        Galvin says that the purpose of this guide is to "distill the overabundance of information on how law and the media interact into one convenient reference manual which deals with the primary issues you are sure to face from one day to the next." She also cautions that "this book is not and does not pretend to be a substitute for the advice of a competent media lawyer." There are chapters on freedom of expression, censorship, libel, privacy and the First Amendment, free press and fair trial, privilege, newsroom searches, access to news sources and records (including detailed information on the Freedom of Information Act), and government regulation of electronic media. A subject and name index is provided. See also Dill's *The Journalist's Handbook on Libel and Privacy* (entry 341) and the National Association of Broadcasters' *Legal Guide to Broadcast Law and Regulation* (1988).

348. Gora, Joel M. **The Rights of Reporters: The Basic ACLU Guide to a Reporter's Rights**. New York: Avon, 1974. 254p. LC 74-21647. ISBN 0-380-00188-8.

The author pulls no punches on the subject of reporters' rights: "This guide sets forth your rights under present law and offers suggestions on how you can protect your rights ... [but] offers no assurances that your rights will be respected." Directed at the non-specialist, this is arranged in question-and-answer format by subject, and is part of a series of American Civil Liberties Union handbooks on rights. There are sections on First Amendment principles, protecting sources, gathering news, publishing news, covering courts, libel and invasion of privacy, and the underground press. Appendices include summaries of state shield laws.

Although this is not a new book, the questions are still valid even if some answers have changed ("If you encounter a specific legal problem in an area discussed in one of these guidebooks, show the book to your attorney"): "Who owns a reporter's notes or materials?" "Can the police arbitrarily deny a press pass to a reporter?" "Apart from national security, are there any other grounds for imposing a prior restraint on what reporters may publish?" "Is radio or television broadcasting of court proceedings allowed?" This book says usually not. "Can the press urge a court to decide a case one way or the other?" "Who comes within the description of a 'public figure'?" "What kinds of reporting deficiencies will result in a finding of actual malice?"

349. **Graphic Artists Guild Handbook: Pricing and Ethical Guidelines**. 5th ed. New York: Graphic Artists Guild, 1984. 194p. index. ISBN 0-932102-05-0.

"This book provides both graphic artists and their clients with a current compilation of the going rates and professional business practices applied throughout the industry." The section on prices and trade customs reveals rates that freelancers and salaried designers and illustrators in various fields command. (On newspapers: "It is worth mentioning again that this is one of the lowest-paying fields of illustration and has its value mostly as a trade-off for the excellent exposure that large daily newspapers provide the beginning talent.") Other chapters offer discussions of pricing artwork, professional relationships and issues, contracts, and ethics. The freelance graphic artist will find this most useful.

350. **Handbook of Magazine Publishing**. 2d ed. New Canaan, CT: Folio Publishing Co., 1983. 790p.

This 800-page "handbook" is a selected compilation of more than 300 *Folio* (entry 518) articles published from 1972-1982. Many "how-to" articles written by *Folio* editors and other specialists are arranged by broad subject, but this arrangement, even in addition to a detailed 10-page table of contents, is not an adequate substitute for a subject index. Sections on advertising management and marketing, selling advertising, circulation management, management, single-copy sales, editorial, printing, and starting a new magazine occupy most of the space, but there also are sections on circulation promotion, fulfillment, graphics, and production. "The Second Edition is a practical guide to understanding the many aspects of a complex, modern industry," according to the preface. "It offers realistic solutions to everyday magazine publishing problems." Another strength of this handbook is the sheer number of two- to three-page articles in each subject section. In the management section, for example, there are 34 articles ranging from "A Magazine Life Cycle and Its Profits" to "How to Destroy a Magazine: Let Me Count the Ways." It is valuable as an overview of the magazine industry as well as a purveyor of advice and tips.

351. Horowitz, Lois. **A Writer's Guide to Research**. Cincinnati, OH: Writer's Digest Books, 1986. 135p. index. LC 86-4052. ISBN 0-89879-222-3.

The beginning researcher is targeted in this "travel guide" to the research process. Unfortunately, there is little discussion of online searching, a research skill useful—and sometimes essential— to the journalist. Instead, there is sometimes simplistic, sometimes cursory treatment of "quick-and-dirty research," original research, and using books, magazines, and newspapers in research. ("Are newspapers really research tools? Indeed they are. Newspapers are time capsules, freeze-frames of life as it existed in a certain time and place.") There are other chapters on research tips, general reference sources ("the old regulars"), indexes, government documents, statistics, pictures, and experts. Horowitz knows her sources and has some excellent advice for novice library users. The serious researcher will want to make a brief stop here, then forge on. Writers will find additional useful research tips in Mona McCormick's *The New York Times Guide to Reference Materials* (Times Books, 1985), Bruce L. Felknor's *How to Look Things Up and Find Things Out* (Morrow, 1988), and *Search Strategies in Mass Communication* (entry 371).

352. **Insurance Handbook for Reporters**. 2d ed. Northbrook, IL: Allstate Life Insurance Company, 1985. 304p.

This highly specialized guide targets not the reporter who needs to buy insurance, but the reporter who covers the insurance business. Chapters on the history and operation of insurance answer general questions about the field. We learn that the ancient Romans had health and life insurance and that the Collegia (Roman benevolent societies) "provided burial insurance and financial help for the sick and aged." Most useful are the separate chapters on automobile, residential, life, health, and commercial insurance, and the glossary of more than 200 terms. Commercial insurance, for example, covers property coverage, liability policy, and even nuclear accident insurance. There are also chapters listing insurance organizations and companies. Allstate intended this handbook to add a "new dimension" to insurance reporting.

353. Kessler, Lauren, and Duncan McDonald. **Uncovering the News: A Journalist's Search for Information**. Belmont, CA: Wadsworth Publishing Company, 1987. 243p. index. LC 86-15930. ISBN 0-534-06954-1.

"Because information gathering is the skill basic to all varieties of mass communication, you are about to read an entire book devoted to its practice." Written for the student, this sometimes-chatty handbook describes techniques for gathering information, research strategies, and reference sources useful to the journalist. The authors emphasize the importance of libraries, and include a chapter on finding facts fast, including locating books, articles, and specialty sources. The "Washington on File" chapter presents a clear picture of how to find a government document. "Institutional Knowledge" tackles federal government sources, and "Issues and Answers" discusses the process of reporting on state, county, and city government. There also are chapters on business, finding and using experts, and press law. The "Electronic Libraries" chapter lists numerous databases useful to the journalist and cuts through database searching jargon. The cost of going online is discussed briefly, but it still deserves more attention. This information can be located in the index under "Computers—Disadvantages of" and in the electronic libraries chapter under "Snakes in Eden." The authors, who teach in the School of Journalism at the University of Oregon, recognize that any discussion of this sort also should include a discussion of ethics in information gathering. Their final chapter "Whom Do You Trust?" and Appendix, "Identifying and Dealing With Ethical Issues," lay a foundation for discussions of credibility and ethics.

354. Kirtley, Jane E., ed. **The First Amendment Handbook**. Washington, D.C.: Reporters Committee for Freedom of the Press, 1986. 64p.

Those who seek a "just the facts" approach to the First Amendment will find this a suitable source. Working journalists seeking information in a minute and students looking for a general overview can brief themselves on surreptitious recording, access to courts and places, gag orders, freedom of information acts, confidential sources, libel, privacy, prior restraints, and copyright. These subjects are then further subdivided. In the section on invasion of privacy, for example, there are discussions of intrusion, publication of private facts, false light, misappropriation, and a "Reporter's Privacy Checklist," consisting of a dozen questions on consent, obtaining information, etc. Obviously, there are sources to turn to for further reading, such as *The Journalist's Handbook on Libel and Privacy* (entry 341), legal textbooks, and communication law textbooks. For a comprehensive discussion of copyright law, consult Donald F. Johnston's *Copyright Handbook* (Bowker, 1982).

The editor reminds the user that "this booklet is not a legal treatise, nor does it attempt to deal with every situation you may encounter. In addition, the law in your state may differ from the general discussions provided here. When in doubt, consult an attorney or contact the Reporters Committee. Our staff attorneys will be happy to assist you."

355. Knapp, Mark L., and John A. Daly. **A Guide to Publishing in Scholarly Communication Journals**. Austin, TX: International Communication Association, 1986. 52p.

Described as a "distillation of the experiences, opinions, pet peeves, and advice from ten scholars and journal editors," this book offers scholarly publishing do's and don'ts from Knapp and Daly as well as Robert Avery, Charles R. Berger, Steven Chaffee, B. Aubrey Fisher, Gustav Friedrich, George Gerbner, and others. The question-and-answer format allows the user to pinpoint specific issues such as "Can I submit the same manuscript to more than one journal at the same time?", "How is my manuscript evaluated?", "What do I do if my manuscript is rejected?", and "I don't understand what the editor wants me to do. What should I do?" The 30 questions are placed in sections on the submission process, reviewing process, and the process of resubmission, revision, and feedback. Appendices contain some examples of journal style requirements, reviewer evaluation forms, and letters of acceptance, rejection, and revise/resubmit. Also included is an example of a "good" review critique. This guide will help those new to scholarly publishing save time and face.

356. Mandell, Judy, comp. and ed. **Magazine Writers Nonfiction Guidelines**. Jefferson, NC: McFarland, 1987. 392p. index. LC 86-43088. ISBN 0-89950-239-3.

Aimed at the novice and freelance writer, this is a collection of official writers' guidelines for more than 200 newsstand and airline magazines and selected periodicals. Mandell says that "this book should help the writer who is uncertain about where to send the piece he or she has written as well as the writer who already has a periodical in mind but doesn't quite know his or her angle." Titles included range from *Fishing World* to *Hustler*. A title and subject index is provided. See also *Writer's Market* (entry 320), which is updated annually.

357. Montgomery, Louis Falls, ed. **Journalists on Dangerous Assignments: A Guide for Staying Alive**. American Committee of the International Press Institute, 1986. 84p.

"You are more important than the story. No story is worth your life."

"Never point your finger; it can be mistaken for a gun."

"Never wear olive green or anything that makes you look like a soldier."

"Always carry a white flag."

Foreign correspondents offer these and other sobering pieces of advice in this thought-provoking book. "The purpose of this manual is to help journalists in dangerous situations to avoid death, injury, jail, expulsion, and other perils." One chapter includes tips and advice ("Journalists should not cross mine fields that have not been deactivated"), while another offers journalists' accounts and "reports from the field." From David Zuccino, *Philadelphia Inquirer*: "I never argued with men holding guns. People in Beirut are always pointing guns at people and you can't take it personally."

There also is a brief discussion of news agencies and their guidelines—or lack thereof—in sending reporters and photographers on dangerous assignments, and information on the Red Cross hotline and tracing service. There is no index, but journalists in need of such information will want to read this cover-to-cover.

358. Morse, Grant W. **Guide to the Incomparable New York Times Index**. New York: Fleet Academic Editions, 1980. 72p. LC 79-87815. ISBN 0-8303-0159-3; 0-8303-0160-7 (pbk).

It takes 72 pages of text and illustrations to explain how to use the index to the "newspaper of record" effectively. Morse says, "Herein one will find what you always wanted to know about *The New York Times Index*, but never dared ask." If one does not close the book after that statement, one will find a brief history of the versatile *Index*, then explanations and illustrations of headings, subdivisions, cross references, entries, and miscellaneous information (biographical, reviews, deaths, etc.). The appendix includes an illustrated step-by-step guide on using *The New York Times* microfilm: copy down full citation, find microfilm reel (illustration: hand closes in on microfilm box), remove reel from box, place on microfilm reader, and turn to correct date, page, and column. It does not, however, show the user how to thread the film on the machine, which is what really terrifies most nonusers of microfilm.

359. **Newsroom Management Handbook**. Washington, D.C.: American Society of Newspaper Editors Foundation, 1985. LC 85-70343. ISBN 0-943086-04-3.

The American Society of Newspaper Editors has produced a looseleaf notebook on newsroom management that is accessible and easily used by even the most harried city editor. According to the introduction,

> Our idea is that if you are well-organized, and have half an hour to solve your crisis, you can read the general discussion before turning to the list of do's and don'ts. If you are both well-organized and prescient, you can order the books on the future reading list. If you're the typical editor, and have ten minutes, you can scan the do's and don'ts—and maybe squeeze in a call to The Newspaper Center.

Divided into sections on "The Editor as Manager," "The Editor as Real Person," and "The Editor as Money Manager," these 25 essays (some of which originally appeared in *ASNE Bulletin* or *presstime*) are written by experts such as Robert Giles, C.K. McClatchy, and Judy Clabes. Subjects include hiring and firing, turnover, labor relations, burnout and stress, management style, and setting salaries. In "The Total Newspaper," Susan Miller tells us that "Real editors yell. They yell at reporters. They yell at copy editors. They yell at everyone in every other department. Real editors are a dying breed." This collection of pithy and well-written articles serves as a realistic overview of potential problems in the newsroom and, fortunately, balances itself with some down-to-earth answers and responses. For more and detailed discussion, see Giles's *Newsroom Management* (entry 464).

360. **Pocket Pal: A Graphic Arts Production Handbook**. 13th ed. Memphis, TN: International Paper Company, 1983. 216p.

In spite of its cutesy name, *Pocket Pal* is a unique and important tool in graphic arts. It satisfies the needs of artists, designers, and students seeking information in a hurry or a portable reference on printing, type, graphic arts photography, platemaking, paper, and inks. There are new sections on electronic prepress systems and quality control. Approximately 450 graphic arts terms such as *mullen tester, soft dot, anti-halation backing, flush cover*, and *fuzz* are defined in the glossary. The table of contents serves as an adequate index. See also the *Graphic Arts Manual* (entry 344), a less portable but far more detailed handbook written in essay format.

361. Polking, Kirk, and Leonard S. Meranus, eds. **Law and the Writer**. 3d ed. Cincinnati, OH: Writer's Digest Books, 1985. 302p. index. LC 79-19500. ISBN 0-89879-170-7.

Though the editors say that "these pages contain the information you need to stay out of the courtroom," this third edition offers only a framework of discussion on press and broadcast law. They do note, however, that "There is no substitute for a lawyer when a writer has legal problems." Twenty-two chapters, written by experts and aimed primarily at freelance writers, cover topics such as libel, advertising law, privacy, copyright law, entertainment law, book contracts, pornography, photography, federal taxes, and retirement funds. For more and directed information on libel and other matters of concern to journalists, see *The Journalist's Handbook on Libel and Privacy* (entry 341). *A Journalist's Primer on Federal Criminal Procedure* (American Bar Association, 1988), a 52-page booklet, might also be useful.

362. Rivers, William L., Wallace Thompson, and Michael J. Nyhan. **Aspen Handbook on the Mass Media 1977-79 Edition**. New York: Aspen Institute for Humanistic Studies, 1977. 438p. index. LC 77-14556. ISBN 0-03-023141-8; 0-915436-67-1 (pbk).

Though it is showing its age, this handbook and directory represents a monumental effort to harness the literature of communications. Subtitled "a selective guide to research, organizations and publications in communications," it is much more than that. First published in 1973, and updated in 1975, this volume is the last edition published. One has only to scan the table of contents to grasp the depth and breadth of information here: communications research in universities and nonacademic institutions, and within organizations; communications organizations (in advertising and public relations, broadcasting, educational and instructional media, film and photography, journalism, new communications technologies, print media); communications law courses; special libraries; communications periodicals (subdivided by subject); books and films on communications; communications bibliographies. All entries are generously annotated. There is a subject and title index.

363. Rogers, Geoffrey. **Editing for Print**. Cincinnati, OH: North Light, 1985. ISBN 0-89879-184-7.

Those involved in book or magazine editing and production will find this a handy reference, but should be forewarned of some glitches. The imprint page takes pains to credit the editor, art editor, designer, art director, editorial director, and those responsible for the copyediting principles text, magazine text, computer text, and origination, imposition, finishing and binding text. But who was responsible for numerous misspellings and other errors in the bibliography? (It's Jacques Barzun, not Barzan.) Who alphabetized the glossaries where *format* comes before *form*, *leading* before *leader*, and *modem* before *milking machine*. There are similar problems with the index. Although there is good advice and instruction throughout the book, one wonders if the sloppy treatment found in some sections carries over to content. In the chapter on editing and typesetting, Rogers writes, "If the copy-editing has been done poorly, the reader is distracted by errors in much the same way that a filmgoer is distracted by poor continuity: the very best of films is spoiled when the hero's moustache appears and disappears between shots!" There is a chapter on fundamentals, including an explanation of what editors do and how books and magazines are produced. Other chapters discuss design, paste-up and print processes, and promotion.

364. Rosen, Philip T. **International Handbook of Broadcasting Systems**. New York: Greenwood Press, 1988. 309p. index. LC 87-29986. ISBN 0-313-24348-4.

Twenty-eight experts examine broadcasting in twenty-four countries in this essay handbook. John Lent takes on Cuba and India; Benno Signitzer and Kurt Luger look at Austria; and Marvin Alisky reports on Chile, Mexico, and Peru. Other included countries are Australia, Belgium, Brazil, Canada, China, the Federal Republic of Germany, Great Britain, Hungary, Israel, Italy, Japan, Kenya, Korea, Nigeria, Saudi Arabia, the Soviet Union, Sweden, and the United States. According to the introduction, "At present no reference work exists where one can readily ascertain what the broadcast structure is in a given nation and how it came to be. By filling this void, we hope that our work will make a substantial contribution to the field of international broadcasting." This they have done.

Most essays include a bibliography, information on history, regulation, economic structure, programming, new technologies, broadcast reform, and a conclusion and/or forecast. What type of information can be found under broadcast reform? In Israel, for example,

> The reaction against the "leftist mafia," a nickname coined for broadcasters, has been strongly felt in programming and personnel appointment policies. A popular TV satirical program was taken off the air in the late 1970s in response to harsh political criticism. The television prime-time weekly news magazine,

broadcast on Friday nights, was cancelled in the mid-1980s on the grounds that the Israeli people should not be exposed to "demoralizing" news on the Sabbath eve.

There is no section on broadcast reform for the Soviet Union; instead, there is "Feedback From the Audience."

365. Rubin, Rebecca B., Alan M. Rubin, and Linda J. Piele. **Communication Research: Strategies and Sources**. Belmont, CA: Wadsworth Publishing Company, 1986. 233p. index. LC 85-10490. ISBN 0-534-05514-1.

Disguised as a textbook for undergraduate and graduate communication students, this also is a fine reference guide to sources in communication, mass communications, social psychology, speech and language, business, and political science. Divided into two sections—strategies and sources—the first part examines literature reviews, research papers, research projects, and online database searching. Section 2 outlines a multitude of general and reference sources, indexes, abstracts, communication periodicals, collections, and government publications. Annotations are descriptive and many answer questions uppermost in the student's mind: How do I use this source? Is there an index? What subjects can I look up? Does it have book reviews? How technical is it? According to the authors,

> our goal is to introduce and explain bibliographic tools that are available for investigating communication topics. In so doing, we hope we will accomplish a secondary goal of reducing the anxiety many students feel when researching a communication topic for the first time or when confronted with so much information that they don't know where to start.

Subject and source indexes were thoughtfully compiled with the student in mind. For further information on databases, the user might consult *Search Strategies in Mass Communication* (entry 371).

366. Sprain, Scott. **Staff Handbook for a Student Newspaper**. Ft. Collins, CO: Colorado Language Arts Society, 1981.

This began as a series of handouts for a high school student newspaper staff. In its new format, it aims at high school newspaper advisers and offers a model for a staff handbook which can be adapted to fit the needs of most high school newspapers. The policies section outlines staff policies, procedures, and responsibilities, along with a production schedule. A reference section includes a stylebook and headline schedules. The learning section discusses rights and responsibilities of the press, interviewing techniques, headlines, proofreading, and writing. The handbook concludes with a set of questions on all material covered.

Sprain also mentions several other items, such as copy editing symbols, evaluation forms, and paste-up terms and procedures, which would be appropriate to include in a staff handbook. He has performed a valuable service by publishing this handbook, but one might question some of his policies. He writes, "Writers who make similar stylebook errors, issue after issue, will write out sections of the stylebook to reinforce their knowledge of the stylebook." This practice may also reinforce the idea that writing is punishment.

367. Tallmadge, Alice. **Covering AIDS: A Handbook for Journalists**. Eugene, OR: School of Journalism, University of Oregon, 1987. 31p.

Reporting and writing about AIDS, while answering privacy and sensitivity concerns, is a subject of much discussion and debate in newsrooms, classrooms, trade journals, and panel discussions. Some newspapers have formed AIDS informational networks; others have named AIDS reporters. The University of Oregon's School of Journalism designed a two-day seminar on covering AIDS, and the result is this handbook. Part 1 is an update and overview of the current situation and number of AIDS cases (arranged by state) as of August 1987. Part 2 is an AIDS stylebook of usage and terms, cautioning the reporter about using "value-loaded expressions." The section on covering AIDS stories lists guidelines, stressing "restraint and careful checking of sources." Other sections discuss covering the gay population, HIV testing, federal and state laws, and communicable and venereal disease statutes. The appendix includes a glossary and source list of journals and organizations. Present and future issues in AIDS coverage are defined and presented as story ideas, although most of those issues—AIDS in schools, worldwide HIV infection, ethics, and including cause of death in obituaries—are already being tested by the media. For example, in October 1987, *The Philadelphia Inquirer* sent reporters and photographers around the world to record the impact of AIDS in various cities on one day. The result was a story called "AIDS: A Day With a Global Killer," and it represents one of the finest efforts to date in detailing the destructive path of the disease from Philadelphia to the Philippines.

Other organizations have also presented special programs and seminars on AIDS, including The Poynter Institute for Media Studies (entry 704) (a report on their "Reporting on AIDS" conference, held in January 1988, will be published). See also an *Annotated Bibliography on Media Coverage of AIDS, Cancer, Swine Flu and Related Topics* (entry 99).

368. **Tapping Officials' Secrets: A State Open Government Compendium**. Washington, D.C.: The Reporters Committee for Freedom of the Press, 1989. 3 vols.

Publication of this source was announced as *Journalism: A Guide to the Reference Literature* was going to press. It is described as a "comprehensive guide to using open meetings and record laws in the 50 states and the District of Columbia, including analysis of the statutes and cases interpreted." The 51 guides are available separately or as a compendium. The Fall 1987 issue of *News Media and the Law* (entry 534), also published by the Reporters Committee for Freedom of the Press, contains a pullout guide entitled "Confidential Sources and Information: A Practical Guide for Reporters in the 50 States."

369. Trimble, Vance H., ed. **Scripps-Howard Handbook**. 3d ed. Cincinnati, OH: E. W. Scripps Company, 1981. **1983 Supplement**. LC 80-54072. ISBN 0-9605484. 400p.

"Scripps-Howard journalism" is the theme of this handbook. "This is not a rigid 'stylebook' in the conventional sense," according to the preface. "It is a guiding set of principles. The emphasis is on the spirit, rather than the mechanics, of doing things. As much as anything, this is a statement of our journalistic faith." This is not a stylebook at all. It consists of sections on the chain's aims and purposes, institutions, newspapers, broadcasting company, and a chronology of important dates in Scripps-Howard history. Much of the book contains brief biographical sketches of Scripps-Howard people, with sections on "Pioneers and Other Personalities," trustees, and general management and staff. The first and second editions were published in 1948 and 1967, and though the editor says this edition has "moved uptown a few blocks" in the areas of size, design, and typography, this volume resembles a reader or textbook and still looks like it was printed in another era. The chapter on "Good Typography" states, "But nothing that has happened, or possibly will happen, has altered the time-honored Scripps-Howard principle that type is a medium for the expression of ideas—not a substitute for ideas. Great newspapers are not created in the composing room." A 1983 supplement is included at the front of this volume, so the user has to flip through more than 20 pages of text to find the contents page of the main volume. Fortunately, there is an index.

370. Ullman, John, and Steve Honeyman, eds. **The Reporter's Handbook: An Investigator's Guide to Documents and Techniques**. New York: St. Martin's Press, 1983. 504p. index. LC 80-52367. ISBN 0-312-67394-9; 0-312-67393-0 (pbk).

According to the editors,

> Some say investigative reporting is nothing more than a trendy name for good, old-fashioned reporting of the hard-nosed, lots-of-shoe-leather school. They may be right. But many of us believe that investigative reporting can be classified and defined.... The three basic elements are that the investigation be

the work of the reporter, not a report of an investigation made by someone else; that the subject of the story involves something of reasonable importance to the reader or viewer; and that others are attempting to hide these matters from the public.

This is the most important book a reporter will find while hacking through the red-tape jungle of records and documents. In all "Documenting the Evidence" sections, one learns why certain records should and can be used, how to use them, and where to get them. A 15-page table of contents testifies to the amount of information here.

Part 1 is "Getting Started." It contains four chapters with detailed information on "Keeping Tabs on Elected Officials," government purchasing, audits, government documents, backgrounding businesses, and the Freedom of Information Act. Part 2 discusses ways of investigating individuals, backgrounding licensed professionals and politicians, how to get birth, death, marriage, divorce, and tax records, and tracing land holdings. "Institutions" is the last and fattest part, focusing on business, labor, law enforcement, courts, health care, and education. Within these chapters, the reporter can find out how to investigate for-profit and not-for-profit corporations, bankruptcies, the Securities and Exchange Commission, Federal Trade Commission, worker health and safety, college sports, etc. The index allows access by subject and title, and there is even a form number index. This book, written by reporters who know what they are talking about, serves fellow working journalists well, and it might teach the journalism student a thing or two about the reporting process.

In contrast is *The Muckraker's Manual* by "M. Harry" (Loompanics Unlimited, 1984):

> Harry's First Law is: There is dirt on everyone. Harry's Second Law is: Anyone can dig up the dirt on anyone else if they want to badly enough.... Harry's Third Law? If Harry can do it, anyone can.... I do not have a college degree—except the two I bought through the mail for $10. Nor have I ever taken a single journalism class or seminar. Nor do I have any so-called "credentials" (except two mail-order ordination certificates). My only professional asset is a fat scrapbook of the investigative reports I've done.

Stay with *The Reporter's Handbook*.

371.   Ward, Jean, and Kathleen Hansen. **Search Strategies in Mass Communication**. New York: Longman, 1987. 274p. index. LC 86-18527. ISBN 0-582-99851-4; 0-582-28596-8 (pbk).

This textbook presents a model for mass communication research that can easily be adapted for use as a handbook. Searching the literature of mass communications can be a strenuous experience, but Ward and Hansen, of the University of Minnesota School of Journalism and Mass Communication, detail and simplify the process. Chapters on "Digging into Institutions," "Approaching Libraries: Tactics and Tools," and "Data-Base Searching in Mass Communication" identify specific reference sources and other library tools and discuss public and private institutions. In addition, there is a selected list of databases for mass communicators, subdivided by newspaper and magazine databases, business, legal and literature, statistical, social sciences and humanities, and science, medical, and technical databases. General and topical tool indexes ease the user into the valuable contents.

8
Stylebooks

Many newspapers adhere to Associated Press style, but have their own rules and guidelines for local issues, names, etc. The best-known and most-used stylebooks are included here, as well as stylebooks, when available, from *Editor & Publisher*'s top 10 daily newspapers according to circulation and the "Ten Best U.S. Dailies" (*Time*, 30 April, 1984). Some design and broadcast stylebooks are listed as well. Also included in this chapter are selected books on English language usage intended primarily for the journalist.

372.   Berner, R. Thomas. **Language Skills for Journalists**. 2d ed. Boston, MA: Houghton-Mifflin, 1984. 249p. index. LC 83-82323. ISBN 0-395-34098-5.

Designed as a journalism textbook, Berner says that in this second edition "a number of changes have been implemented to make the book easier to use as a reference." These changes include the use of subheadings, a glossary, and a list of frequently misspelled words. Berner admits that "grammar is not a sexy topic. 'Investigative journalism' sounds exciting; 'grammar' doesn't. But grammar describes the writing and speaking characteristics of a people. And journalism students should realize that if they want their stories read or listened to, they must adhere to their readers' and listeners' conventions of grammar." Berner meets journalists on their own turf and uses examples of correct and incorrect grammar in newspapers, magazines, and newscasts. Chapters on writing, sentences and paragraphs, functional grammar, conventional grammar, modification, punctuation, and meaning are further subdivided. For example, the chapter on writing includes subsections on "Needless Detail," "Stating the Obvious," "Weak Phrasing," "Prepositional Pile-Up," redundancy, throwaways, etc. So well-organized is the table of contents that the user probably will have no need to consult the index, which is also a model of organization and detail.

Especially useful to the journalist is the discussion of meaning. A single misused word can change the whole tone and meaning of an article or newscast. Here the author explores "high-sounding words and phrases," tampering with meaning, and double meanings, using examples such as "mandatory flotation device," "locational preference," and "combat emplacement evacuator" (a shovel). Berner says, "Ignorance may be an excuse for talking and writing like this, but it is not an excuse for journalists reporting such nonsense." E. L. Callihan's *Grammar for Journalists* (Chilton, 1979) also provides useful information.

373.   Bernstein, Theodore M. **The Careful Writer: A Modern Guide to English Usage**. New York: Atheneum Press, 1965. 487p. LC 65-12404. ISBN 0-689-70555-7.

Even those not prone to reading dictionaries and encyclopedias will delight in *The Careful Writer*. Bernstein, an assistant managing editor of *The New York Times* who died in 1979, was a wordmaster who tempered his criticisms with witticisms. He writes,

> A monologophobe (you won't find it in the dictionary) is a writer who would rather walk naked in front of Saks Fifth Avenue than be caught using the same word more than once in three lines. What he suffers from is synonymo-mania (you won't find that one, either), which is a compulsion to call a spade successively a "garden implement" and an "earth-turning tool." The affliction besets journalists in general and sports writers in particular.... The simple verb "say" never seems to be good for more than one inning; then writers or editors feel they must rush in all kinds of bush league relief pitchers.

He also writes, "Thus, unless one belongs to that tiny minority who can speak directly and beautifully, one should not write as he talks. To do so is to indulge in a kind of stenography, not writing." Bernstein takes a further step and tells us where these guidelines to good usage have come from:

> practices of reputable scholars and writers, past and present ... observations and discoveries of linguistic scholars ... predilections of teachers of English ... observation of what makes for clarity, precision, and logical presentation ... personal preferences of the author—and why not (After all, it's my book) ... experience in critical examination of the written word as an editor of *The New York Times*.

He also wrote the "Bernstein on Words" column.

Arranged in dictionary format, most examples of use and abuse were taken from newspapers. Bernstein also is the author of *Do's, Don'ts, and Maybes of English Usage* (Times Books, 1977), *Miss Thistlebottom's Hobgoblins* (Simon & Schuster [c1971], 1984), *Watch Your Language* (Macmillan, 1965), etc.

374.   Bremner, John B. **Words on Words: A Dictionary for Writers and Others Who Care About Words**. New York: Columbia University Press, 1980. 406p. LC 80-256. ISBN 0-231-04492-5; 0-231-04493-3 (pbk).

Bremner has the journalist in mind as he writes in the introduction, "I have witnessed the steady growth of literary ignorance during a career of more than a third of a century as a professional journalist, a professor of journalism and a newspaper consultant." But he doesn't scold the students of journalism. He blames the teachers, "many of whom either blame their students' previous teachers or pass the buck to later ones. Worse, many young teachers are being taught not to teach grammar. What used to be the first art of the trivium has become trivial." With his position on that issue firmly established, Bremner goes on to define and discuss words and their correct and incorrect usage, and includes "some verbal gamesmanship and excursions into mythology and literary allusion." A "gatekeeper," for example, is " 'communicologese' for editor, a gatekeeper is one who mans a gate to control what copy will get through him and how it will be played. Rarely in the history of the press has an editor ever identified himself as a gatekeeper." The book is arranged in dictionary format.

375.   Campbell, Richard M. **Stylebook**. Toronto, Canada: The Toronto Star, 1983. 148p.

A 1-page introduction set in 14-point type and an understated title are the only introductory materials to 148 pages of *Toronto Star* style. Managing editor Ray Timson writes, "Campbell used every reference book he could find and assessed changes in style recommended by a host of *Star* editors over the years. And then he began writing, and I think you will find passages here that are absolutely delightful and unique among contemporary stylebooks." If stylebooks can be delightful, surely this one qualifies. It would be nice to know, however, which style and usage books and dictionaries he used most frequently. On "Xanthippic," Campbell says, "Xanthippe was the name of Socrates' shrewish wife, and by extension, it applies to any peevish and ill-tempered woman. But you'd be xanthippic too if you had to put up with the Socratic method all day long." There is no index. "No index is necessary," counters Timson. "Everything we have to say about spelling, punctuation, abbreviation, libel, contempt of court, is listed alphabetically." This is true. Campbell has produced a most engaging, frequently humorous, and occasionally brilliant book of Canadian newspaper usage and style. Would that other stylebooks were written with such flair.

376. Cappon, Rene J. **The Associated Press Guide to Good Writing**. Reading, MA: Addison-Wesley, 1982. 140p. LC 82-73305. ISBN 0-201-10320-6.

The *AP Guide to Good Writing* is best described by Cappon himself. This is "extended shoptalk—a continuation of the discussions, formal and informal, with newswriters intent on improving themselves in their craft." Here are Jack Cappon's rules on and gripes about the use and abuse of language. According to the introductory material, however, the book cannot adequately describe "the gurgles and sighs and the groans that rise from behind his desk when he comes upon sentences that are particularly well turned or upon writing that is lazy or pompous or dull." Cappon, AP newsfeatures editor, offers a loosely organized volume with no index, so the user will have to browse, skim, and scan. The table of contents can lead you to general areas of interest, such as news writing, leads, tone, pitfalls, quotes, color ("small, specific detail"), pseudo-color (clichés, etc.), features, and usage.

He concludes with a "Bestiary" section, a "compendium for the careful and the crochety" or "a collection of usages which I regard as bestial." Of "literally," Cappon writes, "Disastrous as a casual intensifier because it means that something is factually and precisely true. The Mets literally slaughtered the Cardinals last night would have left at least nine corpses. I would never use literally in a million years. I mean that figuratively." And on one of his favorite phrases, "pre-dawn darkness": "Hackneyed journalese. Write pre-dawn darkness if you're also prepared to write pre-dusk brightness. It is a poetic phrase that has been worked to death, that's all. A substitute is needed. How about 'ere Aurora rose'? No? Then let us return, simply, to before dawn." Cappon's admonishments are enough to strike fear in the hearts of all. He says, "If you write disinterested when you mean uninterested you are wrong, period. Other entries, I admit, may be open to discussion —but not if I'm handling the copy." This is a lively companion volume to the *Associated Press Stylebook and Libel Manual* (entry 383).

377. **The Chicago Manual of Style**. 13th ed. Chicago, IL: The University of Chicago Press, 1982. 738p. index. LC 82-2832. ISBN 0-226-10390-0.

Though not a newspaper or broadcast style manual, the formidable *Chicago Manual of Style* is used most frequently in book and magazine publishing. First published in 1906, this thirteenth edition is "much more a 'how-to' book for authors and editors than was its predecessor." It answers more questions relating to technology and electronic publishing, and devotes the final section to production and printing. The first two sections are concerned with aspects of bookmaking, such as manuscript preparation, copy editing, proofs, and permissions. The bulk of the book is the detailed style section, with chapters on punctuation, spelling, numbers, foreign languages, quotations, illustrations and captions, tables, abbreviations, documentation, indexes, etc. Also useful is the United States Government Printing Office *Style Manual* (1984) for printers, writers, and editors.

378. Copperud, Roy H. **American Usage and Style: The Consensus**. New York: Van Nostrand Reinhold, 1980. 433p. LC 79-11055. ISBN 0-442-21630-0; 0-442-24906-3 (pbk).

"Disputed points" of usage are compared in this consolidation and revision of Copperud's *A Dictionary of Usage and Style* (Hawthorn, 1964) and *American Usage: The Consensus* (Van Nostrand Reinhold, 1970). Consulted for this consensus were: Bernstein's *The Careful Writer* (entry 373); Margaret M. Bryant's *Current American Usage* (Crowell, 1965); Copperud's own *A Dictionary of Usage and Style* (Hawthorn, 1964); Bergen and Cornelia Evans' *A Dictionary of Contemporary American Usage* (Random House, 1957); Rudolf Flesch's *The ABC of Style* (Harper & Row, 1964); Wilson Follett's *Modern American Usage* (Hill & Wang, 1966); H.W. Fowler's *A Dictionary of Modern English Usage* (Oxford University Press, 1965); and several dictionaries, including *Webster's New*

International Dictionary, Third Edition, Random House Dictionary of the English Language, and the *Oxford English Dictionary*. "I decided that a more useful purpose would be served by comparing the views of these books, and indicating where the weight of opinion lay," writes Copperud.

Entries are arranged in dictionary format, and range in length from a few lines to several pages. If an entry contains only one opinion, then it is the consensus of the authorities. Copperud writes,

> Dictionaries of usage often disagree, but they have one quality in common: prescription. It could not be otherwise, for the authors are saying to the reader, "I know best." Yet correct usage, whatever that may be, is not a matter of revealed truth, but oftener than not reflects taste or opinion.

The entry for *critique* reads as follows: "Criticized by Evans, Flesch, and Fowler as pretentious for criticism, review, notice. This view seems dated and pedantic. Dictionaries give it as standard as a noun, but only Webster lists it as a verb (critique the performance). The use is widespread, however, and will probably gain recognition." Even though this is a consensus, Copperud gives himself the last word.

379. Covey, Rob. **Newspaper Design Stylebook; The Seattle Times**. Seattle, WA: Seattle Times Co., 1983. Various paging. illus. index.

Covey, now art director of *U.S. News and World Report*, compiled a stylebook of newspaper design when he was with *The Seattle Times*. A section on "Ingredients" is divided into chapters on typography, photographs, space, color, design principles, and "putting it all together." The "Formats" section focuses on headlines, body copy, typebreakers, standing heads, special formats, and listings. There is an index and detailed table of contents. For further information on design stylebooks, see the March 1988 issue of *Design: The Journal of the Society of Newspaper Design* (entry 516) and the article on designing a design stylebook.

Covey's book includes a list of six design stylebooks available at the following newspapers: *The Virginian-Pilot and The Ledger-Star; Corvallis Gazette Times* in Oregon; the *Fort Worth Star-Telegram; The Minneapolis Star and Tribune*, now out of print; *Alexandria Daily Town Talk* in Louisiana; and *The Record* in Bergen, NJ. Other design stylebooks worth noting include the Orlando Sentinel's *Design Guide*, and Mario Garcia's *Redesign Stylebook: The Daily Breeze, The Outlook, The News-Pilot* (Copley Los Angeles Newspapers).

380. Crump, Spencer. **The Stylebook for Newswriting: A Manual for Newspapers, Magazines, and Radio/TV**. Corona del Mar, CA: Trans-Anglo, 1979. 112p. LC 79-2440. ISBN 0-87046-052-8; 0-87046-051-X (pbk).

According to Crump, "this guide, unlike the wire services' stylebooks, is intended primarily for the writer associated with a local newspaper, radio/TV news outlet or magazine." Entries are arranged alphabetically and focus more on style than basic English usage because "the journalist should be a person who knows how to use our language because of schooling and aptitude." He also says this book is compatible with the *Associated Press Stylebook* (entry 383) and the *United Press International Stylebook* (entry 391), though its emphasis is on local news. For example, he allows a "more avant garde position" on courtesy titles and provides guides for writing about local sports.

381. **Detroit Free Press Style Book**. Detroit, MI: Detroit Free Press, 1989. 34p.

"The aim is consistency." Those are the first words in this new book of style from Detroit. (Why then is this book called a Style Book on the cover and a stylebook on page 3?) Entries are alphabetical, "arranged to enable all staff members to find answers quickly, and so to spell, capitalize and punctuate the same way; to avoid usages that imply favoritism or bias, and to present our material clearly." The cover is graced by a drawing of a cigar-smoking newsman wielding a pencil and what looks to be a paste jar.

382.   Evans, Harold. **Newsman's English: A Guide to Writing Lively, Lucid and Effective Prose**. New York: Holt, Rinehart and Winston, 1972. (Editing and Design: A Five Volume Manual of English, Typography and Layout). 224p. index LC 77-160163. ISBN 0-03-091349-1.

Harry Evans on "Good English":

> English is a battlefield. Purists fight off invading yes-men, dropouts, hobos, killjoys, stooges, highbrows and coeds. Vulgarians beseech them to trust the people because the people speak real good. Grammarians, shocked by sentences concluding with prepositions, construct syntactical defences up with which we will not put. Officials observe that in connection with recent disturbances there does not appear to have been a resolution of the issue. And journalists race to the colourful scene to report the dramatic new moves.

In other chapters Evans discusses words, language, the structure of news story leads, accuracy, and editing. Other books in this five-volume collection are *Handling Newspaper Text*, *News Headlines, Picture Editing,* and *Newspaper Design*.

383.   French, Christopher W., ed. **The Associated Press Stylebook and Libel Manual**. Rev. ed. Reading, MA: Addison-Wesley, 1987. 330p. LC 80-51657. ISBN 0-917360-03-6.

Most newspapers today either use the *AP Stylebook and Libel Manual* or have designed their own stylebooks, based on AP style, to incorporate local rules and guidelines. In the style section, entries are arranged in dictionary format, and include usage information, correct and incorrect usage, abbreviations, and related topics. Some entries just offer correct spelling and/or capitalization. A "stylebook key" illustrates how entries are organized and explains the significance of entries printed in boldface type, italics, etc.

The libel portion explores defenses and privilege; public officials, figures, and issues; and privacy. It is not, according to the foreword, a textbook on libel and "will make no reader an expert on libel."

Other features include sections on closed courtrooms, captions, and filing wire copy. French writes, "Most of these rules are not dark secrets. They are based on dictionaries, grammar books and local customs and usage." This is not a flamboyant book of word play and display. (If it's entertainment you seek, read the Toronto Star *Stylebook*, entry 375).

All working journalists, journalism students, and newspaper freelancers, however, should own and consult the most current edition of this stylebook. It is *the* book of newspaper style. Do not ignore, however, other books of style and usage such as the incomparable *The Elements of Style* (entry 400). For a lengthy discussion of sexism in writing, an issue most stylebooks fail to address in any detail, see Casey Miller and Kate Swift's *The Handbook of Nonsexist Writing* (Harper & Row, 1988).

384.   Holley, Frederick S. **Los Angeles Times Stylebook**. New York: New American Library, 1979, 1981. 239p. LC 80-28897. ISBN 0-452-00552-3.

Each page of this style and usage book illuminates the blunders and gaffes we make as communicators. Although it emphasizes newspaper style for the *Los Angeles Times* and uses numerous examples from Southern California, "this present volume is intended to be of help to anyone engaged in writing or editing—not just Times staff members, not just newspaper people, not just journalism students." A two-page bibliography lists other style and usage books, many of which are mentioned in this text. There is no index, but arrangement is alphabetical and there are cross-references. There is even an entry for *zzyzx*, which says

> you may not believe it, but it's a good one to end an alphabetical listing with. This community near Baker was founded as a religious and health spa and is now being used as a base for desert studies by a consortium of seven California colleges. It was named with the intention of its being "the last word in the language," and it surely is.

385. Hood, James R., and Brad Kalbfeld, comps. and eds. **The Associated Press Broadcast News Handbook, Incorporating the AP Libel Manual**. New York: Associated Press, 1982. 298p. index. LC 81-12702. ISBN 0-917360-49-4.

Based on the *Associated Press Stylebook and Libel Manual* (entry 383), this book is "intended to provide an overview of how the Associated Press serves its thousands of broadcast members." Part 1 describes AP broadcast services and the AP Radio Network, and includes essays on "Telling the Story," "The Editor's Eye," and libel. Part 2 is the stylebook, arranged in dictionary format.

386. Jordan, Lewis, ed. **The New York Times Manual of Style and Usage**. New York: The New York Times Company, 1976. 231p. LC 75-8306. ISBN 0-8129-0578-4; 0-8129-6316-4 (pbk).

The foreword spells out *The New York Times*'s goals and objectives in publishing this volume. Though "compiled for those who write and edit *The New York Times*," any writer will benefit from this close, thorough, and staid examination of newspaper style and usage. Jordan, then news editor of *The New York Times*, reminds us that *style* here is not literary style. "It is a set of rules or guidelines intended to assure consistency of spelling, capitalization, punctuation and abbreviation in printing the written word." Usage, on the other hand, is "the manner in which words are employed — or most often, the preferred manner of using them when a choice can be made. The intent is to give preference to that which safeguards the language from debasement." This is no small task, but this stylebook does an admirable job in battling word debasement, deterioration, and debilitation. Entries are arranged alphabetically in dictionary format, and range in subject from Burmese names to sequence or tense. Users also are reminded that "in case of conflict, the forms listed in this manual take precedence over the style given in the dictionaries or gazzetteers."

387. Kessler, Lauren, and Duncan McDonald. **When Words Collide: A Journalist's Guide to Grammar and Style**. 2d ed. Belmont, CA: Wadsworth Publishing Company, 1988. 228p. index. LC 87-20962. ISBN 0-534-08574-1.

"When words collide, they can collide like trucks on a highway, causing chaos and damage. Or they can collide like atoms of uranium, releasing power and force. Grammatical errors cause words to collide with disastrous results. Grammatical mastering — craftsmanship — causes words to collide in a creative burst of energy." Interestingly enough, Kessler and McDonald define a *collision* as a "violent contact between moving bodies. An accident between a moving car and a stationary telephone pole is not a collision; it is a crash." *American Usage and Style: The Consensus* (entry 378) says that a collision "must involve two moving objects" but a moving object "may be said to collide with a stationary one." *The Washington Post Deskbook on Style* (entry 404) states that a collision "does not require two moving objects; a car can collide with a tree and waves can collide into rocks"; and then the *Broadcast News Manual of Style* (entry 388) says "there is some shifting from the original usage of collision. Purists (myself included on this one) insist that a collision is the violent coming together of two moving objects. Therefore, an automobile cannot collide with a tree. Recently, some wordsmiths have been saying that sticking to the narrow meaning of the word is sophistry." Kessler and McDonald assure us, however, that words can collide.

Aimed at students, teachers, and professionals, this book is divided into two sections. Part 1 tackles parts of speech, sentence agreement, case, passive voice, punctuation, spelling, and the three Cs — clarity, conciseness, and coherence. Part 2 is a 44-page alphabetical guide to usage and grammar. This spiral-bound book does not replace the *Associated Press Stylebook and Libel Manual* (entry 383) or *The Elements of Style* (entry 400), but is appropriate for any writer needing a refresher course in grammar, or English and journalism instructors seeking an up-to-date and well-organized supplemental textbook. In fact, its best audience will be found in the classroom, where students might actually take the time to complete the grammar, word-use, and spelling exercises. Kessler and McDonald, journalism faculty members at the University of Oregon, also wrote *Uncovering the News: A Journalist's Search for Information* (entry 353) and *Mastering the Message: Media Writing with Substance and Style* (Wadsworth, 1989).

388.   MacDonald, R. H. **A Broadcast News Manual of Style**. New York: Longman, 1987. 202p. index. LC 86-27463. ISBN 0-582-99865-4.

A lengthy introduction sets the tone of this manual of radio and television style and usage. "I was determined to write this book when frustration with existing guides reached an intolerable level," MacDonald writes. "Student newswriting exercises and broadcast copy were so filled with errors that correcting and editing were taking a lot of time." He also says that "to my knowledge, there is no extensive style, format and usage guide for broadcast newswriters." Also published in 1987 was Papper's *Broadcast News Writing Stylebook* (entry 393). MacDonald mentions the *AP Broadcast News Handbook* (entry 385) and says that the information therein is "handy for someone writing to the standardized style of the AP, but is extra baggage for the broadcast newswriter working for a local audience." In this manual, *style* also includes the "more mechanical aspects of news-writing — page formats, how to cue tapes, etc. — for both radio and television."

The usage guide constitutes the bulk of the volume. It is arranged in dictionary format and includes cross-references. The nine appendices range in subject from area codes to codes of ethics. There are sections on style and format, and a section entitled "Getting Words on Paper," with discussions of paragraphs, number usage, pronunciation, and listener problems. There is a brief index.

In a brief discussion of editing, the author once again points out some differences between editing broadcast news and newspapers:

> Copy editing for broadcast news is relatively simple beside the complexities of print media editing. There is one basic idea to keep in mind: some poor soul — you or someone else — is going to have to read this mess aloud before an audience. Therefore, you keep your editing as clean and simple as possible.

He also says, "Never use newspaper editing marks. They mean nothing to a broadcaster and just mess up the copy." The following guides to pronunciation in broadcasting might also be useful: *The Spoken Word: A BBC Guide* (British Broadcasting Corporation, 1981) and Eugene Ehrlich's *NBC Handbook of Pronunciation* (Harper & Row, 1984).

389.   Melton, Rob. **Publications Stylebook: An Authoritative Guide on Matters of Style for the High School Journalist**. Portland, OR: published by author, 1986. 50p. index.

This stylebook "will easily provide the answers to the types of questions high school students have about style. This style guide will also teach them AP style." There are separate sections on copy preparation, abbreviations, capitalization, identification, punctuation, quotations, editing, advertisements, design, headlines, etc. Each rule or guideline within these sections is numbered. The subject index refers users to rule numbers, not page numbers. Quill and Scroll's *Stylebook* might also be useful.

390.   **The Miami Herald Stylebook**. Miami, FL: The Miami Herald, 1985. Various paging.

This thick, looseleaf volume "is designed to bring uniformity to the spelling, abbreviations, symbols, capitalization and other forms of usage in *The Miami Herald*," and is arranged in dictionary format. *The Herald* follows AP and UPI style.

391.   Miller, Bobby Ray, comp. and ed. **The UPI Stylebook: A Handbook for Writers and Editors**. New York: United Press International, 1977. 196p.

H.L. Stevenson, then editor-in-chief of UPI, spells out the aim of this wirebound stylebook: "This new and enlarged edition of the UPI Stylebook does not undertake to be a manual of literary style. Its primary purpose is to achieve consistency in spelling, capitalization, punctuation and usage for newspaper wires." Entries are arranged alphabetically, include correct and incorrect examples of usage, and are brief and straightforward. For example, "zzz," used to represent the sound of a person snoring, is always lowercase.

392.   **Newsday Stylebook and VDT User Manual**. Melville, NY: Newsday. 47p. n.d.

According to the introduction, there are times "when the writer and the rules of writing are at odds, when the splendid sentence or lyrical passage simply cannot coexist with every admonition to do, or not do. Reconciling inspired, but unorthodox, work with the demands of style is no easy matter." This looseleaf book of style is arranged alphabetically. There are separate appendices for the following: bias, colleges and universities, courts, datelines, fractions, military ranks, misspelled and troublesome words, police jurisdiction, sports, community datelines, and hospitals. New entries and style changes are marked.

393. Papper, Robert A. **Broadcast News Writing Stylebook**. Delaware, OH: Ohio Wesleyan University, 1987. 151p.

Papper offers some sensible advice for choosing and using words and "writing for the ear." He also points out some differences between broadcast and print style. "Beyond Strunk's dictum on 'no unnecessary words,' we in broadcast must write with no lapses in thought, with no errant words or phrases, with nothing askew to try the mind's straightforward understanding of what we're trying to say from first word to last." Nineteen chapters in this spiral-bound book address problems in grammar and usage, readability, sentences, phrases, leads, and endings. In a discussion of words, the author writes, "Beware the thesaurus, a frequently evil volume introduced by well-intentioned middle school teachers. The thesaurus provides the disservice of supplying longer and more complicated words of only approximate similarity to the word you're looking up." Also included are chapters on quality and style; definitions, problems and usage (misused and mispronounced words); reference guides to business, government, and legal terms; and listings of professional sports teams.

Papper's book also contains items not found in print stylebooks, such as a pronunciation guide to countries, and a discussion of television and the relationship between words and pictures. Here, for example, is a script of an NBC report on the space shuttle *Challenger*, with description of video. A glossary defines some basic broadcast terms. *Talent* is defined as "people who perform on the air, including newscasters, weather, sports — but not reporters." Though obviously of most use to broadcast journalists and students, Papper speaks to all journalists when he says, "Write as if you had to defend every word you use." See also *A Broadcast News Manual of Style* (entry 388).

394. Petranik, Steven, comp. and ed. **The UPC Style Guide and Technical Manual**. Toronto, Canada: United Press Canada, 1983. 101p.

Petranik states he "depended heavily on the *UPI Style Guide*" (entry 391) when compiling this stylebook, but listed here are rules and guidelines particular to United Press Canada. In a foreword statement about inconsistency and sloppiness, however, the user is jarred by the appearance of an extra "a" in that very sentence. The book is in binder format and is divided into sections on writing, style, rules, procedures, and computer commands (24 pages of "what you can do with your VDT and how to do it"). "I have tried to confine myself to explaining the current, widely-accepted principles of good news writing. Words, constructions and styles are condemned only if they are wrong, clumsy, or better done another way." The 25-page section of style rules is arranged alphabetically. Subjects such as sentence structure, clarity, quotations, leads, sexism, racism, sources, and editing are covered in the writing section. The procedures section addresses subjects ranging from stringers to sports agate.

There is even a brief discussion of newsroom etiquette; journalists, take heed. Petranik advises, "Editors should praise good reporting and writing, and reporters should praise good editing. Use the message wire to compliment your colleagues and to publicize examples of fine writing."

395. Purcell, Edward B. **The Right Word**. Washington, D.C.: The Washington Post, 99p.

Designed as a companion volume to *The Washington Post Deskbook on Style* (entry 404), this guide to proper usage is filled with often humorous thou-shalts and thou-shalt-nots for journalists. Purcell writes, "When writers blur the distinction between two words, a process starts that eventually destroys one of them." He continues, "The language clearly has a hole in its pocket and is losing some of its riches." Purcell's thoughts on "heart condition": "Burton was known to have a heart condition. We all have heart conditions. Mine is satisfactory, thank you, and I hope yours is fine. Use heart ailment, or better, an exact description." On "cliches" he writes, "Occasionally, writers get their cliches wrong, and that is embarrassing: 'the kinds of students who fall between the cracks.' If they fall between the cracks, they do not fall at all. If you're going to avoid using the cliche, avoid the right one: fall through the crack." Perhaps the most valuable lesson is found in the essays on "copspeak": "Our friends in blue do not speak or write English." The evidence? "An altercation ensued" after "entry was gained," by an "unknown suspect" last seen "traveling westbound."

396. Rose, Turner, ed. **U.S. News & World Report Stylebook for Writers and Editors**. Washington, D.C.: U.S. News and World Report, 1983. index. LC 83-24109. ISBN 0-89193-001-9.

Though written with the staffers of *U.S. News and World Report* in mind, this is one of the most comprehensive and well-organized stylebooks available. According to the introduction, "a good style also spells its words in a uniform way and constructs its sentences in recognizable forms, because this indicates that writers and editors know what they are doing and thus gives their products the ring of authenticity." It is divided into chapters on style and content, abbreviation, capitalization, punctuation, figures, foreign currencies, names of persons, church and clergy, medical terms, compound words, slang, etc. There is a detailed index and word list.

397. Sellers, Leslie. **Doing It In Style: A Manual for Journalists, PR Men and Copy-Writers**. London: Pergamon Press, 1968. 321p. LC 68-21107. ISBN 0-8203791-4; 0-8103791-0 (pbk).

Sellers, then production editor of the *Daily Mail*, states that this is "more than a style book—much more. It is the practical newspaperman's Fowler and should have a place at every journalist's bedside as well as in his office." Entries are arranged in dictionary format, with detailed descriptions, definitions, examples, and, of course, a British slant. For example, "The Queen always takes the article, even if she makes the headline difficult by doing so. 'Queen' alone means any old queen, and that upsets people." Entries range from a few sentences to essay-length discussions of newspaper design, misused words, headlines, and picture cropping.

398. Skillin, Marjorie E. **Words Into Type**. 3d ed. Englewood Cliffs, NJ: Prentice-Hall, 1974. 585p. LC 73-21726. ISBN 0-13-964262-5.

A classic work, *Words Into Type* answers almost every question one could think to ask about style, grammar, usage, editing, and production. It goes far beyond the prescribed duties of a stylebook or handbook of usage; it answers to writers, editors, copy editors, proofreaders, and printers, and is an indispensible source in book and magazine publishing. The table of contents is mammoth, with almost 40 entries under "comma" alone. It is divided into sections on manuscript preparation; copy, galleys, and proofs; copy editing; layout and typography; grammar and use of words; and composition of type. The legal chapter has been updated to reflect changes in copyright law. A glossary of printing terms and a 35-page index conclude this comprehensive reference.

399. **St. Petersburg Times Stylebook**. St. Petersburg, FL: Times Publishing Company, 1987. 311p.

The *St. Petersburg Times* has produced a readable, accessible, and well-designed book of style, policy, and good writing. The foreword states that "there was a desire to merge Associated Press style with our own. With AP's permission, we have done that in this book." It also states that "the *Associated Press Stylebook* [entry 383] is copyrighted and our agreement with that organization prohibits the sale of this book." Those fortunate enough to stumble upon a copy will want to add it to their reference collection.

A style and usage guide, arranged alphabetically, fills 250 pages. The appendix offers a wealth of information on Florida counties in which the *Times* maintains bureaus, and other Florida-particular information such as St. Petersburg City Council districts, Florida points of interest, judicial circuits and district courts of appeal. In addition, there are discussions of open government, including the Sunshine Amendment and the legal system. A section on newsroom policies and operation will interest those who wish to incorporate such guidelines into their own stylebooks. Issues such as confidential sources, conflicts of interest, freebies, identification, cash advances, and expense accounts are covered. A summary of library services is even included, a reflection of the important role the news library plays in newsroom operations.

400.   Strunk, William Jr., and E. B. White. **The Elements of Style**. 3d ed. New York: Macmillan, 1979. 85p. LC 78-18444. ISBN 0-02-418230-3; 0-02-418220-6 (pbk).

These fundamentals of style and usage should be absorbed if only because E. B. White says so. In describing some changes he made in the third edition, White says, "Amplification has reared its head in a few places in the text where I felt an assault could successfully be made in the bastions of brevity." He continues, "The reader will soon discover that these rules and principles are in the form of sharp commands, Sergeant Strunk snapping orders to his platoon." There are 11 rules of usage, 22 principles of composition, and 21 style "suggestions." "A Few Matters of Form" discusses the use of exclamations, numerals, and hyphens ("The hyphen can play tricks on the unwary, as it did in Chattanooga when two newspapers merged — the *News* and the *Free Press*. Someone introduced a hyphen in the merger and the paper became *The Chattanooga News-Free Press*, which sounds as though the paper were news-free or devoid of news".) A 26-page chapter on commonly misused words and expressions is arranged in alphabetical order. There is now an index but do not use it: read it all. In the introduction, White writes, "I still find the Strunkian wisdom a comfort, the Strunkian humor a delight, and the Strunkian attitude toward right and wrong a blessing undisguised." If a journalist consults but one book of rules in his career (besides the *Associated Press Stylebook and Libel Manual*, entry 383), pray it is *The Elements of Style.*

401.   **Stylebook: A Guide for Writers and Editors**. Toronto, Canada: The Canadian Press, 1983. 358p. ISBN 0-920009-00-X.

Intended to be of use to "those in journalism and on its fringes but also to anyone looking for help with writing," this is the official stylebook of The Canadian Press. The Press covers Canadian news for its member newspapers and others. Although arranged alphabetically by subject (breaking stories, crimes and courts, polls, punctuation, sports, etc.), users will need to consult the index when searching for specific entries. Euphemisms, for example, can be unearthed in the section labeled "Taste." The index is particularly well-designed and allows easy access to the contents. The foreword states that this formidable, 358-page spiral-bound book has, since the first edition in 1940, been "known irreverently as the *Bible*. The *CP Style Book* (now *Stylebook*) had many of the qualities that justified such a title: it was authoritative, principled, sometimes capricious, a mixture of sombre injunctions and practical rules. Above all, like the *Bible*, it came from a need for guidance in day-to-day conduct." This stylebook is currently being revised.

402.   United Press International. **The UPI Broadcast Stylebook**. New York: UPI, 1979. 64p.

"UPI publishes two stylebooks, one for broadcasters and one for print journalists. But this does not imply that there are two different kinds of journalism. There is only one kind, that kind concerning itself with reporting accurately news that independent journalists consider to be important for everyone to know." In the preface, we read that "broadcast writing is more alive, more imaginative than straight newspaper or print wire style. United Press was the pioneer broadcast service and has always prided itself on the quality of its writing." Proud they may be, but there are journalists out there who would disagree strongly that UPI has cornered the market on imagination and liveliness. Nonetheless, UPI is a "pioneer" and its broadcast stylebook does contain the very basics of broadcast style. The first half of the book aims at broadcast writing, mechanics, guidelines (slugs, measuring copy, etc.), and a section on audio. Also included is a five-page discussion of broadcast style with guidelines on leads, transitions, tenses, and cliches. (Ironically, we are reminded that we should avoid cliches "like the plague." Then, in a discussion of humor in writing, we are told that "humor is fragile stuff. It can be the icing on the cake.") A usage guide in dictionary format makes up the other half of the book. For more in-depth treatment, see *A Broadcast News Manual of Style* (entry 388) or *Broadcast News Writing Stylebook* (entry 393).

403. **The Wall Street Journal Stylebook**. 2d ed. Paul R. Martin, ed. New York: Dow Jones, 1987. LC 86-72581. ISBN 0-87128-652-1.

According to the foreword, "Some old-time editors at *The Wall Street Journal* argued that the lack of a stylebook helped keep the Journal's style freer. That was certainly true, but the effect was a bit like Humpty Dumpty's telling Alice, 'When I use a word it means just what I choose it to mean — nothing more nor less.' " The first edition was not published until 1981. This second edition, arranged in dictionary format, includes new entries and reflects style changes in the 1980s. Many entries are based on *The Associated Press Stylebook and Libel Manual* (entry 383).

404. Webb, Robert A., comp. and ed. **The Washington Post Deskbook on Style**. New York: McGraw-Hill, 1978. 232p. index. LC 77-22958. ISBN 0-07-068398-0.

"Other newspapers have different rules, different audiences, different resources, different needs. But to the extent that common sense informs this stylebook, it can be useful to all," Howard Simons, then managing editor of *The Washington Post*, writes in the preface. "This, then, is what our stylebook is about. It attempts to provide the reporters and editors of *The Washington Post* with common rules of practice about good writing and correct usage, abbreviations and capitalization, punctuation and spelling, headlines and datelines and deadlines and bylines." These common rules are preceded by a section on standards and ethics.

Ben Bradlee discusses issues near and dear to journalists' hearts: conflict of interest, attribution, plagiarism, fairness, opinion, and taste. This is followed by a discussion of newspaper law, libel, privacy, and fairness, and an essay on ombudsmen. This book begins to take on the appearance of a traditional stylebook with an alphabetically arranged chapter on writing and correct usage. In addition, there are chapters on abbreviations, capitalization, numerals, time elements, and spelling. A chapter on "Deskwork" covers copy editing, headline and caption writing, typography, and artwork. The federal government is discussed and outlined briefly, as is local government, which, in this case, includes the District of Columbia, Maryland, and Virginia.

Since this stylebook is arranged primarily by subject, you may have to consult the index to locate answers to specific questions of style and grammar. A bibliography lists general reference books for the journalist's bookshelf, and there is a useful list of English language usage books in the chapter on writing and correct usage.

With Watergate, *The Post* assumed a unique role in journalism and newspapering. In the standards and ethics section, Bradlee writes that "although it has become increasingly difficult for this newspaper and for the press generally to do so since Watergate, reporters should make every effort to remain in the audience, to stay off the stage, to report history, not to make history." He also writes "we fully recognize that the power we have inherited as the monopoly morning newspaper in the capital of the free world carries with it special responsibilities: to listen to the voiceless, to avoid any and all acts of arrogance, to face the public with politeness and candor." These are words for all journalists, in and out of Washington, to heed.

Other newspaper stylebooks worth noting are published by the *Plain Dealer* (Cleveland), *Chicago Tribune, Boston Globe*, etc. Some newspapers such as the *Detroit News* and *Chicago Sun-Times* now use electronic stylebooks.

9
Catalogs

General Catalogs

405. Akeroyd, Joanne V. **Alternatives: A Guide to the Newspapers, Magazines, and Newsletters in the Alternative Press Collection in the Special Collections Department of the University of Connecticut Library**. 2d ed. Storrs, CT: The Library, 1976. 128p. (Bibliographic Series, no. 5). LC 77-620500.

Though dated, this library catalog of approximately 1,500 titles (250 of which were on subscription in 1976) is an excellent general guide to alternative or underground publication titles. In part 1, titles are arranged alphabetically, and list publisher and issuing group. Those included in the *Alternative Press Index* (entry 151) are marked. Part 2 is a subject listing. Akeroyd warns here that "Right wing materials have not all been cataloged, so the list under "Right Wing" is only partially representative of what is in the collection." Titles are arranged geographically (46 states and 21 foreign countries) in part 3. Entries range from *Attitude Check* (Vista, CA: Movement for a Democratic Military, 1970) to *No More Teachers Dirty Looks* (San Francisco, CA: Bay Area Radical Teachers Organizing Collective, 1970-1973). For further information on Connecticut's Alternative Press Collection, see entry 633. Those seeking other alternative publications and collections should consult Danky's *Undergrounds: A Union List of Alternative Periodicals in Libraries of the United States and Canada* (entry 417). Another useful source is Joseph R. Conlin's *The American Radical Press, 1880-1960* (Greenwood Press, 1974).

406. Brigham, Clarence S. **History and Bibliography of American Newspapers, 1690-1820**. 2 vols. Westport, CT: Greenwood Press, 1975. Reprint of 1947 edition with 1,961 additions and corrections, published by the American Antiquarian Society. 1,508p. LC 75-40215. ISBN 0-8371-8677-3.

Brigham, the late head of the American Antiquarian Society, traveled 29 states and the District of Columbia, consulted more than 500 libraries, and studied more than 2,000 newspapers in order to compile this bibliography of early American newspapers. The first installment was published in the Society *Proceedings* in 1913. Though the final installment was printed in 1927, revision began almost immediately. In all, he spent more than 30 years meticulously compiling these geographical lists. A short history of each newspaper is given, as well as dates of publication and locations. Half of the second volume includes lists and indexes. Brigham states, with justifiable pride, that the editors of the *Union List of Newspapers* began their list with the year 1821, because of his 1820 cutoff date. Edward C. Lathem's *Chronological Tables of American Newspapers, 1690-1820: Being a Tabular Guide to Holdings of Newspapers Published in America Through the Year 1820* was published by the Society in 1972.

407. British Film Institute. **British National Film and Video Catalogue**. London: British Film Institute, 1984- . Quarterly, annual cumulations. index. LC 84-37648. ISSN 0266-805X.

This quarterly, formerly the *British National Film Catalogue* (1963-1984), details more than 3,000 video and nonfeature films each year. Arranged by subject, the catalog lists television programs as well as educational and industrial films. Subject and title indexes are provided, and the annual volume offers a production index listing names of producers, writers, editors, artists, and companies. Entries include title, distributor, year of release, and production company. Television entries list sponsor, running time, video format, credits, synopsis, and intended audience. Coverage is worldwide. Other useful BFI catalogs include the *National Film Archive Catalogue* (1980) of nonfiction films and the *National Film Archive Catalogue of Viewing Copies* (1985) (items such as newsreels and nonfiction films available for previewing at the Archive).

408. British Film Institute. **Catalogue of the Book Library of the British Film Institute**. 3 vols. Boston, MA: G. K. Hall, 1975. 2,540p. index. LC 75-332053. ISBN 0-8161-0004-7. **First Supplement**, 1983. 2 vols. ISBN 0-8161-0388-7.

Though emphasis is placed on film studies in the British Film Institute Library, a large collection of books on television from the early 1960s to the present is available. For a listing of periodicals in the BFI, see *Film and Television Periodical Holdings* (entry 409). Useful author, title, subject, and script indexes are provided. Coverage is worldwide.

409. British Film Institute. **Film and Television Periodical Holdings**. Joan Ingram, ed. London: British Film Institute, 1983. 40p. index. ISBN 0-85170-143-4.

More than 1,600 film and television periodicals from 50 countries are available at the British Film Institute. Entries are arranged alphabetically by title and list variations in title, country of origin, language, and holdings. Cross-references and a geographical index are included. For information on other BFI holdings, see the *Catalogue of the Book Library of the British Film Institute* (entry 408).

410. British Film Institute. **TV Documentation: A Guide to BFI Library Services Resources**. Frances Thorpe, ed. London: Library Services, The Institute, 1985. 67p. LC 86-169903. ISBN 0-85170-181-7.

The British Film Institute (see entries 407-409) has produced numerous useful guides to film and television, and this one describes television research resources in the Library Services and Stills, Posters and Designs Collection of the BFI. Short chapters outline library book collections, periodicals, television scripts, special collections, press clippings, television publicity, the Television Stills Archive, and the *British National Film and Video Catalogue* (entry 407).

411. Buechele, Lisa F. **Newsfilm Index: A Guide to the Newsfilm Collection 1954-1971**. Jackson, MS: Mississippi Department of Archives and History, 1985. 539p. index. LC 85-620005. ISBN 0-938896-45-8.

Though the catalog indicates that the newsfilm is "a collection of unedited newsfilm from a television station in Jackson, Miss.," most is footage from WLBT-TV, the NBC affiliate in Jackson. (For further information on the collection and WLBT, see entry 688). A subject index refers the user to record numbers. These records, which comprise the bulk of the index, are arranged chronologically and include a descriptive title, physical location of the film record, technical access information (silent or sound film, etc.), date, length in feet, reel position, and description of event. There is also an index arranged chronologically by year. Film records range from "Linda Joy Lackey, the 1961 Maid of Cotton, arrives in Jackson" to "James Meredith is interviewed upon his arrival in Canton, Miss., ending his 'Walk Against Fear.' " Civil rights materials are marked with an asterisk. Those researching media coverage of the Civil Rights years will find a wealth of material in this index and collection.

412. Burrows, Sandra, and Franceen Gaudet. **Checklist of Indexes to Canadian Newspapers**. Ottawa, Canada: National Library of Canada, 1987. 148p. index. ISBN 0-660-53735-4.

The authors indicate that this is the first comprehensive listing of Canadian newspaper indexes, and is the result of a survey sent to approximately 4,000 libraries, newspapers, archives, and historical societies in Canada. The introduction details scope and methodology, and the book contains a copy of the original survey and letter. Entries are not arranged by newspaper title, but geographically by province, then alphabetically by city and institution. Fortunately, there is an alphabetical list of newspaper titles at the end of the checklist, as well as a geographical index by province and city. Entries in French and English contain address, telephone number, name of index, title of newspaper indexed, institution, frequency and place of publication, dates indexed, format of index, number of entries, and, if available to researchers, restrictions and charges. The National Library also produces a *Checklist of Indexed Canadian Newspapers: A Checklist Based on the Holdings of the Newspaper Division*. Useful guides to indexed newspapers in the United States include the *Lathrop Report on Newspaper Indexes: An Illustrated Guide to Published and Unpublished Newspaper Indexes in the United States and Canada* (Wooster, OH: Norman Lathrop Enterprises, 1979-80) and Milner's *Newspaper Indexes: A Location and Subject Guide for Researchers* (entry 425).

413. Campbell, Georgetta Merritt. **Extant Collections of Early Black Newspapers: A Research Guide to the Black Press, 1880-1915, With an Index to the Boston Guardian, 1902-1904.** Troy, NY: Whitson Publishing Company, 1981. 401p. LC 80-51418. ISBN 0-87875-197-1.

Some sources defy categorization. Campbell's guide could easily be placed with bibliographies and bibliographic guides or indexes, as it has a little bit of everything. She carries on where Armistead Pride and *The Black Press: A Bibliography* (entry 80) left off. This is a bibliographical guide to black newspapers published between 1880-1915 and available in special collections. More than 1,800 newspapers are known to have existed during that time span, and she locates and documents 180 of them. Entries include location of collections, holdings and dates, and availability on microform. In addition, a prototype index of the *Boston Guardian* is included. Campbell notes that "only one extant black newspaper has been indexed for publication. Fittingly, it is an index to the first black newspaper, *Freedom's Journal*." There is no index to other features, but this source is well worth wading through. The foreword, preface, and first chapter contain valuable information regarding the Pride research, and puts the subject matter in historical perspective.

414. Communications Library, University of Illinois, Urbana. **Catalog of the Communications Library**. 3 vols. Boston: G. K. Hall, 1975. ISBN 0-8161-1174-X.

Eleanor Blum, then communications librarian and author of *Basic Books in the Mass Media* (entry 7), says in her introduction that this catalog is the "largest collection of English-language books on the subject assembled as a single unit." That subject is communications, and it includes mass communications, communication theory, advertising, press freedom, popular culture, newspapers, radio, television, cable, magazines, and book publishing. When the catalog was published, the library held more than 12,500 monographs and 400 continuations and journals. A quarterly publication entitled "New Books in the Communications Library," arranged by subject and annotated by current communications librarian Diane Carothers, serves to update this mammoth catalog. Communications researchers would do well to tap this important catalog and collection. *A Selected Bibliography of Publications, 1949-1972*, published by the Institute of Communications Research, University of Illinois (1973), might also be useful.

415. Cox, Susan M., and Janice L. Budeit, comps. **Early English Newspapers: Bibliography and Guide to the Microfilm Collection**. Woodbridge, CT: Research Publications, 1983. 106p. LC 83-6787. ISBN 0-89235-076-8.

English newspapers from 1603 to the mid-1800s at the British Museum and Bodleian Library were microfilmed by the publisher and listed here. Entries, arranged alphabetically by title, contain little else except dates of publication and reel information. Other publications which may be more useful include the *Census of British Newspapers and Periodicals, 1620-1800* (University of North Carolina Press, 1927) and *Guide to Early British Periodicals Collections on Microfilm with the Subject, Editor, and Reel Number Indexes* (University Microfilms International, 1980).

416.   Danky, James P., ed. **Native American Periodicals and Newspapers, 1828-1982: Bibliography, Publishing Record, and Holdings**. Maureen E. Hady, comp., in association with the State Historical Society of Wisconsin. Westport, CT: Greenwood Press, 1984. 532p. index. LC 83-22579. ISBN 0-313-23773-5.

Danky and Hady prepared this guide to periodicals and newspapers by and about Native Americans "in order to assist faculty and students doing research as well as Native Americans seeking their past." They list 1,164 titles, and the State Historical Society, which has the largest collection of Native American publications, houses more than 800. Titles no longer published are included, as are literary, political, and historical journals. Users would do well to read the lengthy introduction, which provides a historical overview and describes scope and methodology. Detailed entries are numbered, arranged alphabetically by title, and list publication dates, frequency of publication, address, telephone number, number of pages in the last issue examined, availability in microform, title variations, holdings, etc. Cover pages of more than 40 Native American publications ranging from *The Medicine Bundle* to *Native Women's News* are included as well. This source wins the prize for accessibility: there are separate subject, editor, publisher, geographical, catchword and subtitle, and chronological indexes. In the introduction, Danky says,

> Daniel F. Littlefield and James W. Parins provided assistance in identifying and locating titles while doing research for their historical guide to the Native American press (*American Indian and Alaska Native Newspapers and Periodicals*, Greenwood Press, 1984 [entry 422]). Many materials were exchanged during the course of the project, but, beyond that, we reaped the benefits of both their scholarship and professionalism.

417.   Danky, James P., ed. **Undergrounds: A Union List of Alternative Periodicals in Libraries of the United States and Canada**. Madison, WI: State Historical Society of Wisconsin, 1974. index. LC 74-8272. ISBN 0-87020-142-5.

According to Danky, "My own definition of an alternative periodical, and this is purposely left very broad, is one that is politically and culturally to the left of center; i.e., a publication that expresses views not normally presented in the daily press." Complete with psychedelic cover art and matching typography, this guide to more than 3,000 titles is more than a checklist—it is the statement of an era. Compiled from lists prepared by nearly 200 librarians, *Undergrounds* is a comprehensive listing of alternative publications in the United States and Canada. Entries are arranged alphabetically by title and include place of publication, publisher, where indexed, format, holdings, and holding institution. There is a geographical index but no subject index, because "the problems inherent in stereotyping alternative publications persuaded me not to attempt this. I also felt that this would have been potentially unfair to the publications and misleading to researchers." Nonetheless, a subject index to this important source, no matter how misleading, would be most helpful. The following sources might also provide useful information: Gail Skidmore and Theodore J. Spahn's *From Radical Left to Extreme Right* (Scarecrow Press, 1987) and the *Utne Reader*, a bimonthly periodical devoted to reprinting the "best of the alternative press."

418.   Dick, Ernest J. **Guide to CBC Sources at the Public Archives**. Ottawa, Canada: Public Archives Canada, 1987. 125p. index. LC 87-174326. ISBN 0-662-54911-2.

Described as a "centralized index" to a decentralized organization, this catalog attempts to list the Canadian Broadcasting Corporation collections in seven divisions of the Archives. The 782 entries are listed in English and French by administrative division (Head Office, English Services Division, etc.). Categories and series are arranged alphabetically within chapters. Entries contain a brief description, program title, administrative unit, PAC division holdings, accession number, extent of holdings, and dates. There are name, book title, program title, and subject indexes. The author cautions that "this guide is not intended to lead a researcher to a particular document or broadcast, but rather to indicate whether the PAC holds potential sources for a particular research project." He also says that "the researcher should be aware that there exist collections in virtually all archives in Canada, not to mention archives outside the country." For further information on the CBC and Public Archives, see entry 691. Also available is the *Inventory of the National Film, Television, and Sound Archives* (Public Archives, 1983), which lists primarily Canadian Film Institute media.

419. Dooley, Patricia L., David Klaassen, and Richard Chapman. **A Guide to the Archives of the National News Council**. Minneapolis, MN: Silha Center for the Study of Media Ethics and Law, University of Minnesota, 1986. 25p. (No. 86031).

The National News Council "officially terminated operations" in 1984, but its archives are rich with records and reports on press freedom, press accountability, and relations between press and public. This is not an official catalog of the collection, but a general description of what can be found at the archives, such as National News Council Records, administrative and financial records, working files (including complaints papers), and audio- and videotapes. A detailed inventory, however, is planned. The NNC was organized as an "independent and private National News Council ... to receive, to examine, and to report on complaints concerning the accuracy and fairness of news reporting in the United States, as well as to initiate studies and report on issues involving the freedom of the press."

420. Gregory, Winifred, ed. **American Newspapers, 1821-1936**. New York: Kraus Reprint Corp., 1967. Reprint of 1937 edition published by the Bibliographical Society of America. 791p.

Picking up where Brigham left off in 1820 (*History and Bibliography of American Newspapers, 1690-1820*, entry 406) Gregory lists newspapers published in the United States and Canada through 1936. Entries are arranged alphabetically by state or province, and subdivided by city and newspaper. Dates of publication, symbol and holdings, and variations of titles are included. Gregory notes that "we have attempted to eliminate all titles already appearing in the previous union lists in this series." Also excluded are fraternal, religious, and labor union publications.

421. Hamilton, Dave. **"A Guide to the Negro Newspapers on Microfilm: A Selected List."** DeKalb, IL: Northern Illinois University, 1972. 56p. ERIC Report ED 062240.

Designed to fill gaps in the 1953 guide to *Negro Newspapers on Microfilm: A Selected List* (entry 439), this 1972 guide to the Negro Newspapers on Microfilm is divided into three sections. More than 200 titles are arranged alphabetically by title in part 1, and entries include dates of publication and reel and title number. Part 2 lists newspapers geographically by state, then city, and part 3 is a listing of microfilm reels and titles. Hamilton writes that "when an investigation by this author revealed that several newspapers appearing on the film had not been included in the (1953) guide, a thorough canvassing was undertaken to discover other possible discrepancies."

422. Littlefield, Daniel F., and James W. Parins. **American Indian and Alaska Native Newspapers and Periodicals, 1826-1924**. Westport, CT: Greenwood Press, 1984. 482p. (Historical Guides to the World's Periodicals and Newspapers). index. ISBN 0-313-23426-4. **American Indian and Alaska Native Newspapers and Periodicals, 1925-1970**. Westport, CT: Greenwood Press, 1986. 553p. (Historical Guides to the World's Periodicals and Newspapers). index. ISBN 0-313-23427-2. **American Indian and Alaska Native Newspapers and Periodicals, 1971-1985**. Westport, CT: Greenwood Press, 1986. 609p. (Historical Guides to the World's Periodicals and Newspapers). index. ISBN 0-313-24834-6.

These three volumes represent as comprehensive a listing and historical and reference guide as there probably ever will be to newspapers and periodicals edited or published by American Indians or Alaska natives. It also includes those publications "whose primary purpose was to publish information about contemporary Indians or Alaska natives," according to the authors. Canada and Mexico are not included. The native press consists of tribal newspapers, nontribal newspapers, intertribal newspapers and periodicals, and literary periodicals; the nonsectarian reform press and independent press concerns itself with reform periodicals and independent newspapers and periodicals; the sectarian press of native-language periodicals and English-language periodicals; and the government-supported press with the Indian school press and Indian agency periodicals. Magazine titles and essays are arranged alphabetically, and contain history (including affiliations with parties, organizations, or tribes), information sources (bibliography, indexing, location), and publication history. The introduction in all three volumes provides a historical overview and prepares the reader for the time period covered. Volume 1 describes more than 200 publications. Volumes 2 and 3 were compiled with the aid of more than 30 contributors. Volume 2 contains more than 500 listings, and the third volume, which takes the user through 1985, lists more than 1,000. Students of Native American journalism are assured of a comprehensive listing of titles when these volumes are used with Danky's impressive *Native American Periodicals and Newspapers, 1828-1982* (entry 416).

Littlefield and Parins caution that this last volume is a "beginning of research ... and not the end." Notes in the *Native Press Research Journal* (edited by Littlefield and Parins) update these volumes. In a 1988 issue, the editors say

> Despite our efforts to be exhaustive in coverage, many titles were not included because they were unknown at the time or, for some reason, copies were not available for examination. Thus as a regular feature of the *Journal*, we include publication histories for titles that are now available from the pre-1985 period. Also as need arises, we include "Publication Histories: Recent Titles."

James E. Murphy and Sharon M. Murphy's history *Let My People Know: American Indian Journalism, 1828-1978* (University of Oklahoma Press, 1981) also contains useful information.

423. Marzio, Peter C., comp. **The Men and Machines of American Journalism: A Pictorial Essay from the Henry R. Luce Hall of News Reporting**. Washington, D.C.: National Museum of History and Technology, Smithsonian Institution, 1973. 144p.

This catalog could soon be a collector's item. Apparently, the Hall of News Reporting in the Smithsonian Institution is slated for termination. According to a January 1989 brief in *presstime*, "Museum officials are considering closing the 16-year-old exhibit, which features a chronological history of the US newspaper business, as part of refurbishing planned for the museum building." A guide in essay format, it is an excellent historical source.

424. Mass Communications History Center, State Historical Society of Wisconsin. **Sources for Mass Communications, Film, and Theater Research: A Guide**. Madison, WI: State Historical Society of Wisconsin, 1982. 176p. index. LC 81-13569. ISBN 0-87020-211-1.

Manuscript collections at both the Mass Communications History Center of the State Historical Society of Wisconsin and the Wisconsin Center for Film and Theater Research of the University of Wisconsin at Madison are described. Entries also include holdings information.

425. Milner, Anita Cheek. **Newspaper Indexes: A Location and Subject Guide for Researchers**. 3 vols. Metuchen, NJ: Scarecrow Press, 1977, 1979, 1982. index. LC 77-7130. ISBN 0-8108-1066-2. (vol. 1); 0-8108-1244-4 (vol. 2); 0-8108-1493-5 (vol. 3).

Though Milner warns the user that "these three volumes are not comprehensive," they are certainly the most comprehensive available. She received approximately 800 responses from the more than 2,800 questionnaires mailed to libraries, newspapers, historical societies, publishers, booksellers, and "selected individuals." Entries in each volume are arranged geographically by state, then country, and include the name of the newspaper, date indexed, and a repository symbol. Each volume also contains listings of repositories arranged alphabetically by symbol. Included here, when available, are subjects covered, reference and photocopy charges (this information may well be dated), catalogs available, interlibrary loans policies, etc. There also are brief sections on American foreign-language newspapers, church publications, specialized subjects, and miscellaneous newspapers. Users should consult all volumes. Information is updated in later volumes but is not duplicated or cumulated.

426. **Motion Pictures, Television, and Radio: A Union Catalog of Manuscript and Special Collections in the Western United States**. Linda Harris Mehr, ed. Boston: G. K. Hall, 1977. 201p. index. LC 77-13117. ISBN 0-8161-8089-X.

Researchers located on the West Coast will find they do not have to travel far to uncover more than 40 special collections in mass media. A project of the Film and Television Study Center, this catalog is arranged by institution. It is important to note that this is a guide only to printed material such as papers, scripts, and photograph collections. No films or television programs are included. Name and subject indexes are provided.

427. Museum of Broadcasting. **The Catalog of the Museum of Broadcasting: The Radio and Television Collections**. Douglas F. Gibbons, ed. New York: Arno Press, 1980. LC 80-23579. ISBN 0-405-13969-1.

428. Museum of Broadcasting. **Subject Guide to the Radio and Television Collection of the Museum of Broadcasting**. New York: Arno Press, 1979. 186p. LC 79-106857.

From "See It Now" to D-Day network coverage, thousands of radio and television programs and scripts are described in these guides. Programming from ABC, CBS, NBC, NPR, and PBS is included. In the subject guide, entries are arranged by broad subject headings, and list accession numbers, title, and date. For easiest access, remember to use both catalogs, as the lack of a key-word index in the subject guide renders it an unwieldy source. When searching, for example, for a program on the Truman Tour of the White House, one would find it indexed under "Architecture, American." The guide does indicate that "more complete program details may be found by consulting the Museum's card catalog."

429. Pride, Armistead Scott. **"A Register and History of Negro Newspapers in the United States, 1827-1950."** Unpublished dissertation. Northwestern University, 1950. 426p. microfilm.

This guide is the result of a 1946 microfilming project of black newspapers published before 1900 in the United States (see entry 439). Of the more than 2,700 newspapers listed here, more than 2,000 have no known holdings in the United States. (The largest collection of black newspapers is located, according to Pride, at the Kansas State Historical Society, but the State Historical Society of Wisconsin also has a sizable collection). Pride cites other useful lists and studies of black newspapers such as Detweiler's *The Negro Press in the United States* (McGrath [c1922], 1968) and Warren Brown's "Check List of Negro Papers in the United States 1827-1946" (Lincoln University, 1946). The first section of the guide offers a regional overview of the black press in essay format. In the second section, entries are numbered and arranged alphabetically by state, then town or city, with information on title and variations, publication dates, holdings and depositories. See also Hamilton's "A Guide to the Negro Newspapers on Microfilm: A Selected List" (entry 421) and "Black Periodicals: A Union List of Holdings in Libraries of the University of Wisconsin and the Library of the State Historical Society of Wisconsin" (1979, ERIC Report ED 192800).

430. **Public Affairs Video Archives**. Catalogs. West Lafayette, IN: Purdue University, The Archives, 1988, 1989. unpaged.

According to the introduction, "the staff of the Archives put in many hours watching tapes, entering descriptions, and correcting errors to produce this catalog. It will, no doubt, contain errors. We attribute them to the growing pains of a new organization monitoring the programming of a network telecasting 17,520 hours per year with no fixed schedule." The first catalog of Cable-Satellite Public Affairs Network (C-SPAN) programming includes entries for all programs aired between September 1987 and June 1988, as well as some pre-September 1987 election coverage, and is divided into two parts.

Entries in part 1 are arranged by two-letter program codes (AP = American Profiles, WH = White House Events, etc.), then chronologically by event date. Other categories include Journalists' Roundtable, News Briefings, Process and Policy, and the National Press Club. Of particular interest are News Briefings, held regularly at the Department of Defense and the State Department. "In these hearings, one can see the government spokesperson answer questions from the press. These are an excellent way to see how questions are asked, answered, and reported in Washington." Entries list format, program title, length, date, event, and names and titles of persons appearing in the videotape.

In part 2, entries are listed by policy category to aid researchers seeking all programs available on a particular topic such as Washington Politics, Academic Forums, Communications, etc. These programs include conferences, speeches, interviews, ceremonies, and other political events. Some programs are listed in both part 1 and part 2. The second volume covers more than 2,000 programs aired from July-December 1988.

431. **Researcher's Guide to British Film and Television Collections**. London: British Universities Film Council, 1981.

Archives and collections in film and television are documented here. National archives as well as regional, television company, and newsreel collections are described. A bibliography and listings of organizations, conferences, and festivals are provided. Also published by the Council is the *Researcher's Guide to British Newsreels* (1983).

432. Riley, Sam G. **Index to Southern Periodicals**. Westport, CT: Greenwood Press, 1986. 459p. LC 85-27232. ISBN 0-313-24515-0.

This index is really a union list of more than 7,000 consumer, medical, literary, legal, religious, business, and general-interest magazines published in the South from 1764-1985. The South includes Alabama, Arkansas, Florida, Georgia, Kentucky, Louisiana, Mississippi, North Carolina, South Carolina, Tennessee, Texas, and, until the Civil War, Maryland. Entries are arranged chronologically and include title, place published, dates, and, when available, repository information. Alphabetical and geographical lists of periodical titles are included. According to Riley, this list "should help dispel the image held by others, notably Northeasterners, of the literary South as a 'Sahara of the Bozart,' a place of genteel lassitude where men and women do not like to write, or think." A companion volume is Riley's *Magazines of the American South* (entry 478).

433. Schreibman, Fay C., comp. **Television News Resources: A Guide to Collections**. Washington, D.C.: Television News Study Center, George Washington University, 1981. 27p. LC 82-146621.

Schreibman lists useful sources for the novice television researcher and includes information on news documentaries and network and local station news archives. This is a guide to American television news sources in 20 collections in the United States. It is not a how-to guide, but a very brief listing of what is out there. There is no index.

434. Smart, James R. **Radio Broadcasts in the Library of Congress 1924-1941**. Washington, D.C.: Motion Picture, Broadcasting, and Recorded Sound Division, Library of Congress, 1982. 149p. LC 81-607136. ISBN 0-8444-0385-7.

Audio recordings of live radio broadcasts aired through 1941 and available in the Library of Congress are described in this guide. Records are arranged in chronological order and list title of broadcast, station call letters, and length of program. There is a title and performer index. Undated records are listed alphabetically in a separate section.

435. State Historical Society of Wisconsin. **Periodicals and Newspapers Acquired by the State Historical Society of Wisconsin Library**. Edited by James P. Danky and Clifford W. Bass. Madison, WI: State Historical Society of Wisconsin, 1974- . Biennial.

In addition to holding the second largest collection of newspapers in the nation (only the Library of Congress has more), the State Historical Society of Wisconsin also maintains numerous nineteenth- and twentieth-century black and labor newspapers. Title, publisher, and subject listings are provided.

436. **UNESCO List of Documents and Publications in the Field of Mass Communication**. Paris: UNESCO. Annual.

This annual list of documents and publications in communication consists of material processed—not necessarily published—during the year and available at UNESCO. The main list is arranged alphabetically by title and consists of a bibliographic description, abstract, language, document code, and fiche number. There are subject and author indexes. UNESCO also publishes *A New World Information and Communication Order: Towards a Better Balanced Flow of Information: A Bibliography of UNESCO Holdings* (1979, supplements).

437. United States Library of Congress, Catalog Management and Publication Division. **Newspapers in Microform: Foreign Countries, 1948-1983**. Washington, D.C.: Library of Congress, 1984. 504p. index. LC 75-644000. ISSN 0097-9627.

According to the introduction, "this catalog necessarily reflects efforts made in the United States to film foreign newspapers." It also advises the user that

> the number of newspapers included here varies widely from country to country. In many developing nations there is no obvious urgency about reducing newspapers to microform, and there is no particular reason why the state library of a central European nation should report its holdings of microfilmed newspapers to the Library of Congress.

Foreign newspapers are separated from newspapers published in the United States (entry 438) in this Newspapers in Microform publication "because the availability of foreign newspapers in microform is so different from that of U.S. newspapers and because the information in each instance generally serves different interests." Domestic and foreign holdings of newspapers are listed, and even those newspapers which cannot be obtained in the United States are included. Entries are arranged alphabetically by country, then by province or city. When available, publication dates are listed. There also is a title index.

438. United States Library of Congress, Catalog Management and Publication Division. **Newspapers in Microform: United States, 1948-1983**. 2 vols. Washington, D.C.: Library of Congress, 1984. index. LC 75-644000. ISSN 0097-9627.

The introduction offers an explanation of Newspapers in Microform's sometimes confusing publishing record. For example, it is important to note that the dates 1948-1983 refer to the years material was cataloged or received at the Library of Congress, not the actual time period the material covers. There also is a brief history of the publishing record of Newspapers on Microfilm. The Library's definition of *newspaper* is broad:

> When a particular question does arise, the Library's editors will accept a publication as a newspaper if it is listed by Brigham or Gregory, appears in the newspaper directories of Rowell or Ayer to 1929, or is described in *Ayer's Directory of Newspapers and Periodicals* [now *Gale Directory*] since 1930 as

having a depth of more than 10 inches (140 agate lines) and a format of at least four columns. This bibliography thus includes religious, collegiate, labor, and other special-interest papers that were excluded in Newspapers on Microfilm.

Entries are arranged alphabetically by state, then city and title. Volume 1 lists newspapers published from Alabama to Oregon; volume 2, Pennsylvania to Wyoming, plus a title index. Publication dates, frequency of publication, variations in titles, and holdings are included. For a listing of foreign newspapers, including those published in Canada, see *Newspapers in Microform: Foreign Countries* (entry 437). The Serials Division of the Library of Congress also publishes a biennial listing of *Newspapers Currently Received in the Library of Congress*.

439. United States Library of Congress, Photoduplication Service. **Negro Newspapers on Microfilm: A Selected List**. Washington, D.C.: Library of Congress, 1953.
Armistead Pride's "A Register and History of Negro Newspapers in the United States, 1827-1950" (entry 429) was one of the forces behind the microfilming project of the Library of Congress and its later publication of Negro Newspapers on Microfilm. In 1946, the Committee on Negro Studies of the American Council of Learned Societies began the project of microfilming the Negro newspapers published in the United States in the last century.

440. **United States Newspaper Program National Union List**. 8 vols. Dublin, OH: OCLC, 1985. ISBN 0-933418-76-0. **United States Newspaper Program National Union List**. 2d ed. Dublin, OH: OCLC, 1987. 44 microfiches.
The United States Newspaper Program identifies, inventories, and preserves newspapers published and held in the United States, and this union list documents location and holdings information through 1987 of newspaper repositories participating in the USNP long-range program. Entries are arranged alphabetically by title, and include publication dates, place and frequency of publication, numerical and chronological designation, variations of title, and bibliographic notes. Local records list repository, format of newspaper, and a chronological summary of issues held in all collections. Geographical, chronological, and language indexes are included, as well as an intended audience index. (James Danky, of the State Historical Society of Wisconsin, defines intended audience terms in the introduction.) Also of interest might be University Microfilms International catalogs such as the annual **Newspapers in Microform, Serials in Microform, Mass Communications: Theses, Books, and Serials** (1975), etc.

Selected State Newspaper Union Catalogs

Numerous newspaper union catalogs exist and are documented in Milner's *Newspaper Indexes* (entry 425). This is a highly selective listing of state catalogs.

441. Anderson, Aileen, ed. and comp. **Kansas Newspapers: A Directory of Newspaper Holdings in Kansas**. Topeka, KS: Kansas Library Network Board, 1984.
According to Eugene Decker of the Kansas State Historical Society, "Only in Kansas could a newspaper be published before there was news to print. Under an elm tree on the town site of Leavenworth, before there were houses or other signs of civilization, the Kansas Weekly Herald began publication on September 15, 1854." Newspapers and special interest publications are listed by county, then city and newspaper. Shoppers are excluded. Entries contain title and variations, notes, holdings and locations, etc. There are town and title indexes, as well as an alphabetical listing of holding locations with address, telephone number, and restrictions. Most of the titles in this list are housed at the Kansas State Historical Society.

442. **A Bibliography of Iowa Newspapers, 1836-1976.** Iowa State Historical Society, 1979. 371p.

"During the 1960s and early '70s there was growing national consensus that the standard bibliographic guide—Winifred Gregory's *American Newspapers, 1821-1936* (entry 420)—had become woefully outdated. The Iowa Pilot Project and the United States Newspaper Project of which it would form a part were the offspring of that consensus." More than 6,500 newspapers and publications of special-interest groups are arranged alphabetically by city or town, then title. Shoppers are excluded. Entries contain title and variations, dates and frequency of publication, notes, holdings and holding institution, physical status, and accessibility to researchers (some collections are available by appointment only).

443. Grove, Pearce S., Becky J. Barnett, and Sandra J. Hansen, eds. **New Mexico Newspapers: A Comprehensive Guide to Bibliographical Entries and Locations.** Albuquerque, NM: University of New Mexico Press, 1975. index. LC 74-84232. ISBN 0-8263-0336-6.

More than 1,200 entries are arranged alphabetically by county, then title and town. Excluded are educational, business, industry, and underground publications. Entries contain frequency and place of publication, language, origin, title variations, and holdings. There are town, newspaper title, and chronological indexes. The dedication reads:

> This volume is dedicated to those valiant editors who endured the adversities of inadequate equipment, uncertain supply lines, personnel, who fought vested interests and made personal sacrifices to record the times in which they lived. These men and women have provided generations to come with a written heritage for study, analysis, praise, criticism, and appreciation. The volume is also dedicated to those who have preserved these precious materials for decades from fire, flood, wind, and rain.

444. Gustafson, Don. **A Preliminary Checklist of Connecticut Newspapers, 1755-1975.** 2 vols. Hartford, CT: Connecticut State Library, 1978. index.

Gustafson describes this as "primarily a work book—a beginning point for a broader and more thorough two, three or four year effort to publish a well researched and attractive Union List of Connecticut newspapers ... it reflects much of what we do *not* know and is issued with a plea for corrections and additions." An attempt is made here to list all newspapers published in Connecticut from 1755-1975, but university newspapers and shoppers are excluded. In addition, the author says that "no definition of a newspaper was applied, however, in compiling the list." The 995 entries are numbered, arranged alphabetically by town, and include title and variations, dates, sources, notes, and holdings. It is indeed a workbook, though to whom it is aimed is questionable. There are two titles per page and a great deal of white space. Gustafson has this to say about his most peculiar index:

> For purposes of this index, names of towns and words such as evening, daily, etc., were (with a few exceptions) omitted from all newspaper titles. The remaining title words were then grouped on the basis of fifty key words—fifty words common to six or more of Connecticut's newspaper titles since 1775. All of those remaining newspapers which could not be indexed under at least one of these fifty key words were then indexed alphabetically on the basis of their own (often unique) key words. The fifty key words index and the alphabetical index form parts one and two of this index. Selected subtitles are also included and are generally indicated by parentheses.

Needless to say, it is better to search newspapers by town, if possible, rather than to brave this unnecessarily complicated index.

445. Gutgesell, Stephen, ed. **Guide to Ohio Newspapers, 1793-1973.** 2d ed. Columbus, OH: Ohio Historical Society, 1976. index. LC 75-225. ISBN 0-87758-004-9.

Entries are arranged alphabetically by city, then title, and include dates of publication, political affiliation, variations of title, and holdings. An index to the Special Press lists title by newspaper type (Communist, Whig, Episcopalian), then by city and title.

446. Kolar, Carol Koehmstedt. **North Dakota Newspapers, 1864-1976**. Fargo, ND: North Dakota Institute for Regional Studies, North Dakota State University, 1981. 448p. index.

House organs and trade, religious, and fraternal publications are excluded, but Kolar says that "inclusion of titles has bordered on the generous, rather than the overly selective." More than 1,300 newspapers are numbered and listed by town. Entries contain titles and variations, and some list editorial succession and location of extant newspaper files. There is a title index.

447. Lingenfelter, Richard E., and Karen Rix Gash. **The Newspapers of Nevada: A History and Bibliography, 1854-1979**. Reno, NV: University of Nevada Press, 1984. 337p. bibliog. index. LC 83-16790. ISBN 0-87417-075-3.

More than 800 newspapers, many of which were published in mining camps, are arranged geographically by town, then chronologically by date. It includes more than 300 new newspaper listings, some founded since 1958, the date of the previous Nevada newspaper union list. Shoppers and organizational publications also are listed. Entries list variations of titles, frequency of publication, editors and publishers, and holdings. An index of editors, publishers, and titles allows easy access. Black-and-white photographs (there is a picture of the *Rawhide Rustler* office in 1908) liven up the text. The introduction places Nevada newspaper publishing in historical perspective:

> The bulk of the newspapers and periodicals founded in Nevada have folded, and the history of the Nevada press can leave one with a sense of tragedy and futility. Indeed, most Nevada editors would seem either to have lacked good judgment or to have suffered more than their share of insanity. Of the roughly 800 publications started in Nevada in the last 125 years, half failed in a year or less, and only 70 were still being published in 1979.

448. Miller, John W. **Indiana Newspaper Bibliography**. Indianapolis, IN: Indiana Historical Society, 1982. index.

All newspapers published from 1804-1980 are chronicled alphabetically by county, then town. Entries contain place and frequency of publication, title and variations, all known editors and publishers, political or special-interest affiliation, holdings information, and publication history. There are indexes of Indiana towns and counties as well as editors and publishers, but none listing individual newspapers.

449. Moore, John Hammond. **South Carolina Newspapers**. Columbia, SC: University of South Carolina Press, 1988. 315p. index. LC 88-4779. ISBN 0-87249-567-1.

Arranged by county, then by town, entries contain a brief publication history and list location of newspaper files. Excluded are shoppers, educational, professional, and fraternal publications. Appendices document out-of-state and foreign newspaper files in South Carolina. There is a bibliography and index.

450. Preston, Dickson J. **Newspapers of Maryland's Eastern Shore**. Queenstown, MD: Queen Anne Press; Centreville, MD: Tidewater Publishers, 1986. 272p. bibliog. index. LC 85-40433. ISBN 0-87033-336-4.

Yet another unusual source, this is not merely a listing of newspapers in Maryland. It is a geographical and historical study of the rural region where small newspapers, mostly weeklies, flourished. The author believed it was important "before it is too late, to chronicle the history of the country editors." Preston, a Washington-based special correspondent for Scripps-Howard Newspapers from 1952-1966, put the finishing touches on this manuscript a few weeks before he died in early 1985. There are chapters on the first shore newspapers, county weeklies, and several time-period studies. The directory attempts to list "every known issue of every weekly newspaper ever published on the Eastern coast of Maryland." Newspaper listings are arranged by county, then listed alphabetically by city or town. Publication history and holdings are included. Almost 100 black-and-white illustrations make this specialized source very special.

451.   Rossell, Glenora E. **Pennsylvania Newspapers: A Bibliography and Union List**. 2d ed. Pittsburgh, PA: Pennsylvania Library Association, 1978. 317p. index. LC 78-71000.
    A computer listing, in microscopic print, of 7,923 titles, this contains no house organs but does describe labor, religious, fraternal, and school publications. "It does not include newspapers for which a prospectus was published but for which no published issue can be located." Entries are arranged alphabetically by town, and cite title and variations, frequency and place of publication, dates, and holdings. There is a county index.

452.   Taft, William H. **Missouri Newspapers: When and Where, 1808-1963**. Columbia, MO: State Historical Society of Missouri, 1964. 205p. LC 64-63090.
    More than 6,000 newspapers are listed alphabetically by city or town, and entries include title, frequency of publication, dates published, and holdings. There is no index.

453.   Wallace, John Melton. **A Check List of Texas Newspapers 1813-1846**. Austin, TX: University of Texas, Department of Journalism, 1966. 89p. index.
    The 125 entries are "not limited to papers known to have been published or proposed. Entries have been provided for papers heretofore believed to have coexisted but which current study indicates were not established; papers that were rumored in contemporary publications." Newspapers are alphabetically arranged by title, and entries include a brief publication history and historical overview in essay format. There is an alphabetical checklist of newspapermen, an index of newspapers by location, and an index of selected newspaper collections arranged by city.

Other noted union lists include Lester J. Cappon, *Virginia Newspapers, 1821-1935: A Bibliography with Historical Introduction and Notes* (D. Appleton-Century, 1936); T. N. McMullen, *Louisiana Newspapers, 1794-1961: A Union List of Louisiana Newspaper Files Available in Public, College, and University Libraries in Louisiana* (Louisiana State University Library, 1965); James L. Hansen, *Wisconsin Newspapers, 1833-1850: An Analytical Bibliography* (State Historical Society of Wisconsin, 1979) and Donald E. Oehlerts, *Guide to Wisconsin Newspapers, 1833-1957* (State Historical Society of Wisconsin, 1958); Roger C. Jones, *Guide to North Carolina Newspapers on Microfilm* (North Carolina Archives, 1984); and William C. Wright and Paula A. Stellhorn, *Directory of New Jersey Newspapers, 1765-1970* (New Jersey Historical Commission, 1977).

10
Miscellaneous Sources

Miscellaneous Reference Sources

This is a chapter which could easily get out of hand. For the user's sake, it does not. Included are items which could not easily fit into the other designated categories of reference materials and information. I admit to taking some liberties and including a few works which are not necessarily referential in nature.

454.   **"The American Journalist."** Library of Congress exhibition.
   During his fellowship at the Gannett Center for Media Studies, Loren Ghiglione developed an idea that will soon be on exhibit at the Library of Congress in Washington, D.C. "The American Journalist" will display several hundred objects and artifacts of American journalism, and will illustrate the role of journalists in fiction, arts, and media in the United States. Ghiglione, publisher and editor of *The News* in Southbridge, Massachusetts, will be guest curator. The exhibit, funded by Gannett and co-sponsored by the American Society of Newspaper Editors, is scheduled to open in April 1990.

455.   Chielens, Edward E., ed. **American Literary Magazines: The Eighteenth and Nineteenth Centuries**. Westport, CT: Greenwood Press, 1986. 503p. (Historical Guides to the World's Periodicals and Newspapers). index. LC 85-24793. ISBN 0-313-23985-1.
   These were the "qualities," the literary magazines challenged and outpublished by the new "cheaper" mass-circulation magazines of the twentieth century. More than 50 contributors profile 92 magazines founded before 1900. "Less important" titles appear in an appendix. Entries are arranged alphabetically, cite information sources, and describe publication history. Chielens mentions the following useful sources: Frank Luther Mott's five-volume *History of American Magazines* (Harvard University Press, 1930-1968), and Jayne Kribbs' *Annotated Bibliography of American Literary Periodicals, 1741-1850* (G. K. Hall, 1977). Chielens also wrote *The Literary Journal in America Up to 1900* (Gale, 1975) and *The Literary Journal in America, 1900-1950* (Gale, 1978), which contains an interesting section on Edgar Allen Poe's "journalistic activities."

456.   Compaine, Benjamin. **Anatomy of the Communications Industry: Who Owns the Media?** White Plains, NY: Knowledge Industry Publications (c1982), 1983. 529p. bibliog. index. LC 83-12012. ISBN 0-86729-069-2.
   Economic and political aspects of the media are examined in chapters on newspapers, television and radio stations, magazines, theatrical films, books, and cable and pay television. This book provides numerous graphs and tables.

457.   Daniel, Walter C. **Black Journals in the United States**. Westport, CT: Greenwood Press, 1982. 432p. (Historical Guides to the World's Periodicals and Newspapers). bibliog. index. LC 81-13440. ISBN 0-313-20704-6.

More of an encyclopedia than a straight bibliographic guide, and less a catalog than a historical guide, this includes descriptive profiles of about 100 black-oriented magazines and journals published in the United States. They are arranged alphabetically instead of chronologically, although there is a chronology of events and journal publications in an appendix. Some essays were written by contributors. In the introduction, Daniel mentions two doctoral dissertations he found useful: Dorothy Deloris Boone's "Historical Review and a Bibliography of Selected Negro Magazines, 1910-1969" (University of Michigan, 1970) and Mary Fair Burks's "Survey of Black Literary Magazines in the United States: 1859-1940" (Columbia University Teachers College, 1975). Coverage begins in 1827, with the founding of *Freedom's Journal*, and carries through to 1982. Profiles include a historical essay, notes, information sources, and publication history. The information sources sections contain a brief bibliography and location sources. This is a valuable statement about black journalism.

458.   Densmore, Dana, ed. **Syllabus Sourcebook on Media and Women**. Washington, D.C.: Women's Institute for Freedom of the Press, 1980. 47p. LC 80-52917. ISBN 0-930470-06-0.

According to the introduction, the purpose of the sourcebook is to provide a collection of syllabi for departments and teachers who want to institute courses on women and the media, and to offer new ideas for existing courses. The table of contents is arranged by subject (general, film, minorities and women, image, art, etc.) and there is a name index as well. Entries usually contain a course description and outline. More than 60 syllabi are listed, some developed by well-known scholars such as Maurine Beasley and Sheila Gibbons.

459.   **Editorials on File**. New York: Facts on File. 1970- . Semimonthly. ISSN 0013-0966.

Of great interest to writers of commentary, columns, and editorials, this semimonthly publication offers background information on editorial subjects and includes an average of 10 current editorials selected from United States and Canadian newspapers. Subject indexes are published monthly and cumulate quarterly and annually.

460.   Evans, Glen, ed. **The Complete Guide to Writing Nonfiction by the American Society of Journalists and Authors**. New York: Harper and Row (c1983), 1988. 872p. index. LC 87-45592. ISBN 0-06-097135-5.

Originally a Writer's Digest publication directed toward the freelance magazine writer, this is a bulky collection of articles on freelancing, research, writing, publishing, and specialized writing. Part 2 focuses on specific areas of nonfiction writing such as science and technology, environment, medicine and health, psychology, religion, women's magazines, food, home and garden, hobbies, sports, travel, business, etc. Articles range from Shirley Biagi's "Ten Types of Magazine Articles" to Alex Haley's "On Becoming a Writer." There is an index.

461.   **Facts on File: World News Digest with Index**. New York: Facts on File. 1940- . Weekly. ISSN 0014-6641.

This is a weekly summary of national and world news events with a cumulated subject index. It also is available online. (See entry 209.) Other useful news digests include *Keesing's Contemporary Archives, Record of World Events* (Marpep Publishing Ltd.), and *Current Digest of the Soviet Press* (American Association for the Advancement of Slavic Studies), to name a few.

462.   Felsten, Judith. **"News Photograph Collections: A Survey of Newspaper Practices and Archival Strategies."** Philadelphia, PA: Temple University Libraries, 1982. Various paging.

This survey, funded by a grant from the National Historial Publication and Records Commission of the National Archives, addresses the unique problems in evaluating and archiving news photographs and news photo file management. The commission

> had in mind a survey of the field and a set of recommendations that would cover the entire archival process: legally transferring collections from newspaper to library; deciding which photographs to keep and which to dispose of; arranging the photos and preparing guides to the collection; identifying preservation problems and starting work on them.

Included are sections on daily newspaper procedures, negative files, print files, and conclusions and recommendations. There also is a brief section on color files when, in 1982, "the amount of color material at most of the newspapers is so small that it hasn't required formal storage or retrieval systems yet." This, of course, is no longer true. Appendices list participating institutions and survey forms. A useful six-page bibliography arranged by subject is provided. There is no index.

463.   Ghiglione, Loren, ed. **Gentlemen of the Press: Profiles of American Newspaper Editors; Selections from the Bulletin of the American Society of Newspaper Editors.** Indianapolis, IN: R. J. Berg, 1984. 435p. ISBN 0-89730-110-2.

More than 100 newspaper editors are profiled in this collection of *ASNE Bulletin* articles published from the mid-1950s through the 1980s. Included are the likes of Vermont Royster, Ralph McGill, Turner Catledge, William Henry Grimes, Norman E. Isaacs, and J. Donald Ferguson. For those seeking individual profiles of women of the press, try Judith G. Clabes's *New Guardians of the Press: Selected Profiles of America's Women Newspaper Editors* (R. J. Berg, 1983), Barbara Belford's *Brilliant Bylines: A Biographical Anthology of Notable Newspaperwomen in America* (Columbia University Press, 1986), or Madelon Golden Schilpp and Sharon M. Murphy's *Great Women of the Press* (Southern Illinois University Press, 1983). Though not biographical anthologies, the following history sources are not to be overlooked: Ishbel Ross's *Ladies of the Press: The Story of Women in Journalism By an Insider* (Harper & Row, 1936) and Marion Marzolf's *Up From the Footnote: A History of Women Journalists* (Hastings House, 1977).

464.   Giles, Robert H. **Newsroom Management: A Guide to Theory and Practice.** Indianapolis, IN: R. J. Berg, 1987. 739p. bibliog. index. LC 87-71124. ISBN 0-89730-181-1; 0-89730-189-7 (pbk).

Giles, executive editor of *The Detroit News*, explains that his book "is based on many of the behavioral-science theories about management," is "both theoretical and practical" and should be "useful as a textbook for students and a reference for publishers, editors, and other practitioners." That it is. In addition to discussions of management theories, styles of management, leadership, newsroom management, conflict, and stress, there are a glossary of terms, a detailed index, and an extensive, unannotated bibliography.

465.   Hohenberg, John, ed. **The Pulitzer Prize Story.** New York: Columbia University Press, 1959. 375p. LC 59-7702. ISBN 0-231-08663-6.

466.   Hohenberg, John, ed. **The Pulitzer Prize Story II: Award-Winning News Stories, Columns, Editorials, Cartoons, and News Pictures, 1959-1980.** 472p. bibliog. index. LC 80-16880. ISBN 0-231-04978-1.

These collections of Pulitzer-Prize-winning journalism prove to be useful references as well as inspiring reading. Other Pulitzer collections include Kendall Wills's annual *Pulitzer Prizes* (entry 336), *The Pulitzer Prize Archive* (K. G. Saur, 1987) and "The Pulitzer Prizes in Journalism, 1917-1985" (entry 501) on microfilm.

467. **International Media Guides**. South Norwalk, CT: International Media Enterprises, Inc. Annual.

Callings its publications "the complete source of worldwide advertising rates and data," International Media Enterprises publishes *Newspapers Worldwide* and *Consumer Magazines Worldwide*. In addition, four geographic business/professional annuals are available: Europe, Asia/Pacific, Latin America, and Middle East. Entries contain region and country, publication name and description, frequency, telephone number, address, currency exchange rate, advertising rates, circulation, language, etc. Publication and geographical indexes are provided. See also Standard Rate and Data publications (entry 483).

468. **The ITC Typeface Collection**. New York: International Typeface Corp., 1980. (distributed by Robert Silver). 572p. LC 80-82969.

There is an abundance of typography guides and printing specimen books available, but few surpass the ITC collection in size or weight. It showcases both text and display families. Other widely used sources are Jean Callan King and Tony Esposito's *The Designer's Guide to Text Type* (Van Nostrand Reinhold, 1980); Sean Morrison's *A Guide to Type Design* (Prentice-Hall, 1986); Frank Romano's *Practical Typography from A to Z* (National Composition Association, 1983); Christopher Perfect and Gordon Rookledge's *Rookledge's International Typefinder* (Beil, 1983); Benjamin Bauermeister's *A Manual of Comparative Typography* (Van Nostrand Reinhold, 1988); *TypEncyclopedia* (entry 116); *The Encyclopedia of Type Faces* (entry 111); J. Ben Lieberman's *Type and Typefaces* (Myriade Press, 1977); *The Type Specimen Book* (Van Nostrand Reinhold, 1974); and Ben Rosen's *Type and Typography* (Van Nostrand Reinhold, 1976), to name a few.

469. **The Journalist-in-Space Project**. National Aeronautics and Space Administration.

NASA issued new guidelines in 1989 for the Journalist-in-Space Project and said that it will be postponed indefinitely. The journalist flight was originally scheduled for the fall of 1986, but was delayed because of the January 1986 *Challenger* accident in which six astronauts and a teacher died. A 1986 *presstime* article reported there were 1,703 applicants.

470. Kahn, Frank J. **Documents of American Broadcasting**. 4th ed. Englewood Cliffs, NJ: Prentice-Hall, 1984. 501p. index. LC 83-11025. ISBN 0-13-217133-3.

The fourth edition of *Documents of American Broadcasting* is completely revised, and contains both a general and legal decision index. According to Kahn (who has earned a law degree since the third edition was published in 1978), this book "remains a collection of primary source materials in the field of public policy formulation in broadcasting and related media. The laws, commission materials, court decisions, and other documents span electronic media development from their prehistory to the 1980s in chronological fashion." Ranging from "The Radio Act of 1912" to "TV in the Courtroom," each document entry includes background information and a brief bibliography.

471. **The Knowledge Industry 200**. Ira Mayer, ed. White Plains, NY: Knowledge Industry Publications, 1987. 421p. ISBN 0-86729-262-8; 0-8103-4254-5 (Gale Research Company edition); ISSN 0736-6795.

Profiles of the 200 leading media companies in the United States, both public and private, are arranged alphabetically. Some changes are evident since the last edition was published in 1983. Outdoor advertising is no longer counted as media, and new categories include syndicated services and computer software. CBS, however, was still number one. Profiles include information such as revenue rank, total number of employees, number of media employees, total assets, media assets, media revenue breakdown, corporate officers, directors, company description, and recent acquisitions/divestitures. The editor comments on the large number of mergers and acquisitions in the industry and says that this book reflects "such major changes through the end of November 1987 in the appropriate profiles." For a statistical analysis of concentration of mass media ownership, see Compaine's *Anatomy of the Communications Industry: Who Owns the Media?* (entry 456).

472. **Law and the Media**. Stuart M. Robertson, series ed. Ottawa, Canada: Canadian Bar Foundation.

This five-book series was written with the Canadian journalist in mind. Included are the following titles: *Journalists and the Law* by Robert S. Bruser and Brian MacLeod Rogers (1985); *The Charter and the Media* by John D. Richard and Stuart M. Robertson (1985); *Defamation Law in Canada* by Gerald A. Flaherty (1984); *A Reporter's Guide to Canada's Criminal Justice System* by Harold J. Levy (1986); and *Privacy Law and the Media in Canada* by Gordon F. Proudfoot (1984). See also Robert Martin and G. Stuart Adam's *A Sourcebook of Canadian Media Law* (Carleton University Press, 1989).

473. **The Media Book**. New York: The Media Book, 1979. 572p.

A wide selection of charts and digests enlivens this dated book of media statistics. According to the introduction, "numbers are only a means to an end. Always, we analyze and interpret, telling the reader why things are as they are and what the implications might be." It offers an overview of mass media, including history, advertising revenue trends, audience basics, reader demographics, ownership trends, television viewing habits, daily consumption patterns, etc. There are separate sections on magazines, Sunday supplements, city magazines, newspapers, television, radio, news, sports, and company media. Unfortunately, there is no index. See also *The Mass Media: Aspen Institute Guide to Communication Industry Trends* (entry 485).

474. Merrill, John C., and Harold A. Fisher. **The World's Great Dailies: Profiles of Fifty Newspapers**. New York: Hastings House, 1980. 416p. bibliog. index.

Profiles of the "great dailies" which, according to Merrill and Fisher, "represent the very best in the world's journalism," are included here. See also the Media Research Institute's *America's Leading Daily Newspapers* (R. J. Berg, 1983).

475. Miller, Sally M., ed. **The Ethnic Press in the United States: A Historical Analysis and Handbook**. Westport, CT: Greenwood Press, 1987. 437p. index. LC 85-31699. ISBN 0-313-23879-0.

Twenty-eight ethnic presses are described in twenty-seven chapters (Latvian and Lithuanian presses are covered in one chapter). The definition of *press* varies from essay to essay. Some only discuss newspapers; others are broader and include broadcasting. Arranged alphabetically by ethnic group and written by specialists, each essay provides an analysis and historical overview. The Italian press "regrettably could not be covered because no specialist was sufficiently free of constraints to undertake the assignment." Black and Native American presses also are omitted, because they "would not reflect the immigration and adaptation processes." Miller goes on to explain that "these chapters focus on groups which typically chose to immigrate to the United States and underwent the subsequent adjustment process."

476. Mott, Frank Luther. **American Journalism; A History 1690-1960**. 3d ed. New York: Macmillan, 1962. 901p.

A classic general-survey journalism text, *American Journalism* also serves as a fine historical reference. The third edition includes a section on the electronic media, albeit the electronic media of the 1950s. The first and second editions were published in 1941 and 1950. There are numerous bibliographical notes. The prolific Mott also authored the five-volume *A History of American Magazines* (Harvard University Press, 1930-1968) covering the years 1741-1930, and edited *Interpretations of Journalism: A Book of Readings* (F. S. Crofts, 1937) with Ralph D. Carey.

Although not generally considered reference works, the following titles are mentioned here simply as further examples of noted general history texts: John Tebbel, *The Media in America* (Thomas Y. Crowell, 1974); Erik Barnouw's three-volume *A History of Broadcasting in the United States*, published by Oxford University Press: *Tower of Babel: To 1933* (1966), *The Golden Web: 1933-1953* (1968), and *Image Empire: From 1950* (1970); Sidney W. Head and Christopher H. Sterling, *Broadcasting in America: A Survey of Electronic Media* (Houghton Mifflin, 1987); Theodore Peterson, *Magazines in the Twentieth Century* (University of Illinois Press, 1964); Edwin Emery and Michael Emery, *The Press and America* (Prentice-Hall, 1984); Willard G. Bleyer, *Main Currents in the History of American Journalism* (Houghton Mifflin, 1927); Frederic Hudson, *Journalism in the United States from 1690-1872* (Haskell, 1969, reprint of 1873 ed.); Isaiah Thomas, two-volume *The History of Printing in America* (B. Franklin, 1972, reprint of 1874 ed.); Robert Rutland, *The Newsmongers* (Dial, 1973); and Anthony Smith, *The Newspaper: An International History* (Thames and Hudson, 1979), to name but a few.

477.   Riblet, Carl, Jr. **The Solid Gold Copy Editor**. Washington, D.C.: Falcon Press, 1972. LC 72-95673. ISBN 0-202-38000-9; 0-202-38001-7 (pbk).

Aimed at newspaper copy editors, this classic textbook outlines what Riblet considers his "method" for writing headlines, editing ("When to Improve It, When to Leave It Alone"), and speed. Numerous examples and lessons are provided. Other copy editing guides, such as Judith Butcher's *Copy-Editing: The Cambridge Handbook* (Cambridge University Press, 1981) and Karen Judd's *Copyediting: A Practical Guide* (William Kaufmann, 1982), focus on book or magazine publishing but may provide some relevant lessons.

478.   Riley, Sam G. **Magazines of the American South**. Westport, CT: Greenwood Press, 1986. 346p. (Historical Guides to the World's Periodicals and Newspapers). index. LC 85-8012. ISBN 0-313-24337-9.

About 90 literary and popular magazines published in the South (Confederate states and pre-Civil War Maryland) since 1764 are profiled. Religious and black journals are not covered, as they also are subjects in this series. Alphabetically arranged essays are well-written, detailed, and frequently humorous. (About *The Rose Bud*, the 1832 weekly claiming to be the first children's magazine: "The Dick and Jane-like copy, carefully presented in syllables of pablum simplicity....") Summaries list journal policies and include bibliographies and publication history. There is a name and title index. Some titles such as *Foxfire* and *Southern Living* are currently published; others such as *Bob Taylor's Magazine, Texas Siftings,* and *Moonshine* are from other eras entirely.

The companion volume is the *Index to Southern Periodicals* (entry 432). Riley, professor of communication studies at Virginia Polytechnic Institute and State University, states that he "tried to choose periodicals that would be of relatively general appeal, avoiding specialized scholarly journals, trade magazines, technical periodicals, and any other category that would presumably be of interest to only a small group of readers." Granted, this is only a sampling of titles, and one might quibble at Riley's choices and criteria for selection, but at last someone has given full attention to the rich magazine literature of the South. Researchers and students alike would be well-advised to take a look.

479.   Rose, Brian, G., ed. **TV Genres: A Handbook and Reference Guide**. Westport, CT: Greenwood Press, 1985. 453p. bibliog. index. LC 84-22460. ISBN 0-313-23724-7.

Though *TV Genres* focuses mostly on entertainment television programming (the western or situation comedy), there are also essays on television news, docudrama, television documentary, sports television, and talk shows. Each genre essay is written by an expert in the field, and includes an overview, historical development, themes and issues, bibliography, and videography.

480.   Slide, Anthony, ed. **International Film, Radio, and Television Journals**. Westport, CT: Greenwood Press, 1985. 428p. (Historical Guides to the World's Periodicals and Newspapers). bibliog. index. LC 84-8929. ISBN 0-313-23759-X.

Film historian Slide gives most of his attention to film journals, but radio and television are adequately represented. In-depth, alphabetically arranged essays of more than 150 journals examine publication history and political orientation. In choosing journals, Slide emphasized research value and states that "the length of the essay indicates the importance of the journal in the eyes of the editor." Most entries are evaluative as well as descriptive, and contain the essay, notes, information sources, and publication history. Essays are signed, and there are more than 50 contributors. The scope is international, and there is a listing of journals by country of publication. Appendices are comprised of essays on fan-club journals, fan magazines, in-house journals, and national film journals. One index lists names and titles only. This is a valuable source, either as a historical overview or selection guide. See also Slide's *Selected Radio and Television Criticism* (entry 481) and *Sourcebook for the Performing Arts* (Greenwood Press, 1988).

481. Slide, Anthony, ed. **Selected Radio and Television Criticism**. Metuchen, NJ: Scarecrow Press, 1987. 203p. index. LC 86-27891. ISBN 0-8108-1942-2.

Slide says that this mixed bag of 100 short articles on television and radio published from the 1920s to the 1950s is for "students and scholars of popular entertainment needing an immediate insight into contemporary commentary on radio and television." Immediate, perhaps, but for insight, this is not the source. Suffice it to say that 30 years' worth of radio and television criticism is crammed into fewer than 200 pages. Slide also edited *International Film, Radio, and Television Journals* (entry 480).

482. Sloane, David E. E., ed. **American Humor Magazines and Comic Periodicals**. Westport, CT: Greenwood Press, 1987. 648p. (Historical Guides to the World's Periodicals and Newspapers). index. LC 86-27155. ISBN 0-313-23956-8.

It could be the American wit and humor opus we have been waiting for: almost 50 contributors, a foreword, preface, and well-crafted introduction complete with historical and comical overview, location codes, in-depth signed profiles of more than 100 magazines, briefly annotated and signed listings of more than 400 magazines, copyright listings, a list of "magazines identified and described, but not examined," genre essays on college humor, scholarly humor (there is such an animal—just look at *The Journal of Irreproducible Results* and *The Worm Runner's Digest*), and humor in American almanacs, a chronological list, selected bibliography, and an index of general subjects, authors, and titles. This comprehensive title represents 200 years of humor magazines. Comic books, college humor magazines, scholarly humor, and humor in almanacs are not included in profile sections. Each in-depth essay contains a short bibliography, location and index sources, and publication history. Journal titles are arranged alphabetically within chapters. Sloane (editor of *The Literary Humor of the Urban Northeast 1830-1890*, Louisiana State University Press, 1983) and his contributors treat humor seriously.

483. **Standard Rate and Data Service Publications**. Skokie, IL: Standard Rate and Data Service.

SRDS sources, used primarily as guides for placing advertising, offer unique statistical snapshots of the mass media. They include *Direct Mail Lists Rates and Data*, and separate monthly *Business Publication, Consumer Magazine, Spot Radio, Spot Television*, and *Newspaper Rates and Data* as well as the quarterly *Print Media Production Rates and Data* and the annual *Newspaper Circulation Analysis* (entry 310). In the same vein, Adweek's *Marketer's Guide to Media* is a quarterly publication containing demographic data on major consumer media. See also *International Media Guides* (entry 467).

484. Stempel, Guido H. III, and Bruce H. Westley. **Research Methods in Mass Communication**. Englewood Cliffs, NJ: Prentice-Hall, 1981. 550p. LC 80-39609. ISBN 0-13-774240-1. A second edition of this title was published as **Journalism: A Guide to the Reference Literature** was going to press.

Stempel and Westley, masters of research methods, have crafted a well-written and organized guide to mass communication research. Students will be relieved to open this book and find virtually a step-by-step guide to survey methods, experiment, content analysis, and history. Twenty scholars contributed chapters on statistics, data processing, ethics, measurement, secondary analyses, etc., and cross-references are provided. Chapters also contain brief bibliographies. In a chapter on "The Logic of Historical Research," David Nord and Harold Nelson discuss journalism history and footnote numerous important historical texts and historiographical accounts. Prior to this source, Nafziger and White's

Introduction to Mass Communications Research (Louisiana State University Press, 1963) and Nafziger and Wilkerson's *Introduction to Journalism Research* (c1949, Greenwood Press, 1968) were also used in the classroom. See also Roger D. Wimmer and Joseph R. Dominick's *Mass Media Research: An Introduction* (Wadsworth, 1987).

485. Sterling, Christopher H., and Timothy R. Haight. **The Mass Media: Aspen Institute Guide to Communication Industry Trends**. New York: Praeger; Palo Alto, CA: Aspen Institute Publications, 1978. 457p. bibliog. index. LC 76-24370. ISBN 0-275-24020-7.

Described by the authors as a "statistical abstract of the communications industries," this guide offers more than 300 tables of data, organized in seven subject categories, on growth of media industries, ownership, economics, employment and training, content trends, media audiences, and United States media industries abroad. These are further broken down into specific media categories (books, newspapers, magazines, radio, television, etc.). A detailed table of contents and subject index allow easy access to a wealth of information. This is a remarkable gathering of data, and even though it is more than 10 years old, it is still useful in carrying out Sterling and Haight's objective: "to provide a single reference source for the most significant statistics describing communication industry trends in the United States since 1900." Too, "there is a strong historical tone" to this guide. Would that it were updated to include the 1980s. Sterling, however, is also editor of the 1984 *Electronic Media: A Guide to Trends in Broadcasting and Newer Technologies* (Praeger).

486. Sullivan, Alvin, ed. **British Literary Magazines: The Augustan Age and the Age of Johnson, 1698-1788**. Westport, CT: Greenwood Press, 1983. 427p. index. ISBN 0-313-22871-X. **British Literary Magazines: The Romantic Age, 1789-1836**. Westport, CT: Greenwood Press, 1983. 491p. index. ISBN 0-313-22872-8. **British Literary Magazines: The Victorian and Edwardian Age, 1837-1913**. Westport, CT: Greenwood Press, 1984. 560p. index. ISBN 0-313-24336-0. **British Literary Magazines: The Modern Age, 1914-1984**. Westport, CT: Greenwood Press, 1986. index. ISBN 0-313-24336-0. (Historical Guides to the World's Periodicals and Newspapers). LC 82-21136.

The prolific Sullivan concludes his four-part reference guide with *The Modern Age, 1914-1984*. Together, these four volumes cover British literary journals published from 1698 to the present time. These volumes are included here because they represent an important publishing history, offer a periodical bibliography, and are probably the most comprehensive sources available on this subject matter. In all, essays for 369 magazines are included, with more than 400 discussed in appendices. Selection for inclusion is based on, according to Sullivan, the importance of editors and contributors, the influence of the magazine, and "to suggest the character of the publishing enterprise in any age, the notably eccentric behavior or policies of some editors and contributors." Such criteria suggest there may be something here for the journalism researcher. Essays contain an information sources section including a short bibliography, indexing and location information, and publication history. The index to each volume contains references to names, titles, and subjects. Unfortunately, there is no cumulative index covering all volumes.

487. Summers, Harrison B., ed. **A Thirty-Year History of Programs Carried on National Radio Networks in the United States, 1926-1956**. New York: Ayer, 1971. (Reprint of 1958 edition). (History of Broadcasting: Radio to Television series). LC 78-161155. ISBN 0-405-03572-1.

Compiled in 1958, this typed and single-spaced source is hard on the eyes, but is an excellent overview of what the editor calls the "rise and the beginning of the fall of network radio." This is a year-by-year account of national radio network programs, but only those officially scheduled during the month of January of each season. Of course, this means that special programs and summer replacement shows are excluded. In addition to variety and music programs, the following are included: magazine-type variety, human-interest programs, informative drama, sports broadcasts, news commentary, public affairs and forums, and daytime news. This volume is part of the History of Broadcasting: Radio to Television series, which also includes *History of Radio to 1926* (1938) and *Bibliography on Educational Broadcasting* (1942).

488. Tebbel, John. **Opportunities in Journalism Careers**. Skokie, IL: VGM Career Horizons, 1982. bibliog. index. LC 81-80754. ISBN 0-8442-6365-6; 0-8442-6366-4 (pbk).

This book is part of a series of career books aimed at high school students and those seeking broad and somewhat simplistic overviews of the industry. Other titles in the same publisher's series include Bervin Johnson and Fred Schmidt's *Opportunities in Photography* (1985), Elmo I. Ellis's *Opportunities in Broadcasting* (1986), and Tebbel's *Opportunities in Magazine Publishing* (1980). Other books which may prove useful are *Graphic Design Career Guide* (Watson-Guptill, 1983) by James Craig; Maxine K. Reed and Robert M. Reed's *Career Opportunities in Television and Video* (Facts on File, 1982); John H. Noble's *The Harvard Guide to Careers in Mass Media* (Harvard University, Office of Career Services, 1987); and Phil Swann and Ed Achorn's *How to Land a Job in Journalism* (Betterway Publications, 1988).

489. Wilhoit, G. Cleveland, and David H. Weaver. **Newsroom Guide to Polls and Surveys**. Washington, D.C.: American Newspaper Publishers Association, 1980. 82p. index.

The authors write, "With the help of this guide and other persons knowledgeable in survey research, we hope that many journalists will better understand, critically evaluate and accurately report surveys and polls." The guide is arranged in sections on evaluating survey questionnaires, interviewing, sampling, and results, and includes a section on reporting those results. This aims at the working journalist. A subject and name index is provided. Wilhoit and Weaver also wrote *The American Journalist: A Portrait of United States News People and Their Work* (Indiana University Press, 1986).

Newspaper and Special Collections on Microform

Though not necessarily standard reference sources, these microforms provide access to important and unique subject collections on the press and journalism, and are thus included.

490. **ABC News Transcripts and Index**. Woodbridge, CT: Research Publications. Available on microfiche.

Complete transcripts of ABC news programs such as "Nightline," "20/20," "World News Tonight," "This Week with David Brinkley," and "ABC News Special" are available from 1969 to the present. The quarterly *ABC News Index* (entry 149) allows access by subject, name, and program.

491. **Black Newspaper Collection**. Ann Arbor, MI: University Microfilms International Research Collections. Available on 2,038 reels of microfilm.

The black newspapers in this collection were published from 1893-1983 and represent, according to UMI, "the most respected voices in black journalism." Included are such newspapers as the *Amsterdam News*, New York; *Argus*, St. Louis; *Call and Post*, Cleveland; *Chicago Defender; Michigan Chronicle*, Detroit; and the *Los Angeles Sentinel*. The *Index to Black Newspapers* (entry 166) indexes 10 key black newspapers and is arranged by name and subject. See also *Negro Newspapers on Microfilm* (entry 497).

492. **CBS News**. Ann Arbor, MI: University Microfilms International Research Collections. Available on microfilm and microfiche.

Complete CBS news and public affairs transcripts from 1975 to the present are available in this collection. In addition, some news broadcast transcripts from 1963-1975 are available on microform. Transcripts range from "The CBS Evening News with Walter

Cronkite" to "60 Minutes." *The CBS News Index* (entry 158), prepared by CBS News, is arranged by name and subject.

493. **Civil War Newspapers.** Ann Arbor, MI: University Microfilms International Research Collections. Available on microfilm.

More than 300 newspapers from 29 states and published from 1861-1865 are included in this collection. "Of special interest are the editions of *Frank Leslie's Illustrated Newspaper*, which published nearly 3,000 pictures of battles, sieges, and other war scenes."

494. **Early American Newspapers.** Ann Arbor, MI: University Microfilms International Research Collections. Available on 1,845 reels of microfilm.

Almost 2,000 reels of microfilm make up this collection of selected newspapers published as early as 1789. Included are the following: *The Albany Evening Journal*, 1830-1873; *The Baltimore American and Commercial Advertiser*, 1799-1902 and 1903-1920; *The Boston Herald*, 1848-1879; *The Boston Transcript*, 1848-1915; *The Philadelphia Public Ledger*, 1836-1934; *The Pennsylvania Freeman*, 1836-1841 and 1844-1854; *The York Recorder*, 1800-1830; and "Iowa Frontier Newspapers," 1838-1859, a selection of newspapers published from Dubuque to Muscatine. Readex also produces a collection entitled *Early American Newspapers* (1704-1820). When complete, it will include all existing newspapers listed in Brigham's *History and Bibliography of American Newspapers, 1690-1820* (entry 406).

495. **Edward R. Murrow Papers, 1927-1965.** Ann Arbor, MI: University Microfilms International Research Collections. Available on 55 reels of microfilm.

Correspondence, personal and professional papers, press clippings, and important broadcasts of broadcast journalist Edward R. Murrow comprise this collection. A guide entitled *Edward R. Murrow Papers, 1927-1965: A Guide to the Microfilm Edition* is available.

496. **Meet the Press, 1957-1986.** Ann Arbor, MI: University Microfilms International Research Collections. Available on microfiche.

This microfiche collection contains full-text transcripts of "Meet the Press," the longest-running television public affairs program. Each fiche holds one transcript. An annual chronology lists programs and provides names and titles.

497. **Negro Newspapers on Microfilm.** Library of Congress.

Approximately 200 black American newspapers from the mid-1800s to the mid-1900s comprise this collection. See also the *Black Newspaper Collection* (entry 491).

498. **Newspapers Along America's Great Trails.** Ann Arbor, MI: University Microfilms International Research Collections. Available on microfilm.

Newspapers published along the famous wagon trails are included in this collection. It contains thousands of newspapers from hundreds of communities along, for example, the Wilderness Road, Santa Fe Trail, Oregon Trail, Chisolm Trail, Cumberland Road, and the Lewis and Clark Expedition. The collection can be accessed by state or specific trail.

499. **Newspapers from the Depression Years, 1929-1938.** Ann Arbor, MI: University Microfilms International Research Collections. Available on 868 reels of microfilm.

Full runs of nine newspapers published during the stock market crash and the Depression years were compiled to make up this massive collection, which includes *The Wall Street Journal, Baltimore Morning Sun, San Francisco Chronicle, New Orleans Times-Picayune, Kansas City Star,* the *Kansas City Times, Charleston News and Courier,* and *Tulsa World.* According to explanatory notes, "Students and researchers can explore the economic machine of Wall Street as it faltered and then faded. The human despair of ruined lives and fortunes is also chronicled." Of course, most newspapers published during this time might reflect that.

500. **Public Television Transcripts**. Woodbridge, CT: Research Publications. Available on microfiche.

Transcripts of programs such as "The MacNeil/Lehrer Newshour," "Adam Smith's Money World," "Bill Moyers' Journal," and "Healthline" from WNET in New York and other public television stations are available in this collection of microfiche. Backfiles date to original air dates. *Public Television Transcripts Index*, a quarterly publication with an annual cumulation, is arranged by subject, name, and title.

501. **Pulitzer Prizes In Journalism, 1917-1985**. Ann Arbor, MI: University Microfilms International Research Collections, 1986. Available on 56 reels of microfilm.

Available in this collection are full-text versions of every copyright-cleared Pulitzer Prize awarded in journalism from 1917-1985. Included are winners in editorial writing, local reporting, public service reporting, cartoons, and foreign correspondence, as well as commentary, criticism, feature writing, and special awards. *The Pulitzer Prizes in Journalism, 1917-1985: A Guide to the Microfilm Edition* offers reel number, chronology, news organization, author, prize category, and subject indexes.

502. **Summary of World Broadcasts by the British Broadcasting Corporation**. Ann Arbor, MI: University Microfilms International. Available on microform from 1973- .

Transcribed news broadcasts from the Soviet Union, Eastern Europe, the Middle East, Far East, and Africa monitored by the British Broadcasting Corporation are included in this collection. Selected files from 1939-1973 also are available. See also entry 199.

503. **Underground Newspaper Collection, 1965-1985**. Ann Arbor, MI: University Microfilms International Research Collections. Available on microfilm.

More than 550 alternative and underground newspapers published during the 1960s through the early 1980s are available in yearly segments. This collection has a cumulative table of contents issued annually. Newspapers such as *The Village Voice* and *The Berkeley Barb* are included.

11
Core Periodicals

504. **American Journalism**. 1982- . American Journalism Historians Association, c/o School of Communication, Box 1482, University of Alabama, Tuscaloosa, AL 35487. Quarterly. ISSN 0882-1127.

With its small circulation and relative newcomer status, this scholarly and readable publication is not considered the premier journalism history periodical. It does offer some creative articles, a large book review section, and an alternative to *Journalism History* (entry 524). Each issue examines a cross-section of Americana, and includes three main articles such as "Mrs. O'Leary's Cow and Other Newspaper Tales About the Chicago Fire of 1871" and "Conservation, Community Economics, and Newspapering: The Seattle Press and the Forest Reserves Controversy of 1897." William E. Huntzicker's "Historians and the American Frontier Press" begins a seven-year series on mass communication historiography in 1988, and the editor expects to publish three essays each year. There are usually five to ten book reviews which vary in quality and timeliness. The last issue of each volume contains an index to that volume.

505. **APME News**. 1964- . Associated Press Managing Editors Association, 50 Rockefeller Plaza, New York, NY 10020. 6 issues/year.

This little magazine, which speaks directly to the newspaper managers and editors, lives in the shadow of *The Bulletin of the American Society of Newspaper Editors* (entry 507). It is not as well-written or organized as the *ASNE Bulletin*, but each colorful and jumbled issue offers an original article or two. Some recent stories include "The Problem With Anonymous Sources," "On the Unqualified Excuses in Newspaper Minority Hiring," "Love and Friendship—And Our Newsrooms," "Assessing Stories on Terrorists," and "Design Revolution Requires Newsroom Reorganization." The Associated Press Managing Editors Association (entry 566) also publishes the *APME Red Book* (entry 324).

506. **Broadcasting**. 1931- . Broadcasting Publications Inc., 1705 DeSales St., N.W., Washington, DC 20036. Weekly. ISSN 0007-2028.

This is the must-read, most-read trade source for current information on the broadcast industry. Television, radio, cable, satellite, and home video are covered, as well as updates on legislation, business news, technology, advertising, and FCC actions. Business and advertising are emphasized. Its graphic similarity to *E&P* (entry 517) is remarkable. Design is less than imaginative, with a tint block here and a mug shot there and large blocks of copy everywhere, but *Broadcasting* is widely indexed, and the numerous classified ads list professional jobs available in radio and television management, sales, announcers, news, programming, and allied fields. The business news of broadcasting also is covered in the biweekly *Television/Radio Age* (Television Editorial Corp.). *Television Digest* (Warren Publishing) is a weekly newsletter focusing on the latest in cable news, consumer electronics, and legislation. For those who seek a Canadian broadcasting magazine, *Broadcaster* is available from Northern Miner Press in Toronto. For information and ideas on news programming, see *The Rundown* (Standish Publishing Company), a weekly newsletter aimed at broadcast executives.

507. The Bulletin of the American Society of Newspaper Editors (ASNE Bulletin).
1941- . American Society of Newspaper Editors, Box 17004, Washington, D.C. 20041. 9 issues/year. ISSN 0003-1178.

For those who find the literature of journalism dull, overresearched, preachy, or simplistic, this trade journal grasps both the ongoing and cutting-edge issues in newspaper journalism and presents a tight, well-written, original, and attractively packaged collection of articles and columns nearly every month. Each issue is usually 30-40 pages long. Topics of great concern to most editors, such as minorities in the newsroom, journalism education, and journalistic ethics, receive a great deal of attention. Recent articles include "Do Newspapers Need Codes to Make Ethical Decisions?", "I Should Have Been a Teacher," "Managing Newspaper Design," "Women Edge Slowly Into Directing Editor Jobs," and "What Constitutes 'Responsible' Press Coverage?" The Society also publishes an annual convention report (entry 325).

Cover art usually deserves a second look in this illustrated magazine. The "In Search of Credibility" cover features an Indiana Jones-like newsman, clutching a vine, and wielding both a bullwhip and carrier's sack of newspapers. Feature editors have their own publication, *Style: The Journal of the American Association of Sunday and Feature Editors* (AASFE).

508. Channels: The Business of Communications. 1981- . C. C. Publishing Inc., 401 Park Avenue South, New York, NY 10016; subscriptions to Subscription Service Department, P.O. Box 6438, Duluth, MN 55806. 11 issues/year. ISSN 0895-643X.

The emphasis of *Channels* (formerly *Channels of Communication*) has come of age during the last few years, as evidenced by the title change in October 1986. The Publisher's Note of that issue states, "No longer dominated by technology as it was five years ago at the time of our birth, the industry is now driven increasingly by programming and finance. For that reason, people in each part of the industry need to understand what's going on throughout the electronic environment." Still, it provides media professionals with useful and timely information on television networks and local broadcasting. See also *Television/Radio Age*, published by Television Editorial Corporation.

509. C:JET (Communication: Journalism Education Today). 1967- . Journalism Education Association, Inc. P.O. Box 99, Blue Springs, MO 64015. Quarterly. ISSN 0010-3535.

This professional journal is on the must-read list of most secondary school journalism teachers and advisers. Five to ten articles plus regular features usually comprise the whole of *C:JET*, but occasionally proceedings of national meetings or special reports, such as "High School Journalism Confronts Critical Deadline" (a report by the JEA Commission on the role of journalism in secondary education), are printed. This journal addresses universal themes such as "Truth, Responsibility, and the Myth of Objectivity" and "Journalistic Responsibility" as well as subjects only an adviser or teacher could love ("Yearbook Journalism Teaching Aids"). See also *Scholastic Editor's Trends in Publications* (entry 544), aimed at both high school and college journalists and advisers.

510. The Coaches' Corner. 1986- . c/o Paul Salsini, 2405 E. Stratford Ct., Milwaukee, WI 53211. Quarterly.

"Writing coaches assist writers in improving their prose. They concentrate on writers and their habits rather than on errors in copy. They range from the full-time newsroom coach, through editors coaching their own writers in a casual way, even to reporters helping each other," says Don Fry, an associate director of The Poynter Institute for Media

Studies, a teacher of writing, and writing coach. If coaches become more permanent fixtures in today's newsrooms, this new quarterly newsletter will gain in stature and import. At this point, it is a low-budget but high-minded publication, written by coaches and others, for coaches and others pursuing good writing. It aims at newspaper writing and reporting, but there is no reason why the principles of good writing cannot be applied to most disciplines. Examples of "good writing," dialogue between reporters and editors, articles on language and grammar, and general news and information about coaching crowd each issue of eight to ten pages. This will be useful in the newsroom and in the classroom.

511. **College Media Review.** 1956- . College Media Advisers, c/o David Nelson, Journalism Department, Southwest Texas State University, San Marcos, TX 78666. Quarterly. ISSN 0739-1056.

Focusing on issues in publishing college newspapers, magazines, and yearbooks, this thin quarterly aims at the college media adviser. Topics covered range from press freedom to newspaper style. A special annual issue entitled "Best Design Ideas" was introduced in 1988. Subscription inquiries should go to Journalism Department, Memphis State University, Memphis, TN 38152.

512. **Columbia Journalism Review.** 1962- . Columbia University, Graduate School of Journalism, 700 Journalism Building, New York, NY 10027; subscriptions to 200 Alton Place, Marion, OH 43302. Bimonthly. ISSN 0010-194X.

Few journalism reviews have been applauded and booed, praised and spanked as much as *Columbia Journalism Review.* Some reviews (*Montana Journalism Review, Access, Cryano's Journal*) just faded away. Others (*MORE, feed/back, Chicago Journalism Review*) went out kicking and screaming. Some continue to move steadily along (*St. Louis Journalism Review* [entry 546] and *Australian Journalism Review*), serving their regions and readers. *CJR*, however has been accused of being petty, petulant, pedantic, and picky. It also has been lauded for single-handedly raising the standards of journalism. In truth, it lies somewhere in between. The contents page spells out, in an excerpt from the magazine's founding editorial, what *CJR* stands for: "To assess the performance of journalism in all its forms, to call attention to its shortcomings and strengths, and to help define — or redeem — standards of honest, responsible service ... to help stimulate continuing improvement in the profession and to speak out for what is right, fair, and decent." Those are difficult words to live up to, but *CJR* has done a satisfactory job. There have been times when the writing was not so lively, and when *CJR* itself should have been listed in the "Darts" section of its own "Darts and Laurels."

Regardless, this is the basic journalism review, with *WJR* (entry 550) following close behind. The four or five main articles in each issue are usually investigative or analytical. Articles in a 1985 issue include "Trashing the FOIA," "Mexico: The U.S. Press Takes a Siesta," "The Beat Nobody Wants," and "That (Too Long?) One-Hour News Show." In 1988, *CJR* covered "When MBAs Rule the Newsroom," "The Baby Bind: Can Journalists Be Mothers?", and "Straight Sex, AIDS, and the Mixed-Up Press." The "lower case" feature on the inside back cover still features press bloopers such as "Acid Rain Linked to U.S. Emissions by Reagan's Aide," from *The New York Times* (9/14/85) and "Reader Requests Tanning Procedure for Hunter's Wife," from *The Express-News* (San Antonio, 8/1/87). Cumulative indexes are available.

Communication Abstracts (see entry 159). This quarterly publication is fully annotated in Chapter 4, Indexes, Abstracts, and Databases.

Communication Booknotes (see entry 96). This bimonthly annotated booklist is fully annotated in Chapter 1, Bibliographies and Bibliographic Guides.

513. **Communicator.** 1946- . Radio-Television News Directors Association, 1717 K Street, N.W., Washington, D.C. 20006. ISSN 0033-7153.

Aiming at news directors, this magazine addresses all aspects of radio and television news and is an important source for the broadcast journalist. Journalistic ethics are examined closely here in columns entitled "News Practices" and "Tough Calls." Each column assesses situations requiring ethical decisions, raises questions, and makes recommendations when possible. Examples of stories in one 1988 issue are: "Robotic Cameras for NBC News Programs," "Staff Benefits Vary Widely," "Tape Recorders and Other Equipment," and "Douglas Edwards: A Voice of Authority and Compassion."

514. **Content**. 1970- . 2759 Carousel Crescent, Suite 602, Gloucester, Ontario K1T 2N5, Canada. 6 issues/year. ISSN 0045-835X.

Canada's journalism review of print and broadcast media keeps a lower profile than *Columbia Journalism Review* (entry 512) or *WJR: Washington Journalism Review* (entry 550), but does its share of investigative reporting. A plain journal, it does not offer many surprises. A recent article, however, entitled "Disabled Journalists: Empathy Overdue," indicates that the magazine explores new territory. Each 28-40 page issue contains five or six articles, a "Mass Media Studies" column, and book reviews.

515. **Critical Studies in Mass Communication**. 1984- . Speech Communication Association, 5105 Backlick Road, Annandale, VA 22003. Quarterly. ISSN 0739-3180.

Mass Communication includes television, radio, newspaper, and film in this scholarly journal for specialists. The three or four research and theoretical articles in each issue focus on any and all aspects of mass communication, and include the "evolution, organization, control, economics, administration, and technological innovations of mass communication systems." Article titles in the March 1987 issue range from "Out of Work and On the Air: Television News of Unemployment" to "The New Validation of Popular Culture: Sense and Sentimentality in Academia" to "Media Consumption and Girls Who Want to Have Fun." Critical book reviews are lengthy, but shorter notes on some books are also included.

David Eason, in a recent Editor's Note, made the following observations in the finest tradition of this journal:

> Sometimes I wonder about our words and our voices. We seem to like words with sharp edges better than soft ones. We write more easily about power than compassion. We talk a lot about narratives, but we don't tell stories very well. We see ourselves as activists, but our prose too often uses passive voice to create a world that undermines the very notion of active agents. We are moralists who justify our criticism with good intentions but are suspicious of such intentions in those we study....

516. **Design**. The Journal of the Society of Newspaper Design. 1979- . The Society of Newspaper Design, The Newspaper Center, Box 17290, Dulles International Airport, Washington, DC 20041. 6 issues/year.

Design cannot decide on a format (it has gone from magazine to tabloid back to magazine in the last few years), or how often to publish (they say six times a year), but each issue since the first in 1979 has been well-designed and packed with the kind of stories and graphics found in few magazines. This is the only periodical devoted exclusively to newspaper design. The masthead reads like a who's who in publication design. Articles are well-written and timely, with emphasis on newspaper color, informational graphics, typography, redesign, computer graphics, and pagination. As one might expect, graphic art is innovative and the color is superb. A wide array of slick, beautiful, and innovative magazines such as *Graphis* (entry 520), *Step by Step Graphics, How, Communication Arts*, and *Print* should be examined when studying publication design and graphics, but *Design* is the only one that consistently answers the professional prayers of newspaper artists and designers. Journalism students and instructors, and especially school and college newspaper advisers, would also do well to consult *Design*.

517. **Editor & Publisher, The Fourth Estate.** 1884- . Editor & Publisher Company, 11 West 19th Street, New York, NY 10011. Weekly. ISSN 0013-094X.

Some jobhunters pick up *E&P* only to scour the hefty classified advertising section, but most newspaper journalists will at least scan the contents each week. That is not as easy as it sounds, because this is not a particularly accessible magazine. The "Index to Issue" lists only regular features and departments, and cluttered layout leads the eye on a roller-coaster ride across the pages. One of the most important trade magazines and "the oldest publishers and advertisers newspaper in America" should look and read a little better.

All aspects of newspaper journalism are covered in news stories, and regular features include information on technology and syndicates. In "Shop Talk at Thirty," an editor, publisher, professor, etc., will air a grievance, offer an opinion, or "talk shop." Recent Shop columns include "Quotes and the Credibility Gap," "Reading: A Lost Art for News People," "Editor Makes a Case Against Drug Testing," and "Let's Admit We Are Fallible." Annual special features include a directory of journalism awards and fellowships, a syndicate directory, color in newspapers issue, etc.

The *Editor & Publisher 100th Anniversary 1884-1984* issue was published in March 1984 and offers a decade-by-decade account of American journalism history. Editor & Publisher, Inc. also publishes the *Editor & Publisher International Yearbook* (entry 285) and *Editor & Publisher Market Guide* (entry 286).

518. **Folio: The Magazine for Magazine Management.** 1972- . Hanson Publishing Group, 6 River Bend, Box 4949, Stamford, CT 06907-0949. Monthly. ISSN 0046-4333.

Despite its title, this slick trade magazine is not just for magazine managers. A wide range of journalistic, design, ethical, publishing, and management issues are headlined in articles entitled, for example, "Good Journalism vs. What Sells," "Supereditor: Make the Myth Work," "Restless Junior Editors Seen as a Growing Problem," "Business Publishers Starting Their Own 'J Schools'," and "Should Editors Meet Advertisers?" Five or six feature stories and regular columns and departments such as "Magazine People," "Magazine Watch," and "Computers in Publishing" combine to make this an upscale, timely, and important management publication. *Folio* also publishes special sections and an annual *Source Book*, which includes names and addresses of publishing suppliers and industry executives. See *Inside Print* (Media Product Enterprises, Inc., Hanson Publishing Group) for advertising-specific articles on newspapers and magazines.

519. **Gazette: International Journal for Mass Communication Studies.** 1955- . Netherlands Press Foundation, Koningslaan 31-33. 1075 AB Amsterdam, The Netherlands; subscriptions to Kluwer Academic Publishers, Distribution Center, Box 322, 3300 AH Dordrecht, The Netherlands. Bimonthly. ISSN 0016-5492.

This scholarly international journal covers mass communications and journalism. Each issue contains three or four lengthy (15-30 pages) articles ranging in subject from communication imperialism to public opinion polling. The following titles were published in a recent issue: "Nigerian Radio News and the New Information Order," "West African Mass Communication Research at Major Turning Point," "The Effects of Profession and Organization on Decision Acceptance Among Radio Newsworkers," and "Newspaper Agenda-Setting Among Elites and Non-Elites in China." This is an important title in international journalism. For another international perspective and current international press news, see *IPI Report*, the monthly bulletin of the International Press Institute.

520. **Graphis.** 1944- . Published by Graphis Press Corporation, Dufourstrasse 107, 8008 Zurich, Switzerland. Bimonthly.

Graphic artists in all fields will find much to covet in this glossy international journal of graphics, design, and applied art. Text is supplied in English, French, and German. Creative and colorful cover art is a prelude to the designs, illustrations, advertisements, and book reviews inside. Graphis Press also publishes an annual of the best examples of advertising art. For examples of graphic design in the United States, see *Print* (RC Publications). *Graphic Arts Monthly* (Cahners Publishing Co., Inc.) is not as pretty as *Graphis* or *Print*, but focuses on news stories and technical aspects of graphic design.

521. **Grassroots Editor**. 1960- . International Society of Weekly Newspaper Editors, c/o Editor, Northern Illinois University, Department of Journalism, DeKalb, IL 60115. Quarterly. ISSN 0017-3541.

Issues in community and weekly journalism are raised in this plain and outspoken journal. Five or six feature articles comprise the bulk of the twenty or so pages allotted for each black-and-white issue. There are few ads and illustrations, so all attention is focused on the generally well-written and succinct articles on publishing, managing, and editing the community and weekly newspaper. Recent articles include "Becoming a 'Secular' Writer," "A Call for Professionalism," and "Telling Truth Isn't Easy." *Publishers' Auxiliary* (entry 540) also addresses the needs of the weekly, and should be examined in addition to this.

522. **The IRE Journal**. 1978- . Published by Investigative Reporters & Editors, Inc., P.O. Box 838, Columbia, MO 65205. Quarterly. ISSN 0164-7016.

There is no better acronym than IRE for the muckraking crew of investigative journalists who crank this tabloid out four times a year. The *Journal* reminds us, however, that "When we refer to investigative reporting, it is meant in the broadest sense. All good reporters, whether full-time investigative reporters or those assigned to government, science, education, finance or other traditional beats, do investigative work." This journal provides consistently accurate, occasionally humorous, engaging, and in-depth articles on reporting and writing the tough stories. One cover story focused on Gary Hart and "How it Happened" while another looked into "Nursing Home Horrors: How to Document the Wrongs." Each issue usually contains a cover story, three or four feature articles, an "FOI Notebook" of court cases and state reports, and regular departments such as opinion and book reviews. Students and professionals can learn from this unique tabloid. Other Investigative Reporters & Editors publications include *The Investigative Journalist's Morgue* (entry 190), and *The IRE Books*, summaries of investigations in the 1980s.

523. **Journalism Educator**. 1945- . Association for Education in Journalism and Mass Communication, 1621 College Street, University of South Carolina, Columbia, SC 29208-0251. (Jim Crook, editor, School of Journalism, Room 330, Communication Building, University of Tennessee, Knoxville, TN 37996-0330.) Quarterly. ISSN 0022-5517.

This nontechnical publication for professors and administrators considers all aspects of college journalism education. An unadorned little journal, with no illustrations or photographs, some articles are less than bombastic. Still, it approaches the real issues in undergraduate journalism education, such as plagiarism, censorship, grading, computers, and internships. Each issue carries five or more articles, and regular features include "Education Forum," "Tips on Teaching," "Keyboard and Blackboard," and "Educators in Transition." A separate *Journalism and Mass Communication Directory* (entry 302) is also published by the AEJMC.

524. **Journalism History**. 1974- . California State University, Journalism Department, Northridge, CA 91330. Quarterly. ISSN 0094-7679.

A spare but important scholarly research journal, *Journalism History* concentrates on historical aspects of journalism and communication in the United States. Special issues have centered on the Constitution, and, in a bold move, the usual black-and-white cover was changed to yellow for the special issue on sensationalism. Each issue includes four or more lengthy articles as well as book reviews, reports on current research, and opinion essays. A cumulative index of the first 10 volumes is available. See also *American Journalism* (entry 504) or, for a less scholarly approach, *Media History Digest* (entry 532). *The*

Journal of Newspaper and Periodical History (World Microfilms Publications) and *Historical Journal of Film, Radio and Television* (International Association for Audio-Visual Media in Historical Research and Education) offer a British slant on selected issues in journalism.

525. **Journalism Monographs.** 1966- . Association for Journalism and Mass Communication, 1621 College Street, University of South Carolina, Columbia, SC 29208-0251. (Jim Tankard, editor, Department of Journalism, University of Texas, Austin, TX 78712). 4 issues/year. ISSN 0022-5525.

As the title indicates, each thin monograph is a thoroughly documented piece of research on some narrow aspect of journalism. More than 100 monographs have been published, such as "Getting the Story Out of Nazi Germany," "The Press Corps and the Kennedy Assassination," "From the Back of the Foxhole: Black Correspondents in World War II," "Egyptian Radio: Tool of Political and National Development," "Magazine Portrayal of Women, 1911-1930," "Hodding Carter's Newspaper on School Desegregation, 1954-1955," and "Literary Newswriting: The Death of an Oxymoron." Though this publication appeals to a special audience, it belongs in most journalism collections.

526. **Journal of Broadcasting and Electronic Media.** 1956/57- . Broadcast Education Association, 1771 N Street N.W., Washington, D.C. 20036. Quarterly. ISSN 0883-8151.

Read *Broadcasting* (entry 506), *Television/Radio Age* (Television Editorial Corp.), and *Television Digest* (Warren Publishing) for the most current news and information in this broad field, and then sit back with the former *Journal of Broadcasting* for scholarly treatment of radio, television, and satellite broadcasting and their effect on the world at large. Recent research articles include "Voice of America and Radio Moscow Newscasts to the Third World" and "Television Coverage of Jesse Jackson's Speech to the 1984 Democratic National Convention." The many book reviews tend to be well-written, and range in length from notes to essays.

527. **Journal of Communication.** 1951- . Oxford University Press, University of Pennsylvania, 3620 Walnut Street, Philadelphia, PA 19104-3858. Quarterly.

Articles in this basic communication journal tend to be less technical than those in other scholarly publications. A basic communication title, this journal is concerned with the "study of communication theory, research, practice, and policy." Articles on "Feminist Scholarship and Communications," "Press Images of Ronald Reagan," "Communications and Diabetics' Self-Care," and "Selling Cigarettes and Health" appeared in one recent issue. The large critical book review section is one of the best features of this journal. "Intercom," an information service, lists topics of future symposia and other items of research interest. See also the *Canadian Journal of Communication* (University of Calgary Press), *Communication Research* (Sage), and the *Journal of Communication Inquiry* (Iowa Center of Communication Study, School of Journalism and Mass Communication, University of Iowa).

528. **Journal of Mass Media Ethics.** 1985- . Department of Communications, Brigham Young University, Provo, UT 84602. Semiannual. ISSN 0890-0523. (In 1990, the **Journal of Mass Media Ethics** will be published by Lawrence Erlbaum Associates.)

Journalistic ethics has become a frequent focus in most trade journals, but this periodical, already one of the most important in the field, devotes itself exclusively to the topic. The journal's stated purpose is "bridging real and imagined gaps between media professionals and academics who have practical and philosophical concerns over the ethical performance of the media." In this it succeeds, with a balanced mix of theoretical, philosophical, and practical articles written by those whose names we associate with media ethics: Clifford Christians, Lou Hodges, Deni Elliott, Bob Logan, and editors Jay Black and Ralph D. Barney, to name a few. The first issue focused on mass media codes of ethics, and other issues since have centered on newsroom ethics, professional ethics, ethics in photojournalism, credibility, and objectivity. Book reviews employ spirited and thought-provoking writing. A monthly newsletter covering journalistic ethics, *Fineline*, is due in 1989, and is published by Barry Bingham, former editor and publisher of *The Courier Journal and Louisville Times*. The annual *Social Responsibility: Business, Journalism, Law, Medicine* (Washington and Lee University), which contains lectures presented at that university, is another useful source.

529. **JQ: Journalism Quarterly**. 1924- . Association for Journalism and Mass Communication, 1621 College Street, University of South Carolina, Columbia, SC 29208-0251. (Guido H. Stempel, III, editor, School of Journalism, Ohio University, Athens, OH 45701). Quarterly. ISSN 0196-3031.

This is the best-read or most-skimmed scholarly research journal in the field for a number of reasons: it is widely indexed; it considers practically every aspect of journalism and communications in the world; each issue contains "Articles on Mass Communication in U.S. and Foreign Journals," consisting of one-sentence summaries of several hundred articles subdivided by subject (thus devising a semblance of a journalism index); and it contains book and textbook reviews, also subdivided by subject, by scholars in the field. Quantitative research is emphasized, and there is also a "Research in Brief" section. There are usually more than 20 articles in each issue, ranging from "Public Accountability or Public Relations? Newspaper Ombudsmen Define Their Role" to "Prior Restraints on Photojournalists" to "Female Roles in Radio Advertising." Three cumulative indexes have been published. Warning: if you photocopy a page or two from the "Articles" section, be sure to jot down the issue and year of the *Journalism Quarterly* issue, because no publication years are included in article citations.

530. **Mass Comm Review**. 1973- . Association for Education in Journalism and Mass Communication, through the Department of Journalism and Mass Communications, San Jose State University, One Washington Square, San Jose, CA 95192-0055. 3 issues/year.

The Mass Communications and Society Division of the AEJMC, which "encourages the study of mass communication as a system," publishes this scholarly research journal. Writing levels vary, but most articles are directed at an academic audience. Large blocks of copy loom before readers, as there are few or no illustrations. A cumulative index for the first 10 years is available. The editorial board and editorial staff consist of an impressive collection of well-known scholars, but the journal reads and looks as if it could use a surge of adrenalin. *Mass Comm Review* publishes three issues each year, but occasionally these three issues are under one cover. Articles in the 1986 volume (vol. 13, nos. 1, 2, 3,) include "Philadelphia Puerto Rican Community Leaders' Perceptions of Spanish-Language Media," "Cable Adult Entertainment: The Next Round of Obscenity Litigation," "Uses and Gratifications of Magazine Readers: A Cross-Media Comparison," and "Promise vs. Performance: Four Public Access Channels in Connecticut, A Case Study."

531. **The Masthead**. 1948- . National Conference of Editorial Writers, 6223 Executive Boulevard, Rockville, MD 20852. Quarterly. ISSN 0025-5122.

Some of the best writing on journalism is located in this straightforward, well-packaged publication. Editorial and commentary writers face unique problems and situations, and *Masthead* addresses those issues. An occasional column called "Editorial Clinic," for example, deals with topics such as "How Do You Handle Hate Letters?" and "The Insulting Letter to the Editor." The 40-60 page quarterly offers reports, features, and editorial cartoons useful to the editorial journalist and journalism student, and there is no doubt it could be used well in the classroom. The only jarring note is an awkwardly labeled "Academic Section" which showcases a token scholarly article.

Target: The Political Cartoon Quarterly, which focused on editorial cartoons, ceased publication in 1987. Other magazines addressing editorial cartoons include, among others, *Bull's Eye: The Magazine of Editorial Cartooning* (Bull's Eye Publications), *Cartoonist Profiles* (Cartoonist Profiles), and *Witty World* (Witty World Publications).

532. **Media History Digest**. 1980- . Media History Digest Corp., c/o Editor & Publisher, 11 West 19th Street, New York, NY 10011. 2 issues/year. ISSN 0195-6779.

Media History Digest may be the *Reader's Digest* of media history. Filled with short general-interest articles, it should appeal to students and others seeking a breezy approach to history of journalism. In an issue on Lincoln and the Media, for example, there are articles on "Why Mary Lincoln Got Such a 'Bad Press,'" "Lincoln's Lensman: Mathew Brady," and John Jakes's "The Message was Freedom; The Abolitionist Struggle Without Anchormen." One of the most unusual regular departments is "Media Hysteria," which has explored "How the Press Made Fun of Ol' Abe" and "Food Ads of Yesteryear—They Ate the Whole Thing." There is even a quiz in each issue, running the gamut from "Newspapers That Hit the Dust" to "Fill in the Bill of Rights." Contributing editors include Everette Dennis, John Lent, Joseph P. McKerns, John Merrill, and Calder Pickett.

533. **Media Law Reporter**. 1977- . Bureau of National Affairs, Inc., 1231 25th Street N.W., Washington, D.C. 20037. Weekly. ISSN 0148-1045.

Supreme Court and important federal and state court decisions pertaining to media law and communications are presented. A topical index, classification guide, tables of cases, and an index digest allow full access to the text of cases on antitrust, broadcast media, disclosure, fair trial and free press, libel, privacy, and prior restraint. There are annual cumulations. For further information, background material, etc., consult publications such as the quarterly *Communications and the Law* (Meckler) or *News Media and the Law* (entry 534).

534. **News Media and the Law**. 1973- . Reporters' Committee for Freedom of the Press, 800 18th Street N.W., Washington, D.C. 20006. 4 issues/year. ISSN 0149-0737.

From "Cameras in the Courtroom" to "Rap Sheet Access," this journal covers broadcast and print media law. Numerous brief articles cover court cases and news events. Be forewarned that this news-flash publication does not contain any in-depth material. Regular and occasional departments include "Press at Home and Abroad," "Prior Restraint and Secret Courts," "Confidentiality, Libel and Privacy," "Federal-State FOI Acts," and "Broadcasting." The Committee produces an annual index, and a cumulative index for volumes 1-10 is available. For texts of cases, consult *Media Law Reporter* (entry 533). *Communications and the Law* (Meckler) might also be a useful source.

535. **Newspaper Newsletter**. 19??- . Morton Research, Lynch Jones & Ryan, 1037 Thirtieth Street, N.W., Washington, D.C. 20007. Monthly.

This monthly newsletter of the newspaper business contains timely reports on financial aspects of newspapering. Information, data, and statistics on newspaper chains, newsprint consumption, acquisitions, circulation patterns, newspaper groups, stock-price performance of newspaper companies, newspaper advertising revenue, and antitrust are presented. John Morton, of Morton Research, is a newspaper analyst with Lynch Jones & Ryan and currently writes "The Business of Journalism" column for *Washington Journalism Review*. *The Journal of Media Economics* (Emerson College) and *Newspaper Financial Executive Journal* (International Newspaper Financial Executives) might also provide useful data.

536. **Newspaper Research Journal**. 1979- . Association for Education in Journalism and Mass Communication; subscriptions and correspondence to E. W. Scripps School of Journalism, Ohio University, Athens, OH 45701-2979. Quarterly.

The Newspaper Division of the AEJMC produces this scholarly journal devoted entirely to the study of newspapers. Various articles consider all aspects of newspapering, including management, circulation, editorial, readership, libel, ethics, and computerization. Each issue contains about 10 articles, 10-12 pages in length, and the quality of writing varies. Articles range from the nontechnical ("Front Page Mug Shots: A Content Analysis of Five U.S. Newspapers in 1986") to the highly technical and/or quantitative ("A Parsimonious Regression Model to Predict Metropolitan Circulation in Outlying Counties"). The book review section is small but satisfying. This is a basic title for print journalism collections.

537. **News Photographer**. 1946- . National Press Photographers Association, Inc., 3200 Croasdaile Drive, Suite 306, Durham, NC 27705. Monthly.

This is not merely a picture magazine, although it is full of black-and-white and color photographs. *News Photographer* is the only publication which aims at the professional photojournalist, but it also could be an educational tool for publishers, editors, news directors, graphic artists, and journalism students. Photos appearing in *News Photographer* can become topics of discussion in journalistic ethics sessions and hands-on photojournalism classes. Each issue contains several features and departments such as "NewsViews" and "Bookbeat." "Pictures of the Month," which tend to evoke a tear or a smile, include "How I Got the Picture" stories.

538. **Nieman Reports**. 1947- . Nieman Foundation, Harvard University, One Francis Avenue, Cambridge, MA 02138. Quarterly. ISSN 0028-9817.

When *Nieman Reports* is mentioned, the name that might come to mind is Lucius Nieman, founding editor and president of the *Milwaukee Journal*, who died in 1935. His wife, Agnes Nieman, upon her death in 1936, willed most of her estate to Harvard University to promote excellence in journalism. The Nieman Foundation awarded its first fellowships in 1938. Fellows spend a year at Harvard, and this publication highlights their work there. The work of past Fellows is published also.

Any subject in journalism is fair game. A recent issue contains "Nicaragua," "In Praise of In-Depth Journalism," "In Support of Public Notice Advertising," "The Wrong People Bring You the Right Problems," "Changing Aspects of Reporting from Abroad," and "Soul-Searching Press Ethics." Each issue contains five or six articles, letters, Nieman Notes, and, consistently, the most thought-provoking and well-written book reviews available on journalism and related topics. Each plain black-and-white issue looks the same. It's what's inside that counts here, but perhaps the Foundation should select a graphic arts Fellow to plan a redesign.

539. **presstime**. 1979- . American Newspaper Publishers Association, 11600 Sunrise Valley Drive, Reston, VA 22091. Monthly. ISSN 0194-3243.

An indispensable source of practical information on newspapers, this official publication of the ANPA focuses on every aspect of newspapering from carrier delivery to employee relations. It is most useful to the editors, managers, and publishers who assemble budgets, deal with postal regulations, purchase equipment, or handle advertising, but the journal also includes general-interest articles on writing and editing, management, and design for classroom and newsroom reading. An issue of 60-80 pages usually contains 10 or more well-written articles by staffers, and reports from regular departments such as advertising, education, circulation, government affairs, news-editorial, postal affairs, etc. All copy is tidy, well-organized, and easy to locate. Even the comic strip "Shoe" is listed in the contents. *presstime* also presents indexes in January and July issues. Cover art and special reports usually emphasize current issues or trends in the business, such as minorities in the newsroom, first-time managers, readers, free circulation, linking computers, retail advertising, and independent newspapers.

540. **Publishers' Auxiliary**. 1865- . National Newspaper Association, 1627 K Street N.W., Suite 400, Washington, D.C. 20006. Biweekly. ISSN 0048-5942.

"The newspaper industry's oldest newspaper" aims at publishers and editors of weekly, community, semiweekly, and small daily newspapers. Most aspects of newspaper publishing are covered, as well as the specific legal, business, and editorial issues confronting weeklies and small dailies. Ed Arnold, author of *Designing the Total Newspaper, Modern Newspaper Design*, and other titles, discusses newspaper design, graphics, and typography in his "Page of the Week" column. Other regular columns include "Classified Advice," "Ad Workshop," "Managing Newspaper People," and "Editor's Notebook." The magazine also publishes an annual "Buyer's Guide" of newspaper equipment and services. See also *Grassroots Editor* (entry 521), which focuses specifically on the weekly paper.

541. **Quill**. 1912- . Society of Professional Journalists, 53 West Jackson Boulevard, No. 731, Chicago, IL 60604-3610. 11 issues/year. ISSN 0480-7898.

These days, *Quill* is far more than a tool of the Society of Professional Journalists. It has become a mix of house organ, journalism review, and journalism news report. Articles are written by those from the academic and professional communities. In one issue, the following articles appeared: "Reporting from Behind the Walls," "Tackling the Teflon Candidate" (about Jesse Jackson), "It's An Okay Life, Being a Hired Gun" (on freelancing), "The Writing Process," and "To Get the Right Job, Ask Questions." Print journalism is emphasized, although articles on broadcasting are included. Media critic Ron Dorfman contributes a regular column, and other columns and departments include "The Ombudsmen," letters, classifieds, and "FOI/FYI" (a monthly report from the First Amendment Center). *Quill* is an attractive, readable, and nicely packaged journalism magazine that examines the ethics of journalism as ably as any journalism review.

542. **Quill & Scroll**. 1926- . Quill & Scroll Society, School of Journalism and Mass Communication, University of Iowa, Iowa City, IA 52242. 4 issues/year. ISSN 0033-6505.

The official magazine of the International Honorary Society for High School Journalists covers all aspects of the high school press, such as the recent *Hazelwood v. Kuhlmeier* decision. Other *Quill & Scroll* articles have centered on AIDS, informational graphics, censorship, libel, and writing. Roland Wolseley, author of *The Journalist's Bookshelf* (entry 102), contributes "The Newest Books in Journalism" column. Articles are written primarily by journalism instructors and media professionals. This is an excellent source for current information on scholarships and careers in journalism. Other sources on scholastic journalism are *Scholastic Editor's Trends in Publications* (entry 544) and *The School Press Review* (entry 545).

543. **Righting Words, The Journal of Language and Editing**. 1987- . Righting Words Corp., P.O. Box 6811, FDR Station, New York, NY 10150. Bimonthly. ISSN 0892-581X.

Copy editors, the "Rodney Dangerfields of journalism," according to a 1987 *Editor & Publisher* article, finally have a respectable journal all their own. This journal of language and editing approaches journalism and allied fields from the perspective of the editor at the copy desk. Although this is a new journal, it has already made strides in a fairly unexplored and murky area of journalism. Examples of recent articles include "Yes, TV Does Have Copy Editors," "Our Presto-Changeo Language," "Gosh, That's Not in the Picture," "Life and Death of a Headline Desk," and "Stylebooks Once Had More Style." Issues consist of five or six feature articles written primarily by copy editors, copy readers, editors, and journalism professors. Regular features include book reviews and brief news notes. The centerfold is the "Heads You Win" column, exhibiting the nation's best headlines.

544. **Scholastic Editor's Trends in Publications**. 1921- . National Scholastic Press Association and the Associated Collegiate Press, 620 Rarig Center, 330 South 21st Avenue, University of Minnesota, Minneapolis, MN 55455. 7 issues/year. ISSN 0745-2357.

The high school press is the focal point of this publication, although an occasional article on college press will sneak in. It is newsy, with information on journalism awards, school magazines and newspapers, workshops, and conventions. Inside features examine photography, computers and desktop publishing, writing, editing, graphics, color, and all aspects of planning, designing, and publishing the school magazine, yearbook, or newspaper. The book reviews are timely, and occasionally pick up on a title that the trade and scholarly journals have missed or ignored. Anyone involved in scholastic publishing and editing will use this along with *Quill and Scroll* (entry 542).

545. **The School Press Review**. 1925- . Columbia Scholastic Press Association, Columbia University, Box 11, Central Mail Room, New York, NY 10027-6969. Quarterly.

By far the most attractive of the scholastic press publications, *The School Press Review* emphasizes writing and editing in the high school press. Examples of articles published during the last few years are: "Opinion Polls Require Caution," "Approaches to

Better Reporting," "The Complete Yearbook," "Running Lively, Relevant News," and "What Student Journalists Are Saying Today." A semi-annual Literary Supplement showcases poetry, fiction, and nonfiction writing of elementary, junior high, and high school students. Students contribute the imaginative cover art, ranging from black-and-white photographs to an ink drawing of a rabbit. This review of 20 or more pages is a useful supplement to *Quill & Scroll* (entry 542) and *Scholastic Editor's Trends in Publications* (entry 544).

546. St. Louis Journalism Review. 1970- . 8380 Olive Boulevard, St. Louis, MO 63132. Monthly. ISSN 0036-2972.

It accurately labels itself "a critique of metropolitan news media," and a self-promotion reads, "It is a newspaper's duty to print the news and raise hell: when it doesn't, people turn to the *St. Louis Journalism Review.*" *The Review* is not a particularly pretty tabloid, but it is a lofty-thinking, intelligently written, and occasionally muckraking example of regional journalism watchdogism. Each issue contains short articles, news sections (labeled "Here," "There," and "Everywhere"), and some longer national pieces. No mass medium is left untouched, as both print and broadcasting are examined.

547. Television Quarterly. 1962- . National Academy of Television Arts and Sciences, 111 West 57th Street, New York, NY 10019. Quarterly. ISSN 0040-2796.

All aspects of television broadcasting are covered in this attractive and readable quarterly, and a substantial number of articles address television news. Articles in one recent issue include: "TV's Black Comfort Zone for Whites," "The Little Studio That Could," "Communications, Competition and Quality" (by Katharine Graham), "Black Eye at Black Rock," and "Bob Dylan, Westinghouse and 'The Meaning of Communism,' " Each issue also includes timely book reviews.

548. UK Press Gazette. 1965- . Bouverie Publishing Company, Ltd., 244-249 Temple Chambers, Temple Avenue, London EC4Y ODT, England. Weekly. ISSN 0041-5170.

This is Britain's answer to America's *Editor & Publisher* (entry 517). Also in the American tradition, the *UK Press Gazette* is just as confusing and cluttered. The only table of contents is the Inside Note on the front cover. Several pages of news and opinion, a section on broadcasting, and Dateline America, news from the United States, are part of this package. The "Appointments Register" lists a number of professional publishing, editing, reporting, and broadcasting positions available.

549. U & lc (Upper and lower case. The International Journal of Typographics). 1974- . International Typeface Corporation, 2 Hammarskjold Plaza, New York, NY 10017. Quarterly. ISSN 0362-6245.

"Funky but chic" is an apt description of this irreverent salute to graphic design and typography. Of course, this tabloid magazine also is a shameless promoter of ITC typefaces, and is sprinkled with corporation news and views. There is even an index to the ITC typefaces used in each issue. But color is used effectively, design is imaginative and eye-grabbing, and each issue is a new adventure in design. On top of all that, it's free. Circulation figures, at last count, topped 200,000, and readership is estimated much higher. Following are sample headlines and explanatory notes lifted from a recent *U&lc* table of contents: "The Letter B. It started as a symbol for shelter," "Meet the Letterheads. Signmaking is not just their job; it's a way of life," "Families to Remember. The Bachs and ITC Kabel— another in our series of genealogic and typographic families," "An Alphabardian Address Book. Never have so many diverse Shakespearean characters appeared in one production," and "Trenchant Messages. From Aesop's mouth to your ear; via Letraset and ITC."

550. WJR: Washington Journalism Review. 1977- . College of Journalism, University of Maryland College Park Campus; correspondence to 2233 Washington Avenue, N.W., Washington, D.C. 20007. Monthly. ISSN 0149-1172.

It might not have the national prestige that *Columbia Journalism Review* (entry 512) enjoys, but *WJR* has managed to carve quite a niche for itself in a few short years. In fact, a headline in the *Bulletin of the American Society of Newspaper Editors* indicates that "Editors Rate *Washington Journalism Review* above *Columbia Journalism Review* in Usefulness, Improvement" (April 1987). Neither professionals nor students should turn their backs on this attentive watchdog of the press. Though it is now more of a national review source, there are still rumbles that *WJR* leans a bit heavily toward Washington, D.C. and East Coast coverage. (This is an issue even though "National" is nowhere in its title).

Four or five main articles are generally thought-provoking, well-researched, and well-written. Print and broadcast journalism receive fairly even coverage. Regular features include "Press and the Law," "The Business of Journalism," and book reviews, as well as annual "Best in the Business" awards in which readers cast their predictable votes for Peter Jennings and others. In 1988, *WJR* introduced a "Take 2" feature, similar to *Columbia Journalism Review*'s "lower case" of newspaper blunders. *WJR* takes it one step further and features both the bad and the beautiful in headlines, quotes, leads, etc. *WJR* also publishes an annual "Directory of Selected News Sources" special section. When examining journalism reviews, do not overlook this one.

551. **World Press Review**. 1961- . The Stanley Foundation, 200 Madison Avenue, New York, NY 10016; subscriptions to Box 1997, Marion, OH 43305. Monthly.

News and feature stories from foreign newspapers and magazines are reprinted in this monthly digest. Articles are culled from publications such as *The Economist, Der Spiegel, Proceso, Hindustan Times, Toronto Star, Le Monde, Jerusalem Post, Izvestia,* and *The Australian.* Each issue offers a cover story ("Whose Palestine?", "Chemical Warfare") with six or seven representative articles, a feature articles section, and regular department news in business, the press, travel, art, books, viewpoints, etc. "The World in Cartoons" is an international sampling of editorial and feature cartooning. When researching the international press, this digest of primary materials is unequaled.

552. **The Writer**. 1887- . Writer, Inc., 120 Boylston Street, Boston, MA 02116. Monthly. ISSN 0043-9517.

Though it favors fiction, *The Writer* is still of some use in a journalistic setting. In addition, it appeals to the fiction writer who may be lurking within the police reporter or journalism professor. It provides helpful hints, how-to articles, and a marketplace of ideas, and is especially helpful to the beginning writer. Articles such as "Writing the Personal Experience Article," "Research Tips to Help You Write," and "Travel Writing from Both Sides of the Desk" can be tailored to meet the needs of the journalist. See also *Writer's Digest* (entry 553).

553. **Writer's Digest**. 1920- . F & W Publications, 1507 Dana Avenue, Cincinnati, OH 45287; subscriptions to 205 West Center Street, Marion, OH 43305. Monthly. ISSN 0043-9525.

The *Digest* touches a lot of journalistic bases, and is a popular general-writing periodical with the same appeal and audience as most Writer's Digest publications. Each 60-80 page issue speaks to both fiction and nonfiction writers involved in print, television, and radio, as well as cartoonists and photographers. It is a cut above *The Writer* (entry 552) in terms of scope and number of how-to-do-it or how-I-did-it stories. The mechanics of writing receive as much attention as the art of writing.

A features section showcases four or five full-length articles ranging from "You and Your Copy Editor" to "Training Your Muse: Seven Steps to Harnessing Your Creativity." Fiction, nonfiction, poetry, and scripts columns address issues particular to those areas. *Writer's Digest,* or "your monthly guide to getting published," should be skimmed each month for useful articles, but be wary of content. For example, a recent issue includes "Writing Tight," a two-page piece by a *USA Today* reporter, who advocates the use of "creative punctuation," with the demons we know as colons and dashes. "My English teachers would shoot me," he says. For grassroots writing and editing advice, see *The Coaches' Corner* (entry 510).

12
Societies and Associations

General Associations

554. **Accuracy in Media**
   1275 K Street, N.W.
   Suite 1150
   Washington, D.C. 20005
   202-371-6710
   A right-wing news media watchdog organization, AIM researches and publicizes the public's complaints of media errors. It also broadcasts a daily three-minute radio program called "Media Monitor," aired on approximately 80 stations, and publishes a weekly column in 100 newspapers. The *AIM Report* is published monthly, and there is an annual index.

555. **American Newspaper Publishers Association**
   The Newspaper Center
   Box 17407
   Dulles Airport
   Washington, D.C. 20041
   703-648-1000
   The ANPA publishes the monthly *presstime* (entry 539), compiles information on the business aspects of newspapering, and conducts seminars, workshops, and conferences. Facilities, including the journalism library (entry 635), are located at the Newspaper Center in Reston, Virginia. Founded in 1887, ANPA's mission statement is as follows: "To advance the cause of a free press, and to ensure that it has the economic strength essential to serve the American people." Its membership includes newspapers in United States and Canada. Other publications include 28 "ANPA News Research Reports" published from 1977-1980. The ANPA Foundation supports the ANPA's educational programs, including the Newspaper in Education Program.

556. **American Society of Journalists and Authors**
   1501 Broadway
   Suite 1907
   New York, NY 10036
   212-997-0947
   An organization of nonfiction freelance writers, the ASJA maintains the Dial-A-Writer Service, a referral service for those seeking writers for special projects. The ASJA also awards the Conscience-in-Media Gold Medal and publishes a newsletter.

557. **American Society of Magazine Editors**
575 Lexington Avenue
New York, NY 10022
212-752-0055
Senior magazine editors are members of this professional organization founded in 1963. See also the Magazine Publishers Association (entry 591).

558. **American Society of Magazine Photographers**
205 Lexington Avenue
New York, NY 10016
212-889-9144
Membership consists of freelance magazine photographers. Founded in 1944, the ASMP conducts seminars, maintains a small library, and publishes the monthly *ASMP Bulletin*. It also publishes the *Stock Photography Handbook*.

559. **American Society of Newspaper Editors**
The Newspaper Center
Box 17004
Dulles Airport
Washington, D.C. 20041
703-648-1144
Newspaper editors who set news and editorial policy for daily newspapers are members of ASNE. Founded in 1922, this organization publishes the *Bulletin of the American Society of Newspaper Editors* (ASNE Bulletin, entry 507) nine times a year and the annual *ASNE Proceedings* (entry 325). There are approximately 1,000 members.

560. **American Sportscasters Association**
150 Nassau Street
New York, NY 10038
212-227-8080
Television and radio sportscasters make up this group which sponsors seminars and workshops for student and other budding sportscasters. The Association provides a placement service and publishes the monthly *Insiders Sportsletter*. It also maintains a biographical archive.

561. **American Women in Radio and Television**
1101 Connecticut Avenue, N.W.
Suite 700
Washington, D.C. 20036
202-429-5102
Radio and television professionals involved in administrative aspects of the broadcasting industry are members. There are more than 50 local groups and five regional groups. Founded in 1951, the AWRT offers awards Certificates of Commendation for local and network programs, and the Silver Satellite award for outstanding work in the broadcasting field. The association operates a placement service, maintains an educational foundation, and publishes the annual *American Women in Radio and TV* and a newsletter.

562. **Asian American Journalists Association**
1765 Sutter Street
Room 1000
San Francisco, CA 94115
415-346-2051
This organization, founded in 1981, focuses on educational and professional achievement of Asian-American print and broadcast journalists as well as press coverage of Asian-American issues. The AAJA publishes a quarterly newsletter and offers a job bank for members.

563. **Associated Collegiate Press**
   c/o Tom Rolnicki
   620 Rarig Center
   330 21st Avenue South
   University of Minnesota
   Minneapolis, MN 55455
   612-625-8335
   Publisher of the *Scholastic Editor's Trends in Publications* (entry 544), the ACP was founded in 1933. It offers rating services for college publications, awards, and workshops.

564. **Associated Press**
   50 Rockefeller Plaza
   New York, NY 10020
   212-621-1500
   This news agency gathers and transmits news reports and photographs by satellite and cable. AP reporters work out of more than 100 United States and 60 foreign news bureaus. More than 10,000 newspapers and broadcast organizations and stations subscribe to AP wire services. The AP was founded in 1848 when six New York papers (the *Sun, Herald, Tribune, Express, Courier and Enquirer*, and *Journal of Commerce*) set up the New York Associated Press or NYAP.

565. **Associated Press Broadcasters, Inc.**
   c/o Wendell Wood
   1825 K Street, N.W.
   Suite 615
   Washington, D.C. 20006
   202-955-7243
   Broadcasting stations which are members of the Associated Press (entry 564) make up this group. The stations work in cooperation with AP, and offer annual awards for news coverage. APB publishes a monthly newsletter.

566. **Associated Press Managing Editors**
   50 Rockefeller Plaza
   New York, NY 10020
   212-621-1552
   Members include managing editors and news and editorial executives of newspapers subscribing to the Associated Press. It sponsors the Public Service Award and Freedom of Information Award. Publications include the bimonthly *APME News* (entry 505) and the annual *APME Red Book* (entry 324), as well as special reports. The APME was founded in 1933.

567. **Association for Education in Journalism and Mass Communication**
   1621 College Street
   University of South Carolina
   Columbia, SC 29208-0251
   803-777-2005
   This important organization of college and university teachers was founded in 1912, and publishes the following: *Journalism Educator* (entry 523), *Journalism Monographs* (entry 525), *Journalism Quarterly* (entry 529), *Journalism Abstracts* (entry 171), and the *Journalism and Mass Communications Directory* (entry 302). The AEJMC conducts research and compiles statistics on various aspects of journalism education. The Accrediting Council on Education in Journalism and Mass Communication (School of Journalism, University of Kansas, Lawrence, KS 66045, 913-864-3973) publishes a listing of accredited programs in journalism and accrediting standards. AEJMC divisions include advertising, communication theory and methodology, history, international communications,

law, magazine, mass communication and society, minorities and communication, newspaper, public relations, qualitative studies, radio-television journalism, secondary education, and visual communication.

568. **Association of American Editorial Cartoonists**
Library for Communication and Graphic Arts
Ohio State University
242 West 18th Street
Columbus, OH 43210
614-461-8510
Dedicated to promoting editorial cartoon art in newspapers, magazines, and syndicates, members of this association are professional editorial cartoonists. It was founded in 1957.

569. **Broadcast Designers Association, Inc.**
251 Kearny Street
Suite 602
San Francisco, CA 94108
415-788-232
Founded in 1978, this is an association for television designers, artists, photographers, illustrators, art directors, and animators. BDA produces an annual of the best in television design (entry 330) and a monthly "Update." There are approximately 800 members.

570. **Broadcast Education Association**
1771 N Street, N.W.
Washington, D.C. 20036
202-429-5355
The BEA, whose membership consists of faculty and graduate students, is dedicated to improving the quality of broadcast education through training, research, and teaching. It provides special training for member stations of the National Association of Broadcasters (entry 595). Publications include the quarterly *Journal of Broadcasting and Electronic Media* (entry 526) and a *Directory of Academic Broadcasting Programs in Colleges and Universities*. It was founded in 1955.

571. **Broadcast Pioneers**
320 West 57th Street
New York, NY 10019
212-586-2000
Those who have worked in the radio or television broadcasting field for 20 years are eligible for membership. The association sponsors the George Foster Peabody Annual Awards, Broadcasters Hall of Fame, and the Broadcasters Foundation. There is a quarterly newsletter. The Broadcast Pioneers Library (entry 642), which houses books, photographs, oral histories, etc., is located in Washington, D.C. Broadcast Pioneers also sponsors the Broadcasters' Foundation for Broadcast Veterans.

572. **Canadian Daily Newspaper Publishers Association**
890 Yonge Street
Suite 1100
Toronto, Ontario M4W 3P4
Canada
416-923-3567
Founded in 1919, approximately 80 Canadian daily newspaper publishers are members.

573. **Canadian Managing Editors Conference**
Box 5020
Ottawa, Ontario K2C 3M4
Canada
613-829-9100
Managing editors of Canadian daily newspapers, magazines, and wire services are members of this organization founded in 1946.

574. **College Media Advisers**
c/o Ron Spielberger
Department of Journalism
Memphis State University
Memphis, TN 38152
901-454-2403

These advisers and directors of college student newspapers, yearbooks, magazines, television and radio stations, and others interested in college media provide a clearinghouse for student media, compile statistics, publish reports, maintain placement service, conduct national surveys of student media, offer awards to advisers, and sponsor journalism competitions and contests. In addition, the CMA, founded in 1954, publishes a newsletter and the quarterly *College Media Review* (entry 511).

575. **Columbia Scholastic Press Advisers Association**
Box 11
Central Mail Room
Columbia University
New York, NY 10027-6969

This professional organization of teachers and advisers, founded in 1927, focuses on the educational development of the student press. The CSPAA publishes the quarterly "CSPAA Bulletin."

576. **Columbia Scholastic Press Association**
Box 11
Central Mail Room
Columbia University
New York, NY 10027-6969
212-280-3311

A national education association and clearinghouse for information on student magazines, newspapers, and yearbooks, the CSPA also evaluates member student publications and offers awards. The CSPA, founded in 1924, publishes the *School Press Review* (entry 545). It is sponsored by Columbia University.

577. **Committee to Protect Journalists**
36 West 44th Street
Suite 911
New York, NY 10036
212-944-7216

Founded in 1981, this organization's goal is to "support and protect journalists around the world who have been subject to human and professional rights violations." Members are journalists and journalism educators. The CPJ maintains online files of attacks on the press.

578. **Community College Journalism Association**
c/o Mary E. Hires
County College of Morris
Cohen Hall, B300
Route 10 and Center Grove Road
Randolph, NJ 07869
201-361-5000

Founded in 1968, this 200-member organization is open to two-year-college journalism educators. Members work to upgrade standards of community college journalism and the certification of two-year journalism programs. It publishes the quarterly *Community College Journalist*. The Journalism Association of Community Colleges (West Valley College, 14000 Fruitvale Avenue, Saratoga, CA 95070, 408-867-2200) is active in California and Arizona.

579. **First Amendment Congress**
Campus Box 287
University of Colorado
Boulder, CO 80309
303-492-6480

Major journalism associations and others in mass communications-related fields interested in First Amendment issues and education are members. It conducts First Amendment congresses on the national, state, and local levels, and publishes a quarterly newsletter.

580. Graphic Arts Technical Foundation
4615 Forbes Avenue
Pittsburgh, PA 15213
412-621-6941

A large organization with membership numbering more than 6,000, it focuses on the international graphic communications community. The GATF conducts research, seminars and workshops, and other educational programs, and maintains a printing and graphic arts library of more than 4,000 volumes as well as a biographical archive. Its numerous publications (such as *Graphic Arts Abstracts*) were recently consolidated to create *GATF World*, which contains a section on graphic arts abstracts.

581. INCA-FIEJ Research Association (IFRA)
Washingtonplatz
D-6100 Darmstadt
Federal Republic of Germany
(6151) 7005-0

Founded in 1961, IFRA focuses on techniques and trends in newspaper publishing and printing. It publishes the monthly *Newspaper Techniques*.

582. Inter-American Press Association
2911 N.W. 39th Street
Miami, FL 33142
305-634-2465

Organized in 1942 to protect press freedom in the Americas, this association's membership aims at Latin American and Caribbean print journalists. It offers scholarships and awards to students and professionals and publishes the monthly "IAPA News."

583. International Association for Mass Communication Research
c/o Professor J. D. Halloran
Centre for Mass Communication Research
University of Leicester
104 Regent Road
Leicester LE1 7LT
United Kingdom

More than 1,000 members in 63 countries focus on journalism training and education and mass media research.

584. International Federation of Journalists
International Press Center
1 Boulevard Charlemagne
Boite 5
B-1041 Brussels
Belgium
(2) 230 6215

Focusing on freedom of the press issues, IFJ was founded in 1952 when it split with the International Organization of Journalists. It has more than 80,000 members internationally in affiliated unions (The Newspaper Guild in Canada and the United States, The National Union of Journalists in the United Kingdom). IFJ publishes a monthly newsletter and the annual "IFJ Information."

585. **International Federation of Newspaper Publishers, Federation Internationale des Editeurs de Journaux**
6 rue du Faubourg-Poissonniere
7510 Paris
France
(1) 45-23-38-88
An international organization of newspaper publishers in 34 nations, concentrating on ethical and economic issues and freedom of the press. It was founded in 1948 and publishes the "FIEJ Bulletin," "FIEJ-DOC," and "FIEJ-NOTES" in French and English.

586. **International Organization of Journalists/Organisation Internationale des Journalists**
Parizska 9
CS-110 01
Prague 1
Czechoslovakia
The IOJ is an international organization of national unions and journalists with Communist orientation. The International Federation of Journalists (see entry 584) was formed when it split with IOJ in the early 1950s. Publications include the monthly *Democratic Journalist*.

587. **International Press Institute**
Dilke House
1 Malet Street
London
WC1E 7JA
United Kingdom
01-636 0703/4
Newspaper editors, editorial directors, and managers of broadcast organizations worldwide who influence news and editorial policy are members. The IPI, founded in 1951, works to safeguard press freedom and improve the flow of news and information. It also conducts research and publishes the monthly *IPI Report*.

588. **International Society of Weekly Newspaper Editors**
Department of Journalism
Northern Illinois University
DeKalb, IL 60115
815-753-1925
This society, membership of which consists of editors and editorial writers employed at weekly newspapers, is responsible for the quarterly *Grassroots Editor* (entry 521) and a monthly newsletter. Founded in 1954, it sponsors the Golden Quill Editorial Award and the Eugene Cervi Award for local reporting and community service.

589. **Investigative Reporters and Editors**
P.O. Box 838
Columbia, MO 65205
314-882-2042
Founded in 1975, this organization includes reporters and editors, journalism educators, and students. It sponsors workshops and seminars focusing on investigative reporting techniques and public documents. Publications include the quarterly *IRE Journal* (entry 522), *The Investigative Journalist's Morgue* (entry 190) and *The IRE Books*. The IRE's Paul Williams Memorial Resource Center (entry 669) contains clip files and transcripts of television, newspaper, and magazine investigative reports. Membership count is 3,000.

590. **Journalism Education Association**
Box 99
Blue Springs, MO 64015
816-229-1666

This professional association of high school journalism teachers, publications advisers, and others interested in secondary school journalism aims to improve the quality and teaching of high school journalism. Founded in 1924, it sponsors journalism competitions, offers awards, and publishes the quarterly "Newswire" and *C:JET* (Communication: Journalism Education Today, entry 509).

591. Magazine Publishers Association
575 Lexington Avenue
New York, NY 10022
212-752-0055

This association, affiliated with the American Society of Magazine Editors (entry 557), consists of magazine publishers. It conducts seminars and workshops, maintains a library on the magazine industry, and oversees the Publishers Information Bureau.

592. Mass Communication Bibliographers
AEJMC
University of South Carolina
1621 College Street
Columbia, SC 29208-0251

Recognized in 1986 as a special interest group of the AEJMC, the Mass Communication Bibliographers organization seeks to improve bibliographic access to the mass communication literature by developing and evaluating reference materials, special collections, and instructional programs. Members also publish a newsletter. Manuscripts should be sent to: Dolores Jenkins, Library West, University of Florida, Gainesville, FL 32611.

593. National Academy of Television Arts and Sciences
110 West 57th Street
New York, NY 10019
212-586-8424

For television professionals actively involved in all aspects of the industry, this association of more than 14,000 members seeks to advance the television arts and sciences through workshops, seminars, and publications, and recognizes innovation and creativity in the industry. It awards the annual Emmy Awards and publishes *Television Quarterly* (entry 547). Its archives at UCLA contain more than 20,000 television programs.

594. National Association of Black Journalists
11600 Sunrise Valley Drive
Reston, VA 22091
703-648-1270

Print and broadcast journalists working in all aspects of news are members of this association founded in 1975. It also is a national job information clearinghouse, and maintains an archive of biographical information. Its published goals are to

> strengthen the ties between the black media and blacks in the white media; sensitize the white media to the institutional racism in its coverage; expand the white media's coverage and balanced reporting of the black community; become an exemplary group of professionals that honors excellence and outstanding achievement among black journalists.

It also publishes a quarterly newsletter.

595. National Association of Broadcasters
1771 N Street, N.W.
Washington, D.C. 20036
202-429-5300

Founded in 1922, members include representatives from television and radio stations and the networks; producers of equipment and programs are associate members. The NAB acts as a watchdog for government censorship and represents the industry on issues in broadcasting legislation. It publishes the weekly "NAB Today" and other publications on radio and broadcast engineering, confers the Distinguished Service Award, Grover Cobb Memorial Award, and Radio Award, and maintains a library (entry 692).

596. **National Association of Hispanic Journalists**
National Press Building
Suite 634
Washington, D.C. 20045
202-783-6228
Formed in 1984 to provide a forum and support for Hispanic journalists, the association works toward fair and unbiased treatment of Hispanics in the media, and encourages the study and practice of journalism by Hispanics. Members are professional journalists, educators, and students. It offers a job placement service as well as seminars and workshops. Publications include a monthly newsletter and an annual *National Directory of Hispanics in the Media*.

597. **National Association of Hispanic Publications**
c/o La Opinion
1436 South Main
Los Angeles, CA 90017
213-748-2141
With 20 state groups and six regional groups, the NAHP consists of publishers and editors of more than 100 Hispanic newspapers and magazines published in the United States. It conducts research, compiles statistics, and works to promote Hispanic media as a "valuable means of communication." The library subscribes to nearly 200 Hispanic newspapers and periodicals. Publications include the quarterly *Marketing Hispanic Print* and the semiannual *National Hispanic Media Directory*.

598. **National Broadcast Editorial Association (NBEA)**
6223 Executive Boulevard
Rockville, MD 20852
301-468-3959
Members of the NBEA include television and radio editorial writers, those who are responsible for editorial policies, and faculty members of journalism schools. The group seeks to improve the quality of broadcast editorials, and confers numerous awards, including the Editorial Excellence Awards and individual awards to television and radio stations airing outstanding editorials. It publishes the bimonthly *Editorialist*.

599. **National Cartoonists Society**
9 Ebony Court
Brooklyn, NY 11229
718-743-6510
More than 500 professional cartoonists are members of this organization founded in 1946. It publishes a monthly newsletter.

600. **National Conference of Editorial Writers**
6223 Executive Boulevard
Rockville, MD 20852
301-984-3015
Aimed at newspaper editorial writers in the United States and Canada as well as journalism educators, this organization is interested in raising the standards of editorial content and quality. It works with the National Association of Black Journalists (entry 594) and the National Association of Broadcasters (entry 595) to award the Wells Award for leadership. It also publishes *The Masthead* (entry 531).

601. **National Federation of Press Women, Inc.**
    P.O. Box 99
    Blue Springs, MO 64015
    816-229-1666
    More than 5,000 professional women and men involved in all aspects of communications are members. The organization, founded in 1937, offers journalism scholarships and an annual award to a woman of achievement in communications. It also publishes a monthly newsletter as well as the monthly *Press Woman*. There are approximately 5,000 members in 51 state groups.

602. **National Newspaper Association**
    1627 K Street, N.W.
    Suite 400
    Washington, D.C. 20006-1790
    202-466-7200
    Founded in 1855, this association's membershp consists of 5,000 editors and publishers of weekly and semiweekly newspapers and daily newspapers in small towns. It publishes the well-read *Publishers' Auxiliary* (entry 540), an annual *National Directory of Weekly Newspapers*, and the biweekly "News Media Update." The National Newspaper Foundation, which is composed of the board of directors of past presidents of the National Newspaper Association, offers educational training, seminars, conferences, journalism awards, and scholarships. It also oversees the National Blue Ribbon Newspaper Evaluation Program.

603. **National Newspaper Publishers Association**
    970 National Press Building
    Room 948
    Washington, D.C. 20045
    202-662-7324
    Membership consists of publishers of daily and weekly newspapers dedicated to promoting the black press. The Association sponsors an annual Distinguished Service Award to a black leader who has contributed significantly to black advancement and achievement. The NNPA was founded in 1940.

604. **National Press Club and National Press Foundation**
    529 14th Street, N.W.
    Washington, D.C. 20045
    202-662-7500
    The Press Club's membership of approximately 4,600 is comprised of print and broadcast journalists and others working in the news media. Nonvoting members include former journalists. The Club sponsors workshops on Washington reporting, seminars, social events, and journalism contests. The purpose of the National Press Foundation is to "further excellence in journalism," and it funds the National Press Club library and NPC journalism awards. The Foundation also awards grants to journalists studying media coverage of major news events, and awards the Sol Taishoff Award for excellence in broadcast journalism and Editor of the Year Award for excellence in print journalism. National Press Club speeches are broadcast on C-Span and indexed in the *Public Affairs Video Archives* catalog (entry 430). It also commissions research projects.

605. **National Press Photographers Association**
    3200 Croasdaile Drive
    Suite 306
    Durham, NC 27705
    919-383-7246
    News photographers and other professionals associated with photojournalism are members of this association of more than 9,000, founded in 1946. It conducts seminars and

an annual television/newsfilm workshop, as well as monthly and annual newsphoto and newsfilm contests. Winners are printed in its monthly publication *News Photographer* (entry 537). The NPPA also maintains a photojournalism library of videotapes, slides, and recordings.

606. National Scholastic Press Association

c/o Tom Rolnicki
620 Rarig Center
330 21st Avenue South
University of Minnesota
Minneapolis, MN 55455
612-625-8335

Publisher of *Scholastic Editor's Trends in Publications* (entry 544), the NSPA evaluates high school newspapers, magazines, and yearbooks. It was founded in 1921.

607. National Sportscasters and Sportswriters Association

Box 559
Salisbury, NC 28144
704-633-4275

Open to (obviously) sportscasters and sportswriters, this group of approximately 1,000 members maintains the National Sportscasters and Sportswriters Hall of Fame and confers awards for excellence in the field. It was founded in 1962.

608. Native American Press Association

c/o Mike Burgess
4391 Sunset Boulevard
Suite 533
Los Angeles, CA 90029

American Indian print journalists and editors are members of NAPA, which was formed in 1984. It publishes a quarterly newsletter, and offers educational programs.

609. Newspaper Association Managers

The Newspaper Center
Box 17407
Dulles Airport
Washington, D.C. 20041
703-648-1000

National, state, and regional newspaper association executives are members. This small group, founded in 1923, sponsors National Newspaper Week.

610. The Newspaper Guild

8611 Second Avenue
Silver Spring, MD 20910
301-684-5545

Affiliated with the AFL-CIO and the Canadian Labour Congress, the Newspaper Guild was founded in 1933 and is the largest union of journalists. It publishes *The Guild Reporter*.

611. Newspaper Research Council

1000 Two Ruan Center
601 Locust Street
Des Moines, IA 50309
515-245-3828

Research directors and marketing professionals in the newspaper industry who work to promote the use of newspaper research are members. The Council is in the process of building a newspaper research center, and currently conducts an annual research workshop. Its numerous publications include a bimonthly newsletter and semiannual "NRC Conference Notes."

612. **Organization of News Ombudsmen**
c/o Art Nauman
Sacramento Bee
21st and Q Streets
P.O. Box 15779
Sacramento, CA 95852
916-321-1000

Newspaper ombudsmen, often called reader advocates or public editors, are those who receive and investigate reader or viewer complaints and attempt to negotiate and settle disagreements. This group of approximately 50 is comprised of both newspaper and television ombudsmen. More than half of them write weekly columns for their newspapers or contribute monthly columns to trade publications. ONO column archives from January 1988 to the present are housed in the Eugene Patterson Library of The Poynter Institute for Media Studies (entry 704).

613. **Overseas Press Club of America**
310 Madison Avenue
Suite 2116
New York, NY 10017
212-983-4655

Foreign correspondents, editors, reporters, and photojournalists who are currently working or have worked overseas are eligible for membership. In addition, working newspeople with three consecutive years' foreign experience, freelance writers, and authors of foreign-affairs books are members. Founded in 1939, this is the only organization devoted exclusively to overseas reporters. It offers several awards, including the Robert Capa Award for exceptional courage and enterprise in photography overseas. Publications include a monthly "Bulletin." According to a December 1988 issue of *Quill*, the Overseas Press Club has been designated a "Historic Site in Journalism," and the Algonquin Hotel in New York (where the group first met informally) is listed as the founding site.

614. **Quill and Scroll Society**
c/o Richard P. Johns
School of Journalism and Mass Communication
University of Iowa
Iowa City, IA 52242
319-335-5795

This international honor society for high school journalism students, founded in 1926, boasts 1 million members and nearly 13,000 chapters in all 50 states and 40 foreign countries. It sponsors the National Writing/Photo Contest, and, through the Quill and Scroll Foundation, funds several scholarships and conducts research. In addition, it publishes *Quill and Scroll* (entry 542), handbooks, and a stylebook. The Quill and Scroll Foundation was established in 1940.

615. **Radio-Television Correspondents Association**
c/o Senate Radio-TV Gallery
U.S. Capitol, Room S-325
Washington, D.C. 20510
202-224-6421

Television and radio correspondents and reporters covering Congress make up this professional organization. Membership numbers about 2,400.

616. **Radio-Television News Directors Association**
1717 K Street, N.W.
Suite 615
Washington, D.C. 20006
202-659-6510
Aiming to improve the standards of electronic journalism, the RTNDA includes heads of broadcast, cable, and network news departments as well as other broadcast journalists, teachers, and public relations practitioners. It sponsors workshops and annual news reporting awards, and maintains a placement service. Publications include the biweekly newsletter "Intercom" and the monthly *Communicator* (entry 513). This professional society was founded in 1946 and lists approximately 3,000 members.

617. **Reporters Committee for Freedom of the Press**
800 18th Street, N.W.
Suite 300
Washington, D.C. 20006
202-466-6312
Dedicated to preserving First Amendment rights for all journalists involved in news media, this voluntary association offers free legal advice to reporters and sponsors in-house internships. In addition, it houses a small media law library and the Freedom of Information Service Center. (Call 800-336-4243 for the FOI Hotline.) Publications include the important quarterly publication *News Media and the Law* (entry 534) and the biweekly "News Media Update."

618. **Society of Newspaper Design**
The Newspaper Center
P.O. Box 17290
Dulles Airport
Washington, D.C. 20041
703-620-1083
More than 2,000 newspaper designers, art directors, artists, editors, and others involved in newspaper design are members of this international organization founded in 1979. It publishes *Design:* Journal of the Society of Newspaper Design (entry 516), the annual *Best of Newspaper Design* (entry 328), and a membership directory. In addition, it offers an online library of design data on CompuServe's JForum.

619. **Society of Professional Journalists**
53 West Jackson Boulevard
Suite 731
Chicago, IL 60604
312-922-7424
Formerly Sigma Delta Chi, The Society of Professional Journalists, this organization is now simply called The Society of Professional Journalists. It publishes the magazine *Quill* (entry 541) and several special reports on ethics and freedom of information. SPJ also sponsors the following awards: Distinguished Service Awards in Journalism, Eugene C. Pulliam Editorial Writing Fellowship, Frank Corrigan Internship at *Newsday*, and the Barney Kilgore Freedom of Information Internships in Washington, D.C. It conducts seminars such as the broadcasting-Taishoff Seminar for television news. (Sigma Delta Chi Foundation coordinates SPJ activities and funds scholarships and awards.) Founded in 1909, it lists nearly 20,000 members and more than 300 active chapters.

620. **Society of Publication Designers**
60 East 42nd Street
Suite 1130
New York, NY 10165
212-983-8585

Approximately 500 designers, graphic artists, art directors, and others involved in design of business and professional publications and newspapers are members of SPD. It publishes a bimonthly newsletter and the annual *Society of Publication Design*.

621. **Special Libraries Association**
   News Division
   1700 18th Street, N.W.
   Washington, D.C. 20009
   202-234-4700
   Members of the Special Libraries Association News Division include librarians and others affiliated with news libraries in newspapers, magazines, and television. A primary objective of the Division is to "develop the usefulness and efficiency of news media libraries." It publishes the quarterly *News Library News*.

622. **United Press International**
   1400 I Street, N.W.
   Washington, D.C. 20005
   202-898-8000
   This international wire service gathers news stories and photographs and disseminates them to member newspapers, radio and television stations, etc. UPI was formed in 1958 when United Press (founded in 1907) and the International News Service (1909) merged. It has more than 6,500 subscribers worldwide, and more than 200 local news bureaus in the United States.

623. **White House Correspondents Association**
   1067 National Press Building
   Washington, D.C. 20045
   202-737-2934
   More than 600 print and broadcast journalists covering the White House are members. It was founded in 1914.

624. **White House News Photographers Association**
   101½ South Union Station
   Alexandria, VA 22314
   703-683-2557
   Newspaper, magazine, wire service, and television news photographers who cover the White House and Congress are members of this association, founded in 1920. It publishes the *White House News Photographer* annual.

625. **Women in Communications, Inc.**
   P.O. Box 9561
   Austin, TX 78766
   512-346-9875
   This national professional organization for women and men involved in all aspects of print and broadcast journalism, communications, public relations, advertising, publishing, and photojournalism, was founded in 1909. WICI publishes *The Professional Communicator* bimonthly and a *Directory of Creative Communicators*. It also offers seminars and workshops.

626. **Women's Institute for Freedom of the Press**
   3306 Ross Place N.W.
   Washington, D.C. 20008
   202-966-7783
   The WIPF was founded in 1972, and focuses on women working in the media and women's issues in the media. It publishes the annual *Directory of Women's Media* (entry 268), *Women in Media: A Documentary Sourcebook*, and *Syllabus Sourcebook on Media and Women* (entry 458), and maintains a small library.

627. **World Press Freedom Committee**
The Newspaper Center
P.O. Box 17407
Washington, D.C. 20041
703-648-1000
Committee members include more than 30 communications organizations which defend press freedom and oppose state control of the media, with emphasis on Third World countries. It offers professional journalistic assistance, seminars, and workshops to Third World journalists.

628. **Youth Communication/National Center**
2025 Pennsylvania Avenue, N.W.
Washington, D.C. 20006
202-429-5292
Youth Communication is a national network of newspapers and news bureaus staffed by teenagers. This organization, founded in 1977, oversees Youth News Service (a news service focusing on issues of interest to young people) and Project Target: Recruiting Minority Youth for Journalism.

Specialty Associations

The following associations and societies, some appealing to more specific and/or narrowly defined activities, interests, and duties of journalists, are listed below. The focus of each is self-evident from its name.

Alpha Epsilon Rho (The National Broadcasting Society)
c/o Richard M. Uray
National Executive Secretary
College of Journalism
University of South Carolina
Columbia, SC 29208
803-777-6783

American Association of Sunday and Feature Editors
Box 17407
Dulles Airport
Washington, D.C. 20041
703-648-1109

American Auto Racing Writers and Broadcasters Association
922 North Pass Avenue
Burbank, CA 91505
818-842-7005

American Federation of Television and Radio Artists
1350 Avenue of the Americas
New York, NY 10019
212-265-7700

American Jewish Press Association
c/o Robert A. Cohn
St. Louis Jewish Light
12 Millstone Campus Drive
St. Louis, MO 63146
314-432-3353

American Sportscasters Association
150 Nassau Street
Room 1124
New York, NY 10038
212-227-8080

Art Directors Club
250 Park Avenue South
New York, NY 10003
212-674-0500

Association of Newspaper Classified Advertising Managers
P.O. Box 267
Danville, IL 61834
217-442-2057

Audit Bureau of Circulations (including the International Federation of Audit Bureaux of Circulations)
900 North Meacham Road
Schaumburg, IL 60173
312-885-0910

Baseball Writers Association of America
36 Brookfield Road
Fort Salonga, NY 11768
516-757-0562

**Broadcast Financial Management
    Association**
701 Lee Street
Suite 1010
Des Plaines, IL 60016
312-296-0200

**Broadcast Promotion and Marketing
    Executives, Inc.**
402 East Orange Street
Lancaster, PA 17602
717-397-5727

Canadian Association of Broadcasters
Box 627
Station B
Ottawa K1P 5S2
Canada
613-233-4035

**Canadian Circulation Managers
    Association**
P.O. Box 200
Owen Sound, Ontario N4K 5P2
Canada
416-376-2250

**Canadian Community Newspapers
    Association**
88 University Avenue
Suite 705
Toronto, Ontario M5J 1T6
Canada
416-598-4277

Canadian Managing Editors Conference
Box 5020
Ottawa, Ontario K2C 3M4
Canada
613-829-9100

Capital Press Club
P.O. Box 19403
Washington, D.C. 20036
202-429-5497

**Catholic Press Association of the United
    States and Canada**
119 North Park Avenue
Rockville Centre, NY 11570
516-766-3400

Chess Journalists of America
46 Robin Hill Drive
Naperville, IL 60540
312-717-1044

Corporation for Public Broadcasting
1111 16th Street, N.W.
Washington, D.C. 20036
202-293-6160

**Department of State Correspondents
    Association**
2201 C Street, N.W.
Room 2310
Washington, D.C. 20520
202-293-4650

Education Writers Association
1001 Connecticut Avenue, N.W.
Suite 310
Washington, D.C. 20036
202-429-9680

Fairness and Accuracy in Reporting (FAIR)
666 Broadway
Suite 400
New York, NY 10012
212-475-4640

Football Writers Association of America
Box 1022
Edmond, OK 73083
405-341-4731

Free Press Association
P.O. Box 15548
Columbus, OH 43215
614-236-1908

Gay and Lesbian Press Association
P.O. Box 8185
Universal City, CA 91608
213-877-1045

Hollywood Foreign Press Association
292 South La Cienega Boulevard
Suite 316
Beverly Hills, CA 90211
213-657-1731

Inland Daily Press Association
777 Busse Highway
Park Ridge, IL 60068-2462
312-696-1140

International Association of Business Communicators
870 Market Street
Suite 940
San Francisco, CA 94102
415-433-3400

International Circulation Managers Association
Box 17420
Dulles Airport
Washington, D.C. 20041
703-620-9555

International Motor Press Association
211 West 56th Street, #26J
New York, NY 10019

International Newspaper Advertising and Marketing Executives
P.O. Box 17210
Dulles Airport
Washington, D.C. 20041
703-620-0090

International Newspaper Financial Executives
P.O. Box 17573
Dulles Airport
Washington, D.C. 20041
703-620-6580

International Newspaper Marketing Association
P.O. Box 17422
Dulles Airport
Washington, D.C. 20041
703-648-1094

International Newspaper Promotion Association
P.O. Box 17422
Dulles Airport
Washington, D.C. 20041
703-620-9560

International Radio and Television Society
420 Lexington Avenue
New York, NY 10170
212-867-6650

International Television Association
6311 North O'Connor Road
LB 51
Irving, TX 75039
214-869-1112

Kappa Tau Alpha
c/o William H. Taft
107 Sondra Avenue
Columbia, MO 65202
314-443-3521

Media Access Project
2000 M Street, N.W.
4th Floor
Washington, D.C. 20036
202-232-4300

Media Alliance
Fort Mason
Building D
San Francisco, CA 94123
415-441-2557

Music Critics Association
6201 Tuckerman Lane
Rockville, MD 20852
301-530-9527

National Alliance of Third World Journalists
P.O. Box 43208
Columbia Heights
Washington, D.C. 20010
202-387-1662

National Association of Farm Broadcasters
P.O. Box 119
Topeka, KS 66601
913-272-3456

National Association of Media Women
1185 Niskey Lake Road S.W.
Atlanta, GA 30331
404-344-5862

National Association of Public Television Stations
1350 Connecticut Avenue, N.W.
Suite 200
Washington, D.C. 20036
202-887-1700

National Association of Real Estate Editors
P.O. Box 324
North Olmstead, OH 44070
216-779-1624

National Association of Science Writers
P.O. Box 294
Greenlawn, NY 11740
516-757-5664

National Entertainment Journalists Association
P.O. Box 24021
Nashville, TN 37202
615-256-4048

National Federation of Community Broadcasters
1314 14th Street, N.W.
Washington, D.C. 20005
202-797-8911

National News Bureau
2019 Chancellor Street
Philadelphia, PA 19103
215-569-0700

National Public Radio
2025 M Street, N.W.
Washington, D.C. 20036
202-822-2000

National Radio Broadcasters Association
2033 M Street, N.W.
Suite 506
Washington, D.C. 20036
202-466-2030

Newspaper Advertising Bureau, Inc.
1180 Avenue of the Americas
New York, NY 10036
212-921-5080

Newspaper Farm Editors of America
c/o Audrey Mackiewicz
Sanduskey Register
312 Valley View Drive
Huron, OH 44839
419-433-5412

Newspaper Features Council
Ward Castle
Comley Avenue
Rye Brook, NY 10573
914-939-3919

Newspaper Food Editors and Writers Association
c/o Dotty Griffith
Dallas Morning News
Communications Center
Dallas, TX 75265
214-977-8417

Outdoor Writers Association of America
2017 Cato Avenue
Suite 101
State College, PA 16801
814-234-1011

Overseas Writers
1067 National Press Building
Washington, D.C. 20045
202-737-2934

Professional Basketball Writers Association of America
c/o Bill Halls
26 Woodside Park
Pleasant Ridge, MI 48069
313-222-2260

Professional Football Writers of America
12042 Mereview Drive
St. Louis, MO 63146
314-997-7111

Professional Hockey Writers Association
c/o Walter L. MacPeek
55 Forest Avenue
Verona, NJ 07044
201-857-2817

Professional Soccer Reporters Association
c/o John Leptich
1717 Waterville Lane
Schaumburg, IL 60194
312-490-0196

Radio-Television News Directors of Canada
7 Brightbay Circle
Thornhill, Ontario L3T 1C2
Canada
416-889-6070

Religion Newswriters Association
c/o Helen Parmley
Dallas Morning News
Communications Center
Dallas, TX 75265
214-977-8489

Society for Collegiate Journalists
c/o Dr. J. Douglas Tarpley
Institute of Journalism
CBN University
Virginia Beach, VA 23463
804-424-7000, x.4247

Society of the Silurians
164 Lexington Avenue
New York, NY 10016
212-532-0887

Society of Typographic Arts
233 East Ontario
Suite 500
Chicago, IL 60611
312-787-2018

Southern Interscholastic Press Association
c/o Beth B. Dickey
College of Journalism
University of South Carolina
Columbia, SC 29208
803-777-6284

Southern Newspaper Publishers Association
P.O. Box 28875
Atlanta, GA 30328
404-256-0444

Suburban Newspapers of America
111 East Wacker Drive
Chicago, IL 60601
312-644-6610

Television Critics Association
c/o R. D. Heldentels
Schenectady Gazette
332 State Street
Schenectady, NY 12301
518-374-4141

Type Directors Club
60 East 42nd Street
Suite 1130
New York, NY 10165
212-983-6042

United Nations Correspondents Association
Press Section, Room C-314
United Nations Secretariat
New York, NY 10017
212-963-7611

United States Basketball Writers Association
c/o Joseph F. Mitch
Missouri Valley Conference
200 North Broadway
Suite 1905
St. Louis, MO 63102
314-421-0339

U.S. Marine Corps Combat Correspondents Association
4250 Pacific Highway
#122-A
San Diego, CA 92110
619-223-2483

13
Selected Research Centers, Archives, and Media Institutes

Newspaper libraries, for the most part, are not included here. Please consult the *International Directory of News Libraries* (entry 298) and *Newspaper Libraries in the U.S. and Canada* (entry 269) for detailed information on news libraries. Archives and papers of individual journalists are excluded. (For further information on archives, see Lucy Caswell's *Guide to Sources in American Journalism History* [entry 15].) Those interested only in broadcasting might also consult *A Directory of Broadcast Archives* (entry 295). Addresses of selected foundations are included here as well. For a comprehensive listing of funds and scholarships, see the *Journalism Career and Scholarship Guide* (entry 303).

629. **ABC News Information Center**
7 West 66th Street
New York, NY 10023
212-887-3796
Research hours: For in-house use only. Not open to public.
A relatively small collection of 6,000 books and vertical clip files, this center was founded in 1945. It focuses on broadcast journalism, news, and documentary.

630. **Academy of Arts and Sciences**
UCLA Television Archives
Department of Theatre Arts
504 Hilgard Avenue
Los Angeles, CA 90024
213-206-8013
Research hours: Tuesday-Friday, 9a.m.-5p.m. Call or write for appointment.
Focusing on television programming, the Television Archives contains more than 20,000 programs representing all genres and time periods. There is a printed catalog of holdings as well as a card catalog organized by title.

631. **Alfred I. duPont/Columbia University Awards in Broadcast Journalism**
701 Journalism
Columbia University
New York, NY 10027
212-280-5047
Research hours: Monday-Friday, 9a.m.-5p.m. Please call or write for appointment.

The duPont/Columbia University Award winners in local news, national news, and public affairs from 1968 to the present are housed here in ¾-inch format.

632. Alicia Patterson Foundation
1001 Pennsylvania Avenue, N.W.
Suite 1250
Washington, D.C. 20004
301-951-8512

The Alicia Patterson Fellowship program is designed for professional journalists seeking to "pursue independent projects of significant interest." One-year grants are awarded.

633. Alternative Press Collection
Special Collections Department
Homer Babbidge Library
University of Connecticut
369 Fairfield Road
Storrs, CT 06268
203-486-2524

Research hours: Monday-Friday, 9a.m.-noon, 1p.m.-5p.m. (during academic year). Call for information.

Founded in the late 1960s, this special collection maintains more than 3,500 newspaper and magazine titles (of those, 400 are current subscriptions), 5,000 books and pamphlets, and nearly 3,000 pamphlet files, posters, buttons, and manuscripts. Publications focusing on the women's movement, civil rights, the peace movement and the Vietnam War, and the environment comprise the bulk of the collection, although publications of the conservative right (*Phyllis Schlafly Report*) and radical right (John Birch Society, Accuracy in Media publications) are well represented. Also located here is the Students for a Democratic Society Radical Education Project of handouts and tabloids which was the core of the original Alternative Press Collection. The main library card catalog and an additional catalog in the Special Collections Department allow access to books and pamphlets. Newspapers and journals are included in the main library's serial holdings list. There also is a printed catalog (entry 405).

634. American Antiquarian Society Library
185 Salisbury Street
Worcester, MA 01609
508-755-5221

Research hours: Monday-Friday, 9a.m.-1p.m.

When studying the history of early American journalism, the Antiquarian Society Library is a key resource. It is the source of Readex Corporation's *Early American Imprints, 1639-1800*, a microform edition of every extant book, pamphlet, and broadside printed in the United States (see Brigham's *History and Bibliography of American Newspapers, 1690-1820*, entry 406). The Society also houses the most comprehensive collection of pre-1921 American newspapers in the United States, and Readex is currently producing this collection on microfilm in a series entitled *Early American Newspapers, 1704-1821*. There also are extensive collections of amateur newspapers, and Bolivian, Chilean, and West Indian newspapers.

635. American Newspaper Publishers Association Library
The Newspaper Center
11600 Sunrise Valley Drive
Reston, VA 22091
703-648-1090

Research hours: Open to public by appointment. Call or write for information (Box 17407, Dulles Airport, Washington, D.C. 20041).

All aspects of newspaper publishing are covered in this collection of books, periodicals, documents, and files. The library also collects special editions of newspapers, including anniversary and final editions. Holdings are especially strong in the areas of newspaper management, history, biography, and press law. In addition, it serves as a clearinghouse for information on newspaper librarianship. See also the American Newspaper Publishers Association (entry 555).

636. **American Press Institute**
11690 Sunrise Valley Drive
Reston, VA 22091
703-620-3611
Founded in 1946, this nonprofit organization offers five-day and nine-day seminars for working newspaper journalists in "all phases of newspaper operation," including writing and editing, graphics, photography, circulation, advertising, management, copy editing, marketing, and promotion. In order to attend an API seminar, one must be nominated by a principal executive or his or her newspaper. A recent catalog listed more than 35 seminars, including those offered in programs in Canada and on the East Coast.

637. **Annenberg School of Communication**
University of Pennsylvania
3440 Market Street
Philadelphia, PA 19104
215-898-7041
Research hours: Archives not open to public.
Though the archives are for in-house use only, the Annenberg School has made significant contributions to the literature of television by reporting on the social aspects of broadcasting. The library (3620 Walnut Street, C-5, Philadelphia, PA 19104, 215-898-7027) is open to the public for reference use only, and arrangements must be made in advance. Here one can find several special collections such as annual reports of United States public television stations and major communications companies. The book and periodical communication collection emphasizes methodology and research.

638. **Bettman Newsphotos, UPI and Reuter Photo Libraries**
902 Broadway
New York, NY 10010
212-777-6200
Research hours: Call or write in advance for appointment.
Bettman Newsphotos, part of the Bettman Archives, offers the photographic collection of United Press International from 1907 to the present; International News Photos, 1912-1958; Acme Newspictures, 1923-1960; Pacific and Atlantic Photos, 1925-1930; and Reuters from 1985 to the present. In addition, the Bettman Archives contains the Underwood and Underwood Collection of feature and news photography from 1880-1955 and the *New York Daily Mirror* collection from 1947-1961. Professionals in communications, advertising, film, and television may research in Bettman offices or they may request pictures by mail, telephone, or telex. There is a research fee.

639. **Billy Rose Theatre Collection**
Performing Arts Research Center
New York Public Library
111 Amsterdam Avenue
New York, NY 10023
212-870-1639
Research hours: Monday and Thursday, 10a.m.-7:45p.m.; Tuesday and Saturday, 10a.m.-5:45p.m.; Wednesday-Friday, noon-5:45p.m. Photo research closes at 5:30p.m. Monday-Saturday. Researchers should call or write for appointment.

This is the official repository of the American Television Society's archives, although better known for its comprehensive collection on film studies. There are clip files on radio and television programs, and books include standard works on broadcasting history.

640. **Black Press Archives, Moorland-Spingarn Research Center**
Howard University
Washington, D.C. 20059
202-636-7239
Research hours: Monday-Thursday, 9a.m.-8:45p.m. Call for information.
The Black Press Archives is a repository for hundreds of black newspapers. In addition to the black newspapers received on subscription, the Archives also works in cooperation with publishers who send copies of their newspapers to be microfilmed.

641. **British Film Institute, Library Services**
127 Charing Cross Road
London WC2H OEA
United Kingdom
Research hours: Call or write for information. A BFI membership may be required for extended use.
The British Film Institute offers one of the largest collections available on television. In addition to books and reports, there are more than 1,600 periodicals (the library currently receives more than 400 titles) on all aspects of television. A card catalog provides access by subject, author, title, personality, and program. Special collections include material on the BBC series "Twenty Four Hours," and the Labour Party Media Policy Committee. The collection is described in *TV Documentation: A Guide to BFI Library Services Resources* (entry 410).

642. **Broadcast Pioneers Library, Broadcasting Industry Reference Center**
1771 N Street, N.W.
Washington, D.C. 20036
202-223-0088
Research hours: Monday-Friday, 9a.m.-5p.m. Call or write for appointment.
Numerous special collections on radio and television broadcasting history can be found here, ranging from the Communications Bar Association Archives to the *St. Louis Post-Dispatch* Photo Collection. Also located here is the Group W Collection containing the Washington News Bureau Sound Archive. There are oral histories, interviews with broadcasters and photographers, more than 3,000 books, and 2,000 pamphlets. The library publishes a quarterly newsletter and a holdings list. See also Broadcast Pioneers (entry 571).

643. **Canadian Broadcasting Corporation, Reference Library**
365 Church Street
Station A, Box 500
Toronto, Ontario M5W 1E6
Canada
416-975-3244
Research hours: Open to serious researchers studying the CBC or Canadian broadcasting. Call or write for information.
Radio and television broadcasting is the focus of this collection of more than 12,000 books, 200 journal subscriptions, and 8,000 newspaper clip files. For further information on the CBC, consult the National Archives of Canada (entry 691). The Canadian Radio and Television Division Library in Ottawa (613-997-4225) may also provide useful information.

644. **CBS News Audio Archives**
524 West 57th Street
New York, NY 10019
212-975-6489
Research hours: The archives are closed to all outside researchers. For internal use only.
More than 200,000 audiotapes of CBS News special reports, political conventions, daily news broadcasts, and Presidential addresses are located here. Because these materials are for in-house use only, researchers should consult the Motion Picture, Sound, and Video Branch of the National Archives (entry 689).

645. **CBS News Reference Library**
524 West 57th Street
New York, NY 10019
212-975-2877
Research hours: Serious researchers may call or write for appointment.
Founded in 1940, this library holds CBS News program transcripts. In addition to thousands of clip files, there are approximately 30,000 books in the news library covering radio, television, current events, and government. Services such as photocopying and interlibrary loan are provided.

646. **Center for Communication, Inc.**
30 Rockefeller Plaza
Floor 53
New York, NY 10020
212-836-2000
Research hours: Monday-Friday, 9a.m.-5p.m.
The Center, founded in 1980, is a nonprofit organization supported by the communications industry. Its aim is to bring together students in university communication programs with leading media professionals. It offers one-day workshops and seminars in advertising and marketing, broadcasting, design, photography, journalism, new technology, public relations, publishing, theater, and film. The Center publishes a small catalog listing seminar transcripts and videotapes available. In the past, seminars have ranged from "Vietnam Revisited: How CBS Covered the War" to "The Editorial Page: What to Cover: Choosing a Point of View."

647. **Center for Foreign Journalists**
11690-A Sunrise Valley Drive
Reston, VA 22091
703-620-5984
Research hours: Monday-Friday, 9a.m.-5p.m. Call for information.
The Center, founded in 1985 by Thomas Winship, former editor of the *Boston Globe*; James D. Ewing, international press consultant; and George A. Krimsky, former news editor of World Services for the Associated Press, provides workshops, seminars, and consulting and information services for foreign journalists. In addition to acquainting visitors with the United States media, the Center offers orientation programs for American journalists interested in the media overseas. Workshops range in length from three days to four weeks, and may focus on fundamentals of reporting and writing or specialized reporting techniques. The Center also publishes the *CFJ Directory* (entry 275).

648. **Center for Investigative Reporting**
530 Howard Street
2d Floor
San Francisco, CA 94105
415-543-1200

Founded in 1977, this nonprofit organization conducts workshops and seminars on investigative reporting. Center publications include *The Bhopal Syndrome, Raising Hell: How the Center for Investigative Reporting Gets the Story*, and *Raising Hell, A Citizen's Guide to the Fine Art of Investigative Reporting.*

649. **Center for War, Peace, and the News Media, New York University**
     10 Washington Place
     4th Floor
     New York, NY 10003
     212-998-7960
     This organization, founded in 1985, focuses on media coverage of arms control and United States-Soviet Union relations. According to the Center, its "extensive monitoring activities have already established its archive of international security reporting, both print and broadcast, as the largest outside of the Pentagon." The Center publishes the bimonthly *Deadline*, conference proceedings, and occasional papers such as "Uneasy Allies: The Press and the Government During the Cuban Missile Crisis" and "Narrative Strategy and Nuclear News."

650. **Communications Library, University of Illinois**
     122 Gregory Hall
     810 South Wright Street
     Urbana, IL 61801
     217-333-2216
     Research hours: Call or write for information.
     One of the finest communications collections in existence, this library collects books and periodicals on advertising and public relations as well as broadcasting, mass communications, magazines, newspapers, communication, photography, and typography. Emphasis is on television systems and programs, history, and communication theory and effect. The D'Arcy Collection, advertisements appearing in magazines and newspapers from the late 1800s to 1960 (clips from 1960 to 1980 will be added at a later date), is located here. Communications librarian Diane Carothers annotates a quarterly acquisitions list, "New Books in the Communications Library," and distributes it to interested organizations and individuals. Library holdings are listed in a large catalog (entry 414).

651. **Council for the Advancement of Science Writing**
     4 Billingham Street
     Somerville, MA 02144
     617-625-2791
     This nonprofit educational organization focuses on the quality of science and medical writing as well as the relationship between the media and scientific community. The council of scientists and journalists organizes seminars, fellowships, and other programs, and publishes *A Guide to Careers in Science Writing*. Journalists seeking training in science writing may wish to contact the Council.

652. **Dow Jones Newspaper Fund**
     P.O. Box 300
     Princeton, NJ 08540
     609-452-2820
     The Dow Jones Newspaper Fund publishes the *Journalism Career and Scholarship Guide* (entry 303).

653. **Editor & Publisher Library**
     11 West 19th Street
     New York, NY 10011
     212-675-4380
     Research hours: By appointment only. Call or write for information.

Founded in 1884, this small collection houses bound volumes of *Editor & Publisher* (entry 517) from 1900 to the present. In addition, there are books on the newspaper industry and subscriptions to approximately 90 journals.

654. **Eric Sevareid Journalism Library**
School of Journalism and Mass Communication
University of Minnesota
121 Murphy Hall
206 Church Street, S.E.
Minneapolis, MN 55455
612-625-7892
Research hours: Open to public. Call or write for information.
The Eric Sevareid papers on 29 reels of microfilm are available here. There also are books, periodicals, pamphlets, and theses on mass communications, newspaper and magazine journalism, broadcasting, media management, graphics, and international communication. All holdings are listed in the main library's catalog.

655. **Foundation for American Communications**
Journalism Program
3800 Barnham Boulevard
Los Angeles, CA 90068
213-851-7372
Established in 1976, the Foundation offers programs in journalism and business, and provides seminars and forums "to help improve the quality of information flowing from sources through the news process to the public." According to FACS, its scope of programs for journalists "has widened to include the law, journalism ethics, international affairs, science, agriculture and environmental issues." It publishes reports and manuals such as *Media Resource Guide* and *Human Heart Replacement: A New Challenge for Physicians and Reporters*.

656. **Freedom of Information Center**
P.O. Box 858
Columbia, MO 65205
314-882-4856
Research hours: Monday-Friday, 8a.m.-5p.m.
Located within the University of Missouri School of Journalism, the FOI Center studies on a daily basis "actions by government, media and society affecting movement and content of information." Established in 1958, the FOI Library acts as a First Amendment clearinghouse, and indexes and files information and documentation on access laws, press freedom, libel, student press, and censorship. Journalists with research questions and problems may contact the Center.

657. **Fund for Investigative Journalism, Inc.**
1755 Massachusetts Avenue, N.W.
Washington, D.C. 20036
202-462-1844
The Fund for Investigative Journalism awards grants to professional journalists "to enable them to report abuses of authority or the malfunctioning of institutions that harm the public."

658. **Gannett Center for Media Studies**
Columbia University
Journalism Building
2950 Broadway
New York, NY 10027
212-280-8392
Research hours: Open to Gannett professionals only but will mail information (reports, brochures, etc.) on request.

An institute for advanced study of mass communication, the Gannett Center "seeks to enhance media professionalism, foster greater public understanding of how the media work, strengthen journalism education and examine the effects on society of mass communication and communications technology." It is operated by the Gannett Foundation and publishes the *Gannett Center Journal*, a newsletter, and numerous occasional papers, working papers, and conference reports.

659. Gannett Foundation

Lincoln Tower
Rochester, NY 14604
The Foundation operates the Gannett Center for Media Studies and awards minority, research, professional, and career development grants in journalism.

660. Gannett Urban Journalism Center

Medill School of Journalism
Northwestern University
Evanston, IL 60201
312-908-5692
Research hours: Open only to affiliates of Northwestern.
With financial support from the Ford Foundation and Gannett Newspaper Foundation, the Urban Journalism Center offers continuing education and training seminars in management for professional journalists. There are off-campus seminars and conferences, and short courses for publishers and editors.

661. George Arents Research Library for Special Collections

E. S. Bird Library
Syracuse University
Syracuse, NY 13244-2010
315-423-2585
Research hours: Restrictions apply. Call or write for information.
This massive collection of rare books (more than 120,000 volumes), manuscripts, and audio archive includes manuscripts on news photography, newspapers, editing, reporting, columnists, foreign correspondents, and personalities in radio and television. The papers of journalist and photographer Margaret Bourke-White, for example, are housed here. The American Literature collection also includes papers of nonfiction authors.

662. George Foster Peabody Collection

Media Library
School of Journalism and Mass Communication
University of Georgia
Athens, GA 30602
404-542-7462
Research hours: Monday-Thursday, 8a.m.-10p.m.; Friday, 8a.m.-5p.m.; Saturday, 9a.m.-5p.m.; Sunday, 1p.m.-10p.m.; Archival material available Monday-Friday, 8a.m.-5p.m.; Saturday, 9a.m.-5p.m. Call or write for appointment.
The George Foster Peabody Radio and Television Awards for Distinguished Achievements and Meritorious Public Service program was begun in 1940, and more than 17,000 radio and television programs' entries in the contest since then are stored here. The collection is restricted to use by scholars. There is an in-house card catalog.

663. Gilbert M. and Martha H. Hitchcock Center for Graduate Study and Professional Journalism Development

University of Nebraska
Lincoln, NE 68588
402-472-3045
Research hours: Most of the collection is available in the university library, but researchers may call for appointment with the Center.

In addition to financing the graduate program in the College of Journalism, the Center focuses on professional development of Nebraska's working journalists. It is named for Gilbert Hitchcock, a United States senator from Nebraska and founder of the *Omaha World-Herald*. The Center offers workshops in advertising, broadcasting, and newswriting, and supports some research projects.

664. **Graduate School of Journalism Library, University of California, Berkeley**
140 North Gate Hall
Berkeley, CA 94720
415-642-0415
Research hours: Restrictions apply. Call or write for information.
A 225-volume collection of major authors (significant journalists or authors who have written significantly on the subject of journalism) is included in this small collection of books, periodicals, and theses on print journalism, photojournalism, and broadcasting. Some of those major authors include Walter Lippman, H. L. Mencken, Lincoln Steffens, David Halberstam, George Orwell, and A. J. Liebling. Books by and about the authors are included.   .

665. **H. L. Mencken Library**
National Press Club
National Press Foundation
529 14th Street, N.W.
Washington, D.C. 20045
202-662-7523
Research hours: Scholars may use on a fee basis. Call or write for information.
This print and broadcast journalism collection, founded in 1984, contains more than 5,000 books and the archives of the National Press Club (entry 604). There also are special photograph collections.

666. **Hoover Institution on War, Revolution and Peace**
Stanford University
Stanford, CA 94305
415-723-2058
Research hours: Monday-Friday, 8a.m.-5p.m.; Saturday, 9a.m.-5p.m.
There are numerous special collections at the Hoover Institution, including the papers of Herbert Solow, editor of *Fortune* from 1945-1964; papers of Mark Sullivan, editor of *Collier's Weekly* from 1912-1919 and columnist for the *New York Herald-Tribune* from 1923-1952 (includes correspondence, diaries, speeches, writings, memorabilia 1883-1952, 62 manuscript boxes, etc.); and the papers of Karl von Wiegand, Hearst newspaper foreign correspondent 1917-1961. The New Left Politics Collection contains underground and alternative newspapers.

667. **Institute of Communications Research**
College of Communications
University of Illinois, Urbana-Champaign
Urbana, IL
217-333-1549
Research hours: The Institute does not have a separate library collection, but researchers may consult with faculty and use the university library by appointment.
The Institute administers the doctoral program in communications and conducts research in communications, with emphasis on cultural and media studies, effects of mass communications, and the political economy of communications. This is one of the most distinguished research centers in the country.

668. **Institute of Culture and Communication**
CPCC
Resource Materials Collection
John A. Burns Hall
Room 4063
University of Hawaii
Honolulu, HI 96848
808-944-7345
Research hours: Restrictions apply. Call or write for information.
Researchers interested in mass media and international relations will want to consult this collection of approximately 14,000 books, 12,000 documents, and various reports and conference papers. Other subjects covered in this collection include communication and economic development and multicultural issues.

669. **Investigative Reporters and Editors, Inc., Paul Williams Memorial Resource Center**
University of Missouri
Box 838
Columbia, MO 65205
314-882-2042
Research hours: Restrictions apply. Call or write for information.
This is a unique collection of books on and examples of investigative reporting. Investigative reports and articles from United States and Canadian newspapers, magazines, radio, and television are housed here. For more information on IRE, see entry 589.

670. **The Joan Shorenstein Barone Center on the Press, Politics and Public Policy**
The John F. Kennedy School of Government, Harvard University
79 John F. Kennedy Street
Cambridge, MA 02138
617-495-8269
Focusing on the interaction and intersection of media and government, this academic center conducts research, provides mid-career fellowships, publishes reports, and sponsors a public lecture series. It was established in 1986 and named for political journalist Barone, who was producer of "Face the Nation" and "The CBS Evening News with Dan Rather" in Washington.

671. **The John Temple Collection**
Journalism Centre
University of Queensland
St. Lucia. 4067. Queensland
Australia
Australian journalist John Temple died in 1984 and the University of Queensland established this collection in his name. According to Bruce Grundy, coordinator of Journalism Studies, in a 1984 issue of *Australian Journalism Review*, "The intention of the Collection is to provide books, films, videotapes, audiotapes and examples of good journalism of all kinds for students to study, analyse or simply digest. Donations to help set up the collection are being sought from journalists, media organisations and the public."

672. **Journalism/Law Institute, School of Journalism, Michigan State University**
East Lansing, MI 48824
517-353-6405
Research hours: Call Todd Simon for information.
The Institute was established to address and research common areas of concern to the mass media, courts, and the legal profession. It also sponsors seminars and workshops on First Amendment issues.

673. **Journalism Library (Weil), Indiana University**
Ernie Pyle Hall
Seventh Street
Bloomington, IN 47405
812-335-3517
Research hours: Call or write for information.

In addition to housing the Ernie Pyle collection of columns and memorabilia, the Indiana University Journalism Library contains more than 14,000 volumes on journalism and mass communication. The library also holds the Roy Howard Archive. This is one of the most comprehensive journalism collections to be found, with exceptional holdings in media law, broadcasting, and print journalism. It would behoove serious researchers to schedule some time in Indiana.

674. **Journalism Library and Library for Communication and Graphic Arts, Ohio State University**
242 West 18th Avenue
Columbus, OH 43210-1107
614-292-8747; 614-292-0538
Research hours: Open for reference use only. Call or write for information and hours.

A large journalism collection, this library subscribes to more than 80 newspapers and 200 journals. There are more than 24,000 books on radio, television, newspapers, magazines, photography, motion pictures, and public relations. The Library for Communication and Graphic Arts is named for Milton Caniff, the 1930 Ohio State graduate who created the "Steve Canyon" comic strip. (The School of Journalism also sponsors the Kiplinger Graduate Program in Public Affairs Reporting.)

675. **Journalism Library, School of Journalism, University of Missouri**
117 Walter Williams Hall
Columbia, MO 65201-5149
314-882-7502
Research hours: Monday-Thursday, 8a.m.-10p.m.; Friday, 8a.m.-5p.m.; Saturday, 1p.m.-5p.m.; Sunday, 1p.m.-10p.m.

Serious researchers should not bypass this substantial journalism collection. With more than 21,000 books and subscriptions to 450 periodicals on broadcasting, newspapers and magazines, media management, photography, and typography, it is among the most comprehensive. According to the March 1989 *Mass Communications Bibliographers' Newsletter*, the University of Missouri "recently completed a project to preserve on microfilm issues of underground newspapers not known to have been preserved on film." The Freedom of Information Center (entry 656) is a division of the library.

676. **Journalism Library, William Allen White School of Journalism, University of Kansas**
210 Flint Hall
Lawrence, KS 66045-2800
913-854-4755
Research hours: Call for information.

This collection focuses on newspaper journalism, mass communications, broadcasting, and graphic arts.

677. **Knight Foundation**
One Cascade Plaza
Eighth Floor
Akron, OH 44308
216-253-9301

The Knight Foundation funds the John F. Knight Fellowships for Professional Journalists, the Knight-Bagehot Fellowships in Economics and Journalism, and the Knight Science Journalism Fellowships.

678. **Library of Congress, Manuscript Division**
Washington, D.C. 20540
202-707-5387
Research hours: Monday-Saturday, 8:30a.m.-5p.m.
The papers of Roy W. Howard (1883-1964), president and chairman of the board of Scripps-Howard, are filed here and cover the years 1923-1964. There are more than 85,000 items in this collection. Also housed here are papers of Joseph Wood Krutch, Joseph Alsop of *The New York Herald-Tribune*, and Stuart Hensley.

679. **Library of Congress, Motion Pictures, Broadcasting and Recorded Sound Division**
Thomas Jefferson Building
Room 1053
2nd Street and Independence Avenue, S.E.
Washington, D.C. 20540
202-287-5840
Research hours: Call or write for appointment.
The American Forces Radio and Television Service (AFRTS) Collection contains disc recordings transferred to the Library as early as 1945, as well as selected wartime broadcasts. The complete AFRTS radio program package is available from 1967 on. The NBC Radio Collection contains broadcast recordings of NBC radio programs, 1933-1970, which are duplicated at The Museum of Broadcasting (entry 690). There also are recordings, videotapes, and films of "Meet the Press" from 1949-1975, papers of its producer Lawrence E. Spivak, CBS News programs and documentaries from 1950 on, more than 18,000 documentary and entertainment television and kinescope titles, and more than 1 million radio recordings, including NBC News programs from 1937 on. A catalog entitled *Radio Broadcasts in the Library of Congress, 1924-1941: A Catalog of Recordings* (entry 434) is available.

680. **Library of Congress, Prints and Photographs Division**
Washington, D.C. 20540
202-707-6394
Research hours: Monday-Friday, 8:30a.m.-5p.m.
Look magazine's photographic files (1937-1971) and *U.S. News and World Report*'s files (1955-1985) are maintained here. In addition, there are thousands of negatives, transparencies, and prints from the Farm Security Administration documentation project and more than 100,000 negatives from the first news photograph service (Bain News Service). The International Center of Photography in New York also collects materials of interest to photojournalists.

681. **Library of Congress, Serial and Government Publications Division**
Washington, D.C. 20540
202-707-5647
Research hours: Monday-Friday, 8:30a.m.-9p.m.; Saturday, 8:30a.m.-5p.m.; Sunday, 1p.m.-5p.m.
The Library of Congress maintains one of the largest collections of newspapers in the world. Included are 850,000 unbound issues, 75,000 bound volumes, 270,000 microfilm reels, 12,000 microprint cards of early American newspapers 1704-1820, and 1,500 titles currently received (500 from the United States and 1,000 from foreign countries). It publishes a biennial catalog entitled *Newspapers Received Currently in the Library of Congress*. There also is an Alternative Press Collection of approximately 350 titles from more than 25 states containing alternative or underground American newspapers from the mid-1960s to the present.

682. **The Media Institute**
3017 M Street, N.W.
Washington, D.C. 20007
202-298-7512
Research hours: Monday-Friday, 9a.m.-5p.m.
This nonprofit research facility was founded in 1976 "to encourage and promote the development of knowledge and understanding of American media and communications." Research is conducted on news coverage and First Amendment issues. The conservative Institute also publishes *Business and the Media*, and sponsors occasional seminars for journalists.

683. **Media Laboratory**
Massachusetts Institute of Technology
20 Ames Street
Cambridge, MA 02139
617-253-0300
Research hours: Call for information.
This center for advanced study and research in new information technologies and communications media opened in 1985. The Media Lab's "interdisciplinary laboratory" consists of groups in electronic publishing, learning research, advanced television, computer music, spatial imaging, graphics, human-machine interface, telecommunications, film and video, computer graphics and animation, and computers and entertainment. Projects include NewsPeek, an electronic newspaper composed of wire service news and television news broadcasts.

684. **Media Management and Economics Resource Center, School of Journalism and Mass Communication, University of Minnesota**
111 Murphy Hall
206 Church Street, S.E.
Minneapolis, MN 55455
612-625-9531
Research hours: Call for information.
Established in 1985, this center gathers and disseminates information on teaching media management and economics to media professionals and students. It is the first computer-based resource of its kind. The Center also has produced a media management bibliography (entry 21).

685. **Media Research Bureau, School of Journalism, University of Missouri, Columbia**
P.O. Box 838
Columbia, MO 65205
314-882-3396
Research hours: Call or write for information regarding services and charges.
This nonprofit center offers audience and market research services to print and broadcast media and advertising companies. In addition, it assists faculty and graduate students in media research projects. Research methods employed include surveys, telephone interviews, and Q-studies. The MRB also conducts research projects for the *Columbia Missourian* and *Weekly Missourian*, such as readership surveys and circulation analyses.

686. **Media Resource Service, Scientists' Institute for Public Information**
355 Lexington Avenue
New York, NY 10017
800-223-1730; 212-661-9110 in New York state
Research hours: Call or write for information on telephone hours.
This free referral service for expert sources in the areas of science, technology, and medicine maintains an online file of more than 20,000 experts. The Service takes calls from

any member of the working press (use the toll-free number), and is sponsored by the Scientists' Institute for Public Information, a nonprofit organization interested in improving "public understanding of science and technology." Users of this service should keep in mind that

> no one is excluded from the MRS files, because SIPI does not believe it has the authority to decide who qualifies as a scientific expert and who does not. However, the MRS questionnaires ask for detailed descriptions of educational background, positions held, areas of specialization, society and committee memberships, and recent publications. This information usually speaks for itself.

The MRS was founded in 1980.

687. **Media Studies Project, Woodrow Wilson International Center for Scholars**
Smithsonian Institution Building
Washington, D.C. 20560
202-357-2429
Established in 1988, this project focuses on media research, with emphasis on newspapers, magazines, and television, and offers research fellowships. Publications include the *Wilson Quarterly* anthology.

688. **Mississippi Department of Archives and History**
Special Collections Section
Newsfilm Collection
P.O. Box 571
Jackson, MS 39205
601-359-1424
Research hours: By appointment only. Call or write for information.
More than 1.5 million feet of television newsfilm from 1954-1971 is held in these Mississippi archives. Most is footage from WLBT, the NBC affiliate in Jackson, thus offering documentation of the Civil Rights years. This collection is all the more important because WLBT was the only commercial television affiliate in the United States to lose its FCC license on the grounds that its news coverage of blacks was biased and otherwise unfair. The Archives can provide videotaped copies of newsfilm for classroom use, and interested persons are asked to contact the Archives. There is a published guide to the collection, *Newsfilm Index: A Guide to the Newsfilm Collection, 1954-1971* (entry 411). The Archives continues to collect WLBT newsfilm.

689. **Motion Picture, Sound, and Video Branch, Special Archives Division, National Archives and Records Service**
Washington, D.C. 20408
202-786-0041
Research hours: Monday-Friday, 8:45a.m.-5p.m. Call in advance for appointment.
News and documentary programs constitute the bulk of this collection. Coverage for ABC is from 1977-1982, NBC from 1976-1982, and CBS from 1974 to the present. For a comprehensive collection of network news from 1968 to the present, consult the Vanderbilt Television News Archives (entry 723). Special collections include the following: ABC Radio News and Public Affairs Collection, 1943-1972 (27,000 items); National Radio News and Public Affairs Collection, 1935-1972 (3,000 items); National Public Radio and Public Affairs Collection, 1971-1976 (7,000 items); and the Foreign Broadcast Intelligence Service Collection, 1941-1946 (30,000 items). Researchers may bring their own recording equipment and record items from research room machines for no charge. Individuals may also request tape duplications, for which there is a fee. It is important to note that only recordings in the public domain may be copied unless the researcher has a permission release form for recording of restricted items. Several catalogs guide the user through the varied collections.

690. **Museum of Broadcasting**
   1 East 53rd Street
   New York, NY 10022
   212-752-4690
   Research hours: Serious researchers should call or write for appointment.
   The Television Information Office Library was moved to the Museum of Broadcasting in 1989 after the National Association of Broadcasters voted to cease TIO operations. The TIO collection of 5,000 books and nearly 300 journals focuses on all aspects of television, with emphasis on network programming and social issues. The history of radio and television from the 1920s to the present is chronicled in the Museum's collection of more than 10,000 television programs, 10,000 radio programs, and 2,000 books. The Museum published a catalog entitled *Subject Guide to the Radio and Television Collection of the Museum of Broadcasting* (entry 428). There also is a card catalog. There are plans to move to a larger facility.

691. **National Archives of Canada**
   395 Wellington Street
   Ottawa, Ontario K1A ON3
   Canada
   613-995-1311
   Research hours: Monday-Friday, 8a.m.-4:45p.m.
   Formerly the Public Archives of Canada, the National Archives houses many of the Canadian Broadcasting Corporation's records. The CBC is Canada's principal broadcasting agency and its records are scattered. Some can be found at the Head Office in Ottawa, others at the English Services Division in Toronto or the French Services Division in Montreal. There also is a Regional Broadcasting Division and Radio-Canada International. Fortunately, there is a guide to the collections, *Guide to CBC Sources at the Public Archives* (entry 418), which guides the user through the Federal Archives Division, Manuscript Division, National Map Collection, National Photography Collection, National Film, Television and Sound Archives, etc. Special collections range from the Shugg Collection (Orvill Shugg was the first supervisor of the "CBC Farm Broadcasts" in 1939) to Tuesday Night, a collection of kinescopes and videotapes of the weekly current affairs program. See also the Canadian Broadcasting Corporation Reference Library (entry 643).

692. **National Association of Broadcasters, Library and Information Center**
   1771 N Street, N.W.
   Washington, D.C. 20036
   202-429-5490
   Research hours: Tuesday-Friday, 2p.m.-4p.m. Call or write for appointment.
   Radio and television broadcasting are covered in more than 9,000 volumes and 230 periodicals. The NAB (entry 595) publishes a biennial broadcasting bibliography, *A Guide to the Literature of Radio and Television*.

693. **National Jewish Archive of Broadcasting**
   The Jewish Museum
   1109 Fifth Avenue
   New York, NY 10028
   212-860-1886
   Research hours: Open only to researchers by appointment. Call or write in advance.
   The bulk of this film and tape collection focuses on news and documentary programs of interest to the Jewish community. Emphasis is on the Depression years, World War II and the Holocaust, Israel, television and radio's Golden Age, the Korean War, and the Vietnam War.

694. **National Library of Canada**
   395 Wellington Street
   Ottawa, Ontario K1A 0A9
   Canada
   613-995-9481
   Research hours: Monday-Friday, 8:30a.m.-5p.m.
   The largest collection of Canadian newspapers in Canada is maintained here, as are many ethnic newspapers.

695. **National Press Foundation**
   1282 National Press Building
   Washington, D.C. 20045
   202-662-7350
   The National Press Foundation sponsors short seminars for professional journalists as well as fellowships for Spanish-language study in Mexico.

696. **National Public Radio Broadcast Library or Library and Audio Archive**
   2025 M Street, N.W.
   Washington, D.C. 20036
   202-822-2064
   Research hours: Restrictions apply. Call or write for appointment.
   More than 50,000 NPR audiotapes are located here. The Broadcast Library keeps five years of NPR programs; then they are sent to the Library of Congress and the National Archives. There is a computer printout catalog of NPR programs.

697. **NBC News Archives**
   30 Rockefeller Plaza
   Room 902
   New York, NY 10112
   212-664-3797
   Research hours: Open only to buyers of newsfilm and tape.
   More than 200 million feet of NBC newsfilm and 50 million feet of stock-shot footage, as well as NBC news and documentaries from the 1940s to the present, are housed here. Researchers may purchase newsfilm, but all research and sale footage must be approved by NBC. Those interested in this service must write in advance for an appointment and include references and the purpose of the study. It is important to note that scholarly access to NBC material is provided through the Museum of Broadcasting (entry 690) and the Library of Congress. Videotapes of NBC evening newscasts from 1968 to the present can be obtained from the Vanderbilt Television News Archives (entry 723).

698. **NBC Reference Library**
   30 Rockefeller Plaza
   New York, NY 10112
   212-664-5307
   Research hours: Open only to NBC, General Electric, and RCA employees, and professional librarians. Open to researchers on fee basis. Call or write for information.
   The NBC Reference Library was founded in 1930 and contains more than 15,000 books and 200 periodicals on broadcasting, current events, politics, and New York City. The professional staff will perform computer searches for a fee.

699. **New Directions for News**
   School of Journalism
   University of Missouri, Columbia
   P.O. Box 838
   Columbia, MO 65205
   314-882-3167
   Research hours: Call for information.

Called a "research and problem-solving think tank for newspapers," this new organization "seeks to bring innovative changes to newspapers by focusing the resources and analyses of a think tank to increase newspapers' readership, reader intensity and contribution to the nation," according to a Missouri Professional Programs Bulletin. Its statement of purpose, published in part in the *ASNE Bulletin* in July/August 1987, states that "it will be a unique institution aimed at exploring new approaches and new visions of practical benefit to key personnel in the profession. The activities will center on monitoring, interpreting, redefining and demonstrating the best new work and thought for American newspapers." NDN was developed from a project on newspaper coverage and content by Dorothy Jurney at George Washington University in 1983. NDN's executive director is Jean Gaddy Wilson. Its first roundtable, "Reaching Tomorrow's Readers," was held in 1989.

700. **Newspaper Management Center**
c/o Ed Bassett
Medill School of Journalism
Northwestern University
Evanston, IL 60208
312-491-5091
This new teaching and research facility, founded in 1989, is funded by the Knight Foundation. It grew out of a Knight study by John M. Lavine, professor of media management and economics at the University of Minnesota. One of its goals is to develop a management training program for mid-level newspaper managers. In addition, seminars for top executives and new managers are planned. It is a joint project of Northwestern's Medill School of Journalism and J. L. Kellogg Graduate School of Management, and is designed to complement newspaper training programs at organizations such as American Press Institute and The Poynter Institute for Media Studies.

701. **Nieman Foundation**
Walter Lippman House
Harvard University
One Francis Avenue
Cambridge, MA 02138
617-495-2237
The Nieman Foundation funds Harvard University's academic-year Nieman Fellowships for journalists.

702. **Nieman-Grant Journalism Reading Room**
University of Wisconsin
2130 Vilas Communication Hall
821 University Avenue
Madison, WI 53706
608-263-3387
Research hours: Open to researchers. Call or write for information.

The 350-volume Thayer Law of Mass Communications Collection is located here, as are other books and periodicals on international communications, journalism, mass communications law, public opinion, reporting, research, and photojournalism. The Mass Communications Research Center, located in a separate facility at the University of Wisconsin, conducts research on all aspects of communications and provides opportunities for graduate students to conduct their own projects.

703. **Pacifica Radio Archive, Pacifica Tape Library**
Pacifica Radio Network
Pacifica Foundation
5316 Venice Boulevard
Los Angeles, CA 90019
213-931-1625
Research hours: Researchers may call for appointment.

More than 20,000 audiotapes are housed here, with emphasis on news, information talk, documentary, and political programs. A substantial portion of the collection focuses on alternative radio and the Vietnam War. There is a card catalog for post-1976 holdings and a key-word index for pre-1976 materials. The Library also publishes a catalog.

704. **The Poynter Institute for Media Studies**
801 Third Street South
St. Petersburg, FL 33701
813-821-9494
Research hours: Not open to public. Journalists and researchers should call or write for information.

A nonprofit educational institution, the Institute (formerly Modern Media Institute) was founded in 1975 by Nelson Poynter, the late publisher of the *St. Petersburg Times* and chairman of the Times Publishing Company. There are more than 30 seminars each year in the four centers of writing, graphics and design, ethics, and media management. Most seminars are aimed at professional journalists. The Eugene Patterson Library contains more than 8,000 books, 300 periodicals, 400 videotapes, 40 newspapers, and numerous vertical files on all aspects of print and broadcast journalism, ethics, graphics and design, color, newsroom management, etc. Special collections include Organization of Newspaper Ombudsmen columns and the NewsLeaders videotape series. NewsLeaders consists of 26 videotaped interviews with leading print and broadcast journalists, as well as unedited tapes, which are time coded and indexed. The Institute publishes *Best Newspaper Writing* (entry 327) annually in cooperation with the American Society of Newspaper Editors.

705. **Public Affairs Video Archives**
Purdue University
Stewart Center G-39
West Lafayette, IN 47907
317-494-9630
Research hours: Monday-Friday, 8a.m.-5p.m. Call for information.

In the fall of 1987, Purdue University began recording programs on both channels of the Cable-Satellite Public Affairs Network (C-SPAN). Researchers may view tapes at the archive, and educational institutions may purchase any unedited two-hour VHS tape for $30. The videotapes are not to be used for commercial or political activities. Contact the Video Archives for further information. Researchers interested in all aspects of public affairs, Senate proceedings, congressional hearings, press conferences, and presidential debates that C-SPAN regularly covers will want to consult this new archive. A computerized index is in the works. Archives catalogs (entry 430) are available.

706. **Public Broadcasting System Archives**
475 L'Enfant Plaza, S.W.
Washington, D.C. 20024
202-488-5227
Research hours: Monday-Friday, 9a.m.-5p.m.

This collection of the National Educational Television (NET) programs from 1953-1970 is a gold mine for those researching noncommercial television. The collection ends in 1970 when NET became PBS. There is a holdings list as well as a printed catalog and card catalog. There also is computer access by title.

707. **Radio Advertising Bureau**
Marketing Information Center
304 Park Avenue South
New York, NY 10010-4302
212-254-4800
Research hours: Special permission required. Call or write for information.
Founded in 1951, the Bureau archives *Broadcasting Yearbook* from 1935 to the present, as well as a small collection of books and periodicals on radio, advertising, and competitive media. There also is a tape library of more than 30,000 commercials located in a separate department.

708. **Radio Quebec**
Centre Des Resources Documentaires
800, rue Fullum
Montreal, PQ H2K 3L7
Canada
514-521-2424
Research hours: Not open to the public.
Special collections include Radio-Quebec production and administrative documents (some in French) from 1968 to the present. Television, graphic arts, and communications are emphasized, in addition to Canadian history. More than 4,000 television programs are available on videotape. The Centre also indicates it has more than 3 million feet of film. Maintained by the Societe de Radio-Television du Quebec, the Centre is not open to the public, but does participate in interlibrary loan.

709. **Roy O. West Library**
DePauw University
Greencastle, IN 46135
317-658-4800
Research hours: Monday-Thursday, 7:45a.m.-12:30a.m.; Friday, 7:45a.m.-11:30p.m.; Saturday, 9a.m.-11:30p.m.; Sunday, noon-12:30a.m.
The archives of the Society of Professional Journalists (entry 619), the largest professional journalism organization in the country, are located here. SPJ was founded in 1909 by students at DePauw.

710. **Science Journalism Center**
School of Journalism
University of Missouri, Columbia
P.O. Box 838
Columbia, MO 65202
314-882-2914
Research hours: Call for information.
The Center was founded in 1986 as an independent organization to help journalists research and prepare science and biomedical news stories. The resource library of more than 3,000 abstracts of newsclips is online (entry 232) and journalists are encouraged to use this free service. The Center also conducts workshops for journalists and journalism educators. See also the Media Resource Service (entry 686).

711. **Scripps Howard Foundation**
1100 Central Trust Tower
Cincinnati, OH 45202
513-977-3035
The Foundation offers scholarships to undergraduate and graduate communications students.

712. **Sigma Delta Chi Foundation**
53 West Jackson Boulevard
Suite 731
Chicago, IL 60604
312-922-7424
The Sigma Delta Chi Foundation funds Project Watchdog (public understanding of freedom of the press), the First Amendment Center, and the Pulliam Award for editorial writers. It also sponsors a lecture series.

713. **Silha Center for the Study of Media Law and Ethics**
School of Journalism and Mass Communication
University of Minnesota
111 Murphy Hall
206 Church Street, S.E.
Minneapolis, MN 55455-0418
612-625-3421
Research hours: Call or write for information. Researchers must fill out an application form.
Mass communication law and ethics are interests of this center, which holds conferences, lecture series, and symposia. The Center's publication series includes National News Council publications from 1973-1978, and lecture, bibliography, and report series. It also houses the archives of the National News Council. Bibliographies published by this center include *Mass Media Law* (entry 30) and *Two Bibliographies in Ethics* (entry 17). The Center was established in 1984.

714. **Smithsonian Institution**
Washington, D.C.
202-357-1300
Research hours: Monday-Sunday, 10a.m.-5:30p.m.
The Henry R. Luce Hall of News Reporting exhibit opened in 1973. It portrays the history of the news media and includes historical newspaper pages, teletypes, cartoons, typesetting equipment, newsreels, and exhibits of radio and television news. Luce (1898-1967) was the founder of the newsweekly *Time*. Exhibit organizer and curator Peter C. Marzio also compiled an exhibit guide entitled *The Men and Machines of American Journalism: A Pictorial Essay from the Henry R. Luce Hall of News Reporting* (entry 423).

715. **State Historical Society of Wisconsin Library, Newspaper and Periodicals Section**
816 State Street
Madison, WI 53706
608-262-3421
Research hours: Monday-Thursday, 8a.m.-9p.m.; Friday-Saturday, 8a.m.-5p.m.
This is the home of the second largest collection of newspapers in the United States, with titles published in every state and Canadian province. Newspapers are available in bound volumes and micro-formats. It also houses the largest collections of Native American newspapers and United States and Canadian underground or alternative newspapers (more than 4,000) in North America, and has one of the largest collections of black newspapers, Asian-American newspapers, Canadian newspapers, and Hispanic-American newspapers. Their catalog, *Periodicals and Newspapers Acquired by the State Historical Society of Wisconsin Library*, is published biennially. James Danky, newspaper and periodicals librarian, is one of the finest resources available, and is the author of numerous newspaper bibliographies.

716. **State Historical Society of Wisconsin, Mass Communications History Center**
 816 State Street
 Madison, WI 53706
 608-262-3338
 Research hours: Call for information.
 The Mass Communications History Center provides scholars access to private collections, papers of journalists, and unpublished materials relating to the development of mass communications and the media. It was established in 1955, holds nearly 700 special collections, and published *Mass Communications, Film, and Theater Research: A Guide.*

717. **Sterling Memorial Library, Manuscripts and Archives**
 Yale University
 New Haven, CT 06520
 203-432-2798
 Research hours: Monday-Friday, 8:30a.m.-5p.m.
 Researchers interested in twentieth-century journalism should consult this collection which houses, among others, the papers of Walter Lippman (1889-1974), a founder of the *New Republic, New York Herald-Tribune* columnist and winner of the Pulitzer Prize in 1958 and 1962 for international reporting, and Dwight MacDonald (1906-1982), author and writer for *The New Yorker* from 1951-1971. The university library also maintains an extensive collection of American colonial and English eighteenth- and nineteenth-century newspapers.

718. **Student Press Law Center**
 Suite 504
 1735 I Street, N.W.
 Washington, D.C. 20006-2402
 202-466-5242
 Focusing on First Amendment rights of high school and college students, the Student Press Law Center is a clearinghouse of information on press freedom. Publications include the "SPLC Report" and *Law of the Student Press.* It was founded in 1974.

719. **Sulzberger Journalism Library**
 304 Journalism Building
 Columbia University
 Broadway and 116th Street
 New York, NY 10027
 212-280-3860
 Research hours: Sunday, 10a.m.-5p.m.; Monday-Thursday, 9a.m.-10p.m.; Friday, 9a.m.-7p.m.; Saturday, noon-8p.m. Open to faculty and students.
 The Sulzberger Journalism Library holds more than 14,000 books, 60 periodical subscriptions, and numerous clip files.

720. **Technical and Education Center of the Graphic Arts**
 Information Service
 Rochester Institute of Technology
 One Lomb Memorial Drive
 Rochester, NY 14623
 716-475-2791
 Research hours: Call for information.
 Books on graphic arts, and photographic and applied art, with emphasis on the science and technology of printing, make up the bulk of this collection. Also available are more than 250 periodicals, reports, brochures, and theses. The Graphic Arts Research Center produces the *Graphic Arts Literature Abstracts* (entry 164).

721. **Television News Study Center/Media Resource Center**
Gelman Library
George Washington University
2130 H Street, N.W.
Washington, D.C. 20052
202-994-6378
Research hours: Monday-Thursday, 9a.m.-9:45p.m.; Friday, 9a.m.-4:45p.m.; Saturday, noon-5:45p.m.; Sunday, noon-7:45p.m. Call for appointment.
The Television News Study Center was designed to provide access to the Vanderbilt Television News Archive (entry 723). Playback facilities are available, as are numerous television news-finding aids. The Center published *Television News Resources: A Guide to Collections* (entry 433).

722. **University of California Research Library, Department of Special Collections**
405 Hilgard Avenue
Los Angeles, CA 90024
213-825-4879
Research hours: Monday-Saturday, 9a.m.-5p.m.
The Los Angeles *Daily News* morgue, with 200,000 negatives and 20,000 prints, with indexes, is located here. The collection also includes more than 1 million negatives and 300,000 prints from the *Los Angeles Times* morgue. In addition, the Social Sciences Collection houses a collection of numerous underground newspapers.

723. **Vanderbilt Television News Archive**
Jean and Alexander Heard Library
Vanderbilt University
Nashville, TN 37240-0007
615-322-2927
Research hours: Monday-Friday, 8a.m.-5p.m.; Saturday by appointment. Call or write for appointment.
Researchers interested in broadcast history and the evolution of television news will want to schedule some time at Vanderbilt. All network television evening news programs (18,000 hours) and selected special news programs (5,000) from August 5, 1968 to the present are stored on videotape in these archives. The evening news programs are indexed monthly in the *Television News Index and Abstracts* (entry 185). Special collections include Democratic and Republican national conventions, press conferences, and Watergate hearings. "Face the Nation," "Meet the Press," and "Issues and Answers" from 1970 on can also be found here. The Archive will duplicate entire news broadcasts or compile items from various broadcasts per user request. No tapes are sold, but all are offered on a loan basis. Contact the Archive for further information on services and charges.

724. **Washington Journalism Center**
2600 Virginia Avenue, N.W.
Suite 502
Washington, D.C. 20037
202-337-3603
The Washington Journalism Center focuses on innovation in journalism education and public affairs reporting. It sponsors conferences for journalists in Washington, concentrating on major issues in the news, and offers the Thomas L. Stokes Award for best reporting or comment on energy, the environment, etc., in a daily newspaper.

725. **William Allen White Library**
Emporia State University
Emporia, KS 66801
316-343-5203
Research hours: Monday-Friday, 8a.m.-5p.m.; Saturday, 1p.m.-5p.m.; Sunday, 2p.m.-11p.m.

The William Allen White Collection contains books by and about White (1868-1944), items from his personal library, manuscripts, photographs, articles, memorabilia, and letters. White was editor and owner of the *Emporia Gazette* in Kansas and winner of the Pulitzer Prize in 1922 for editorial writing.

726. **William Randolph Hearst Foundation**
90 New Montgomery Street
Suite 1212
San Francisco, CA 94105
415-543-4057
The Hearst Foundation funds the annual Journalism Awards Program for undergraduate journalism students in the United States.

727. **Wisconsin Center for Film and Theater Research**
816 State Street
Madison, WI 53706
608-262-3338
Research hours: Monday-Friday, 10a.m.-4:30p.m. Call or write for appointment.
This Center also collects materials in television, and has some holdings in news programs and documentary. There is a published catalog, entitled *Sources for Mass Communications, Film and Theater Research* (entry 424), as well as a card catalog.

728. **World Press Institute**
c/o Macalester College
1600 Grand Avenue
St. Paul, MN 55105
612-696-6360
Founded in 1961, the World Press Institute sponsors work and travel programs in the United States for foreign journalists. It is privately funded by media, corporate, and individual donations.

In addition to the libraries and collections mentioned above, the Boston Public Library, Chicago Public Library, New York Historical Society, University of Illinois Urbana/Champaign, The Center for Research Libraries (Chicago), Harvard University, and University of Washington Libraries maintain extensive newspaper collections. Other journalism collections or newspaper archives can be found at the Centre for Mass Media Studies at the University of Western Ontario, BBC Enterprises, the Chicago Historical Society, Detroit Public Library, Houston Public Library, Newbury Library (Chicago), Orange County Library, Princeton University, University of Georgia, Duke University, University of Texas, University of Louisville, Memphis State University, Minnesota Historical Society, Historical Society of Pennsylvania, the University of Florida, Mississippi State University, Emory University, the New York Public Library, University of Iowa, and University of Virginia, to name a few.

Important newspapers which have ceased publication can be found at Boston University, Free Library of Philadelphia, Temple University, and elsewhere.

Queensborough Public Library houses the important *New York Herald Tribune*.

Other media institutes or programs in communications which should be mentioned include the Annenberg Washington Program in Communication Policy Studies, Duke University's Center for the Study of Communications, the University of Michigan's Howard R. Marsh Center for the Study of Journalistic Performance, the Journalism Resources Institute of Rutgers University, and the University of Maryland's Knight Center for Specialized Journalism.

Appendix

Database Service Suppliers and Vendors

American Library Association (ALA)
50 East Huron Street
Chicago, IL 60611
312-944-6780

BRS (Bibliographic Retrieval Service),
BRS After Dark
BRS Information Technologies
1200 Route 7
Latham, NY 12110
518-783-1161
800-345-4277
TWX 710-444-4965

BRS/Colleague
555 East Lancaster Avenue
4th Floor
St. Davids, PA 19087
215-526-0128
800-468-0908

CISTI
Canadian Online Enquiry Service
(CAN/OLE)
National Research Council Canada
Ottawa, Ontario K1A 0S2
Canada
613-993-1210
Telex 0533115 CA

CompuServe Information Service
5000 Arlington Centre Boulevard
Columbus, OH 43220
614-457-8600
800-848-8990
TWX 810-482-1709 CPS A COL

Datacentralen
Retororvej 6-8
25000 Valby
Copenhagen
Denmark
45 (1) 46 81 22
Telex 27 122 DC DK

DATA-STAR
D-S Marketing Ltd.
Plaza Suite
114 Jermyn Street
London SW1Y 6HJ
England
44 (1) 930-5503
800-221-7754
Telex 94012671 STAR G

DataTimes Corporation
14000 Quail Springs Parkway
Suite 450
Oklahoma City, OK 73134
405-751-6400
800-642-2525

Dialcom, Inc.
6120 Executive Boulevard
Rockville, MD 20852
301-881-9020
800-435-7342
TWX 710-825-9601

Dialog Information Services, Inc.
3460 Hillview Avenue
Palo Alto, CA 94304
415-858-3785
800-334-2564
800-387-2689 (in Canada)
Telex 334499 DIALOG
TWX 910-339-9221

DIMDI
Weisshausstrasse 27
Postfach 420580
5000 Cologne 4I
Federal Republic of Germany
49 (221) 47 24 1
Telex 8881364 DIM D

Donovan Data Systems
Berger House
7 Farm Street
London W1X 7RB
England
44 (1) 629-7654

Dow Jones and Company, Inc.
P.O. Box 300
Princeton, NJ 08543-0300
609-520-4000

ESA/IRS
Via Galileo Galilei
00044 Frascati
Italy
39 (6) 94 18 01
Telex 610637 ESRIN I

Executive Telecom System, Inc.
The Human Resource Information Network
9585 Valparaiso Court
Indianapolis, IN 46268
317-872-2045
800-421-8884

Finsbury Data Services
A Reuter Company
68-74 Carter Lane
London EC4V 5EA
England
44 (1) 248-9828
Telex 892520 FINDAT G

G. CAM Serveur
Tour Maine-Montparnasse
33 Avenue du Maine
75755 Paris Cedex 15
France
33 (1) 45 38 70 72
Telex 203933 GCAMSER F

Harris Media Systems Limited
2161 Yonge Street
Suite 806
Toronto, Canada M4S 3A6
Canada
416-487-2111

Infomart Online
164 Merton Street
Toronto, Ontario M4S 3A8
Canada
416-489-6640
800-268-8817
Telex 0622111

Interactive Market Systems
55 Fifth Avenue
New York, NY 10003
212-924-0200
800-223-7942
Telex 66251

IST-Informatheque, Inc.
1611 Boulevard Cremazie East
Montreal, Quebec H2M 2P2
Canada
514-383-1611
800-361-4777

Knowledge Index
Dialog Information Services, Inc.
3460 Hillview Avenue
Palo Alto, CA 94304
415-858-3785
800-334-2564
800-387-2689 (in Canada)
Telex 334499 DIALOG
TWX 910-339-9221

Management Science Associates, Inc.
6565 Penn Avenue at Fifth
Pittsburgh, PA 15206-4490
412-362-2000

Market Science Associates
1560 Broadway
Third Floor
New York, NY 10036
212-398-9100

Mead Data Central (NEXIS, LEXIS)
P.O. Box 933
Dayton, OH 45401
513-859-1611
800-227-4908

NewsNet, Inc.
945 Haverford Road
Bryn Mawr, PA 19010
215-527-8030
800-345-1301

ORBIT Search Service
Pergamon ORBIT InfoLine, Inc.
8000 Westpark Drive
Suite 400
McLean, VA 22102
703-442-0900
800-456-7248
Telex 901811

PROFILE Information
Sunbury House
79 Staines Road West
Sunbury-on-Thames
Middlesex TW16 7AH
England
44 (932) 761444
Telex 8811720 DSOLVE G

QL Systems Limited
901 St. Andrew's Tower
275 Sparks Street
Ottawa, Ontario K1R 7X9
Canada
613-238-3499

Science Journalism Center
University of Missouri
P.O. Box 838
Columbia, MO 65205
314-882-2914

The SOURCE
Source Telecomputing Corporation
1616 Anderson Road
McLean, VA 22102
703-734-7500
800-336-3366
800-572-2020 (in Virginia)

TECH DATA
Information Handling Services
Department 406
15 Inverness Way East
P.O. Box 1154
Englewood, CO 80150
303-790-0600
800-241-7824
Telex 4322083 IHS UI

Telesystemes-Questel
83-85 Boulevard Vincent Auriol
750 13 Paris
France
33 (1) 45 82 64 64
800-424-9600 (in United States)
Telex 204594 TELQUES F

Telmar Group, Inc.
902 Broadway
New York, NY 10010
212-460-9000

U.S. Telecom, Inc.
315 Greenwich Street
New York, NY 10013
212-925-0667
Telex 650 1746064

VU/TEXT Information Services, Inc.
325 Chestnut Street
Suite 1300
Philadelphia, PA 19106
215-574-4400
800-323-2940

West Publishing Company
50 West Kellogg Boulevard
P.O. Box 64526
St. Paul, MN 55164-0526
612-228-2500
800-328-0109
800-328-9833

Western Union Telegraph Company
1 Lake Street
Upper Saddle River, NJ 07458
201-825-5000
800-527-5184
Telex 642491

Wilsonline
H.W. Wilson Company
950 University Avenue
Bronx, NY 10452
212-588-8400
800-367-6770
800-462-6060 (in New York)

Windsor Systems Development, Inc.
545 Fifth Avenue
Suite 400
New York, NY 10017
212-697-5390

Author-Title Index

This index lists titles of works given full annotations, titles of organizations listed in chapters 12 and 13, and authors, editors, compilers, and corporate bodies associated with the publications of the works included. Numbers cited in the index are entry numbers, with the exception of the roman numerals for entries found in the front matter.

Subject Index

This index covers entries for all reference works, periodicals, and organizations named in annotations in this book. Numbers cited in the index are entry numbers, with the exception of roman numerals for entries found in the front matter.